Fulbright Papers

PROCEEDINGS OF
COLLOQUIA

SPONSORED BY THE
UNITED STATES-UNITED KINGDOM
EDUCATIONAL COMMISSION:
THE
FULBRIGHT COMMISSION
LONDON

Volume 2

Ethics and international relations

The Fulbright Programme of Educational Exchanges, which has been in operation since 1946, aims to promote mutual understanding between the United States of America and other nations. It now operates in more than 120 countries, with forty-three bi-national commissions involved in its administration. In the United Kingdom the Commission aims to offer qualified British and American nationals the opportunity to exchange significant knowledge and educational experience in fields of consequence to the two countries, and thereby to contribute to a deeper mutual understanding of Anglo-American relations and to broaden the means by which the two societies can further their understanding of each other's cultures. Among its activities the Commission promotes annual colloquia on topics of Anglo-American interest; the proceedings are published in this series.

1. *Lexicography: an emerging international profession*
ed. Robert Ilson

2. *Ethics and international relations*
ed. Anthony Ellis

3. *Orphan diseases and orphan drugs*
ed. J. M. Walshe and I. H. Steinberg

Ethics and international relations

edited by
ANTHONY ELLIS

MANCHESTER
UNIVERSITY PRESS

IN ASSOCIATION WITH
THE FULBRIGHT COMMISSION, LONDON

COPYRIGHT © THE US – UK EDUCATIONAL COMMISSION 1986

Published by MANCHESTER UNIVERSITY PRESS
Oxford Road, Manchester M13 9PL., U.K.
Wolfeboro, N.H. 03894–2069, U.S.A.

in association with THE FULBRIGHT COMMISSION,
6 Porter Street, London W1M 2HR

British Library cataloguing in publication data

Ethics and international relations.—(The
    Fulbright papers. Proceedings of
    colloquia; v. 2)
    1. International relations—Moral and
    ethical aspects
    I. Ellis, Anthony   II. Series
    172'.4   JX1391

Library of Congress cataloging in publication data applied for

ISBN 0-7190-1974-5 hardback

Printed in Great Britain by
Robert Hartnoll (1985) Ltd
Bodmin Cornwall

Contents

Foreword

This volume records the proceedings of the second Fulbright colloquium – on Ethics and International Relations – which was held at the University of St. Andrews, Centre for Philosophy and Public Affairs, from Friday 28 September to Monday 1 October 1984.

The idea of a colloquium to mark the opening of the Centre came from the Principal and Vice-chancellor of St. Andrews, Dr Steven Watson, who saw such an international conference as a valuable way of bringing experts in the field of philosophy and public affairs in the United States into contact with their European counterparts. The US–UK Educational Commission warmly welcomed this initiative as entirely consonant with its aim of promoting Anglo-American cultural understanding.

In meeting this aim the Fulbright Commission has traditionally concentrated on transatlantic exchanges of students and scholars, and over 10,000 Britons and Americans have benefited from this programme since the Commission was established in London in 1948. More recently the Commission has extended its responsibilities to cover a wide range of educational activities, and its programme now includes the sponsorship of conferences such as that at St. Andrews, where discussion on subjects of Anglo-American interest, with participation from both sides of the Atlantic, can take place.

The colloquium on Ethics and International Relations attracted an attendance of some seventy participants, drawn from Academe, the legal profession and public life in Great Britain, the United States and Canada. As will be seen from the contents of this volume, the subjects ranged over a wide area and the presentations produced lively discussion. The opinions expressed are, of course, personal to the contributors and do not necessarily reflect the views of the Commission. Nevertheless, the Commission believes publication of the proceedings will be welcomed by a wide audience and hopes this will generate increased interest in the subject of Ethics and International Affairs in its Anglo-American context.

John E. Franklin, Executive Director
United States–United Kingdom Educational Commission:
The Fulbright Commission, London

Introduction

It has often been thought that international relations lie outside the sphere of morality, and this in two ways. First, it may be held that the *practice* of international relations is, just as a matter of fact, unconstrained by moral considerations. But more radically, it may be held that moral considerations simply have no proper application in this sphere.

This second, more radical, view has been held for a number of reasons. Many writers have deduced it from what they held to be the nature of morality. So it may be held, for instance, that morality is a matter of *personal* relations, and so it is a confusion to think that it could govern the behaviour of states and their representatives. Or it may be held that morality is a matter of feeling, whereas politics, and international politics, should be a matter of hard, rational calculation. Or again, it may be thought that morality is of its nature opposed to self-interest, and that the behaviour of states should be governed by self-interest.

The second view is sometimes thought to follow from the first in one way or another. One simplistic line of reasoning is that since states never have as a matter of fact allowed their behaviour to be constrained by moral considerations there is no point in trying to formulate or propagate their moral obligations. More sophisticatedly, it may be pointed out that there is a deep problem about the scope of moral obligations of members of a group in which a sufficiently large number of the members do not fulfil their obligations; and that this is the case in international relations. More subversively, it may be claimed that the lesson we learn from international relations is that where agents, generally states in this case, have no higher authority to govern their behaviour (such as, in the case of individuals, the law or received social mores) then considerations of self-interest make them behave in a more or less sensible way – as sensible anyway as that in which individuals, whose behaviour is moulded by morality, generally behave. So morality itself may be seen to be an illusion, or a hoax perpetrated by the ruling class for their own ends. Those who are less impressed by the behaviour of states may, of course, draw the conclusion that the absence of moral thought here is precisely the problem.

There is little in this volume about the first claim, that international relations are, simply as a matter of fact, not governed by moral considerations. It is in any case a mainly historical question. The interest of most of those participating in the conference centred ultimately on normative questions.

Brian Barry asks whether morality can properly govern the dealings of states with each other at all. For one thing, states have always pursued their own national self-interest; and perhaps they have a duty to do so. For another, it seems that no state could be obligated to comply with international norms in the absence of an authority which could ensure that, by and large, other states complied. And Peter Ingram, in his contribution, argues that the existence of any such authority would leave states less than sovereign and hence, he argues, not states at all as we at present understand the term. (Not that he finds this an uncongenial prospect; he looks forward to a redistribution of power away from states to other bodies as a staging post on the way to the existence of a single world authority.) Barry argues that there are precise analogues to these difficulties in the case of ordinary morality within society, but that they do not suffice to show that the behaviour of individuals should not be governed by morality. Nor should they in the case of states. And once we see that states are subject to the demands of morality, we shall be struck by the fact that the international system has virtually nothing corresponding to the Western liberal democracies' systems of economic intervention and redistribution that protects citizens from violent fluctuations in the market, or from personal misfortune. And that is not a state of affairs, Barry argues, that would be accepted by any impartial, reasonable spectator. And we may therefore conclude that it is not morally acceptable.

Barry leans heavily, as other philosophers have done, on the notions of impartiality and reasonableness. Robert Fullinwider points out that much work still needs to be done here (a criticism which Barry would for the moment, I am sure, accept), and argues that economic redistribution will accompany only a change of consciousness – a move from the *impartial* point of view to the *fraternal*.

James Sterba, in his paper, also makes much use of the notion of the *reasonable,* arguing that libertarians who oppose welfare rights misunderstand their own position: welfare rights can in fact be given a libertarian justification. Like Barry, in effect, he concludes that rich countries have a strong moral obligation to aid poor ones.

Moorhead Wright also arrives at that conclusion, but via a different route, one suggested by the work of Barrington Moore, Jr. A society is based on an implicit social contract whose purpose is the accomplishment of certain ends, and which generates rough agreement on what constitutes unjust treatment. Substantial inequality may often be justified but there is no adequate justification for the economic disparity in wealth between the rich countries and the poor ones.

David Scarrow, in his paper, does not dissent from the view that a nation may have moral duties towards other nations, though he does try to show that such judgements are not as simple as some have thought, and that talk of *rights* in this area is not at all straightforward.

Hugh Lehman is also concerned with the relations between rich and poor countries, but in a different way. It is a common practice for transnational corporations to establish manufacturing operations in Third World countries because of the greatly reduced labour costs in such countries; this seems to conflict with the principle of equal pay for equal work. But Lehman argues that this principle has a restricted scope, and that in fact the practice need involve no conflict with any acceptable moral position.

Thomas Donaldson is concerned with this issue too, but as part of a wider question: How should a multinational company respond to the different standards, legal and moral, that obtain in the various countries in which it has operations? And in particular, may it adopt lower standards in a 'host country' because they are normal there? Donaldson argues that it may, but only in certain well defined contexts.

A concern with the role of impartiality in morality may, though it need not, lead one to a way of thinking which James Fishkin, in his contribution, calls 'Systematic Impartial Consequentialism'. With its particular emphasis on the equal value of everyone's interests, this way of thinking finds it hard to give an adequate justification for the personal commitments which make up a good deal of our moral life, and Fishkin holds that it won't do as a self-sufficient account of morality. But might it be the right way of thinking for *social* choice? Even here, Fishkin argues, the adoption of SIC is morally unthinkable.

Fishkin's respondent, Antony Flew, is even more scathing than Fishkin himself about such an approach to morality or politics. Brian Baxter, in his paper, also tries to resist this way of thinking, by exploring the notion of the personal. But SIC is not a straw man; it had no scarcity of supporters in discussion.

Anthony Kenny, in his paper, is concerned with the strategy of nuclear deterrence, arguing that it is wholly unacceptable; it is both intolerably wasteful and risky, but also murderous – murderous in that it involves a willingness on our part to commit mass murder. No *use* of nuclear weapons could be sufficiently devastating to underpin the deterrent threat, while sufficiently discriminating to be capable of non-murderous execution (a claim discussed in considerable detail by Henry Shue in his contribution). Can it be replied to this that whilst the *use* of nuclear weapons would be immoral, their possession as a deterrent is not? Kenny argues that as a matter of political fact, nuclear weapons cannot act as a deterrent unless there is a deeply rooted willingness to use them; and that willingness is absolutely immoral. On the other hand, it may be legitimate to retain them as bargaining counters if all authorisation to use them were publicly withdrawn. A number of participants in the conference felt that this would involve bad faith.

Arthur Hockaday, Kenny's respondent, emphasises that any intention, or willingness, to use nuclear weapons is conditional, and that the morality of such intentions is partly a function of the value of their *objectives*. The conditional intention that in certain circumstances we will use nuclear weapons is formulated, and conveyed to the potential adversary, with the objective of securing that he will not commit the actions postulated in the condition and that consequently the intention will not be activated. Of course, if the intention is in the end activated then this will involve great evil; but it may none the less be the right course.

Jeff McMahan is concerned with the question whether a state, or any other powerful body for that matter, may legitimately intervene in the affairs of another state, and if so when. He argues that there is a presumption against such intervention, against, that is, the coercive external interference in the affairs of a population organised in the form of a state. If the state is illegitimate, then the presumption will be weak, but if the state is legitimate, then it will be very strong; but in either case, it may be overridden. But since the conditions which have to be satisfied before an intervention is justified are extremely complex, we should adopt, for declaratory purposes, a very restrictive form of the principle. As Neil MacCormick points out, this is similar to what we do in many other difficult legal cases, such as that of assisted euthanasia, where many people think that to enshrine the correct principle, if we knew it, in the law, would do more harm than good; as it is, any particular transgression of the law can be dealt with on its merits.

The conference was divided into six sessions: four plenary sessions and two open sessions. There was vigorous discussion at all of these, but it has been possible to reproduce discussion only from the plenary sessions; and that has been ruthlessly edited.

The Centre for Philosophy and Public Affairs would like to express its gratitude to the Fulbright Commission for making the Conference, and this volume, possible. I should also like to thank Alice Anne Ellis for help with the proof reading and the preparation of the index; and Janet Kirk and Anne Cameron for an enormous amount of secretarial work.

St. Andrews   Anthony Ellis,
1985   Lecturer in Moral Philosophy
                                                  and Academic Director of the
                          Centre for Philosophy and Public Affairs,
                                             University of St Andrews

Theories of justice and international relations: the limits of liberal theory

JAMES FISHKIN

University of Texas at Austin

For the last decade the revival of liberal political philosophy has been based on a single basic paradigm which I will call systematic impartial consequentialism (or SIC): (1) states of affairs are evaluated by an impartial procedure granting equal consideration to everyone's interests; (2) first principles ranking those states of affairs are selected by the procedure; (3) the moral requirements specified by the first principles apply to everyone within jurisdiction of the procedure; (4) the first principles apply without further exceptions or qualifications so as to provide a systematic solution without any recourse to intuitionistic balancing. This kind of theory is *systematic* because the principles deduced from the procedure apply rigorously. It is *impartial* because the procedure grants equal consideration to everyone's interests. It is *consequentialist* because the rankings apply directly to states of affairs (typically distributions of some valued commodity) rather than, say, to actions or virtues, as in some other kinds of theory. Rawls's theory[1] (and its extensions by Beitz[2] and Richards[3] to international and personal choice respectively) offers a prime example; Ackerman's theory,[4] recent resuscitations of utilitarianism (particularly by Peter Singer[5]) provide other prime examples. All these theories provide instances of the same basic strategy of argument.

This paradigm cannot plausibly be offered as an adequate self-sufficient account of morality. But, at the level of social choice, this aspiration has appeared plausible for SIC (at least for ideal theory) because its application has been restricted to *intra*-national justice. I will argue, first, that, at the level of individual choice, its limitations become obvious from the famine relief debate. Second, I will argue that at the level of social choice, parallel limitations become obvious once international (rather than merely intra-national) justice is considered.

International relations provide a context where this paradigm routinely breaks down. Impartial consequentialism can be applied beyond the borders of the nation-state, I will claim, but not *systematically*. Other moral factors which are incommensurable in that we cannot make sense of them from within the paradigm of SIC must be balanced against the paradigm's conclusions, if anything like a plausible theory is to result. The necessity for this kind of unsystematic result for the ethics of international relations will be profoundly disappointing to many. In fact, I have argued elsewhere that, unless we learn to expect less from political theory, results of this kind place liberalism at risk for a legitimacy crisis.[6] I will return to this issue at the end.

What is left out of systematic impartial consequentialism? Two kinds of agent-centred claims: special obligations and plausible limits on moral demands. Both are claims that look, from the impartial perspective, to be biased, selfish and perhaps chauvinistic or ethnocentric because they yield more than equal consideration for some people. The point can be made at two levels of choice – individual and social.

The first kind of claim that is left out is exemplified, at the level of individual choice, by the controversy between Charles Fried[7] and Bernard Williams[8] over Fried's speculation (in *An Anatomy of Values,* a speculation since recanted[9]) that perhaps morality would require that he flip a coin between his wife and a perfect stranger in a lifeboat situation. Within the generally Rawlsian paradigm he emphasised in that book, Fried could not conceptualise giving more than equal consideration to his wife (compared to the stranger) as anything other than bias. He offered the coin flip as one procedure embodying equal consideration to resolve the problem.

Fried's difficulty arises because an obligation to one's wife is a special obligation and there is no fundamental basis within the SIC paradigm for anything other than general obligations. We normally assume that I have obligations to my wife and family and, for example, to persons I have contracted with or promised, based on shared conventions and a previous history of action. My wife and I have obligations to each other that we do not owe total strangers.[10]

Try to bring such special obligations within the framework of SIC. If I take the perspective of Rawls's original position, or the perfectly sympathetic spectator of the classical utilitarians or of Ackerman's neutral dialogue, the stranger's claims stand on the same footing as my wife's. Of course some instrumental, long-term considerations of the effect on institutions (such as marriage and the family) might be brought in to break ties. But such considerations have a derivative place: they loom so small that Fried suggests a coin toss to break ties, instead.

The interesting cases arise when the good to a stranger may be great compared to the sacrifice to a loved one that is minor. Let us assume that each small contribution to famine relief will facilitate the delivery of foodstuffs to additional starving refugees.[11] From the perspective of any plausible variant of SIC, I must compare the small sacrifice for me and for my family compared to the large benefits to others, total strangers, whose interests must be counted equally. Within this framework, the impartial consideration of interests continually ranks states of affairs more highly where great benefits to impoverished strangers are produced at minor cost to affluent Westerners. If one attempts to interpose an obligation to devote resources, at the margin, to one's family rather than to an impoverished stranger, there is no basis within the SIC framework for blocking the inference that the impartial consideration of interests requires priority to the stranger whose needs are far greater. The special ties that are most important to most of us look like favouritism, nepotism or bias from this perspective. An impartial spectator must weigh equally the disutility or utility to my family member or to a stranger; the agent in Rawls's original position (extended by Richards to individual choice) does not know whether he will be a starving refugee or a member of my family. Similar conclusions follow for a participant in Ackerman's neutral dialogue where the winning argument is always 'I'm at least as good as you are, therefore I should get at least as much'. The pronoun 'my' in my references to my family carry no weight from any of these impartial perspectives – which consider the interests of my family only as the interests of *someone's* family.

My special obligations to my country – and my country's special obligations to me – are similarly difficult to bring within the SIC paradigm, The basic assumption – equal consideration for everyone's interests – has an embarrassing tendency to ignore national borders, just as it ignores family borders and other roles defining special obligations. The original position, Ackerman's neutral dialogue or the perfectly sympathetic spectator of the classical utilitarians, have all been interpreted as embodiments of the moral point of view. Hence Ackerman is forced to admit that Mexicans on one side of the border should have the same right to live in the liberal state as Americans on the other.[12] And Beitz has, notoriously, extended the Rawlsian framework to yield a global maximin principle such that the world community is obligated, so far as it can, to maximise the minimum share of primary goods for anyone (or any representative person) anywhere in the world. Peter Singer's famine relief argument similarly places utility to displaced Bengalis on the same footing as utility or disutility to affluent Westerners. If the cost to the latter is not significant while the benefits to the former are great, we are obligated to continue giving – perhaps down to near-Bengali levels ourselves.[13]

Within this paradigm, once persons outside the boundary are considered at all, there is no basis for giving them anything less than equal consideration – for anything less looks like bias or ethnocentrism. Weighting the interests of Americans ten or fifteen times that of Mexicans looks indefensible within this perspective.[14] And if the impartial procedure is an embodiment of the moral point of view, how can morality leave them out?[15]

The problem is that special obligations (whose place within morality many of us would defend) have no foothold for entering at any fundamental level. Persons with interests must be equally considered – my wife or a stranger, my countryman or a foreigner. If we try to bring in special obligations as a factor to be balanced *against* the results of SIC, the point to emphasise is that we are bringing in a factor from outside the paradigm. It is, in this precise sense, incommensurable. It is not a factor that can be assimilated to the procedure but one that must be weighed against it – and weighed against it without the benefits of any such systematic procedure, i.e. weighed, to use Rawls's term, 'intuitionistically' and in that sense unrigorously.

Hence the first factor that defies assimilation within SIC is the moral claim of special rather than general obligations. In addition, SIC provides no basis for the kinds of limits on moral demands we commonly presuppose in secular Western moral culture. In *The Limits of Obligation* I explored two:

(a) *The cut-off for heroism* Certain levels of sacrifice cannot be morally required of any individual.
(b) *The robustness of the zone of indifference* A substantial proportion of any individual's actions fall appropriately within the zone of indifference or permissibly free personal choice.

The first limit is merely the notion that sufficient sacrifice (including sufficiently great risk of sacrifice) renders an act that might otherwise be obligatory 'beyond the call of duty'. It is more than can reasonably be demanded or required; performing such an action is unusually noble or heroic, but failing to perform it is not morally blameworthy. In that sense it becomes discretionary in a way that distinguishes it from the moral requirements defined by duties and obligations. Morally speaking, our actions can be classified into three broad classifications: (1) *the zone of moral requirement,* defined by duties or obligations: it is right or morally praiseworthy that we conform to these requirements and wrong or morally blameworthy that we fail to; (2) *the zone of supererogation,* defined by actions 'beyond the call of duty' and any other discretionary actions that it would be praiseworthy for us to perform but not wrong were we to fail to perform them; (3) *the zone of indifference,* defined by actions that fall under no morally prescriptive classifications of right or wrong, good or bad: it is neither praiseworthy that we perform them nor blameworthy that we fail to perform them. The zone of moral indifference defines an area of permissibly free personal choice where we can, morally speaking, do as we please. The second limit specified above is merely the claim that it is appropriate that a substantial proportion of our actions fall into this classification.

It is an unspoken assumption of the way most of us live that morality is reserved for special occasions. Many, if not most, of the actions we normally perform over the course of the day are not performed out of duty or obligation and they are not heroic; raising no moral issues one way or the other, they are morally indifferent.

Perhaps it is not defensible that we should live this way. There are traditional ways of life, and some modern religious sects as well, that regard every minute aspect of life as determined by moral dictates of one sort or another. But the way of life we commonly take for granted in modern, secular Western moral culture clearly is quite different and conforms to the assumption. We might regard this second limit, the robust zone of indifference, as a corollary of the first, the cut-off for heroism. For any of us to give up virtually *all* of the normal activities whose appropriateness we take for granted and replace them with actions determined by duties or obligations would constitute a very substantial sacrifice, a sacrifice of the sort that might be characterised as 'beyond the call of duty'. It would constitute a substantial sacrifice precisely because it would require us to give up an entire way of life. More particularly, if we were each to give up our present activities and replace them entirely with actions prescribed by duty or obligation, our particular interests would be sacrificed in that our present projects, our plans of life, would have to be relinquished or abandoned. Hence the robust zone of indifference assumption can be rationalised as a particular demarcation of the cut-off for heroism (but not, of course, the only relevant kind of sacrifice rendering acts beyond the call of duty).

When an individual moral agent employs SIC to determine his or her *individual* obligations to contribute to famine relief, or to other collective actions intended to eliminate great suffering, any plausible consideration of claims or interests quickly yields conclusions that overwhelm the two limits just defined.

When the state of the world is such that a strictly impartial consideration of all relevant claims or interests yields a *requirement* that a given agent act, let us call that *an obligation-determining situation.* Given the empirical assumptions standard in the famine relief debate, each small contribution will lower only incrementally and imperceptibly the number of obligation-determining situations facing each of us. Under the conditions of imperfect moral cooperation that commonly apply, and given the state of the world at present, there are enormous numbers of human beings who are available to make moral claims on us of the most basic sort. If I were to give, say, *half* my income to famine relief, it would still be the case that *another* small contribution of $5 or $10 would, even at that cumulative level of sacrifice, be small in its comparative effects on me – as those effects might be compared, with strict impartiality, to the benefits to those helped. Hence, by a strictly impartial consideration of interests, I could reasonably be faced with *further* requirements to contribute and further requirements to act. These requirements would follow from the condition of the countless refugees waiting to be helped by someone. Yet, I believe, if I were to go so far as to give half my income, I would already have triggered any plausible construction of the cut-off for heroism. Yet strict impartiality easily requires that I continue giving after that point. By a strictly impartial consideration of claims, the fact that I have already acted does not insulate me from further moral demands. And in a world of imperfect moral co-operation, where others fail to do their full share, I should continue to conclude that more persons will be helped if I act than if I do not.

This famine relief problem brings home a more general difficulty. If any given agent is faced with a large enough number of obligation-determining situations, the interests at stake for the agent, however small for each required act, may accumulate so as to overwhelm any reasonable construction of the cut-off for heroism and of the robust sphere of indifference. The resources, time, effort, and interests sacrificed will, at some point, add up to more than could reasonably have been demanded as a matter of obligation. Let us term this the 'overload' problem. The central point, for our purposes, is that a strictly impartial consideration of interests disconnects an agent's present obligations from his or her own past history of action. Provided that one is capable of further sacrifice, one is eligible for further moral demands, just like any other person in the interests of bringing about the impartially preferred state of affairs. Given the number of obligation-determining situations produced by the number of worthy recipients throughout the world, each of us, when we consider the problem with strict impartiality as isolated individuals, arrives at obligations that can, quite reasonably, be interpreted as overloading the two limits we have assumed.

The argument just outlined requires only the following components:

(1) strict impartiality in the consideration of individual obligation, (2) assumptions about individual claims or interests that give priority to the claims of starving refugees over those at stake for (comparatively) affluent Westerners in the consideration of marginal contributions, (3) the empirical assumptions about famine relief that specify that further contributions will have the desired effects, and (4) the two limits on appropriate moral demands, the cut-off for heroism and the robust zone of indifference.

It seems clear that (1), (2), and (3) together overwhelm (4). The result seems paradoxical because we find ourselves in the position of being obligated to be heroic. Peter Singer's position in this debate seems startling because he consistently refrains from assuming anything like (4), the limits on moral demands. His position is a consistent challenge to the way most of us think about morality and to the way most of us live (if both presume something like the limits mentioned above) because he would simply require us to act in ways we normally regard as heroic.

The strength of his position is that he is operating entirely from within the SIC paradigm. Within that paradigm there is no fundamental basis for the limits we have posited (they might, for example, have a purely instrumental basis if requiring less leads to less cynicism so as to yield more benefits). SIC moves directly from equal consideration of interests in ranking states of affairs to the general obligation to bring about some of those states of affairs. The obligation applies to all those who can further those preferred states of affairs provided that the sacrifices they incur – when considered impartially – do not lead to those states of affairs no longer being preferred because of the altered state of those performing the actions.[16] This means that there is continuing moral pressure from SIC to require further contributions at the margin if I compare the interests at stake for starving refugees and affluent Westerners. From the impartial perspective, the limits on moral demands we have assumed look like an effort to give more than equal consideration to the affluent – to let them off the hook when there is a great deal that they could do that would be required by an impartial consideration of everyone's interests.

The limits were formulated above for individual choice; but the same issue arises for social choice. How much should any particular country be required to sacrifice its interests (and those of its citizens) for the sake of an impartially preferred global state of affairs? Whether or not there is any systematic basis for it, we commonly assume *some* upper limit on sacrifice. And under normal conditions[17] we commonly assume some collective analogue to what I called the robust sphere of indifference – that citizens of a given country are morally justified in going about their business without having the bulk of their actions morally determined for them by requirements of justice or obligation emanating from outside, from other parts of the world.

In a world whose population is expected to double before 2050 with the growth coming almost entirely from the impoverished, it should be clear that any rigorous application of SIC across national boundaries would lead to enormous moral demands for redistribution and other sacrifices facing any given affluent nation-state. Just as overload arises for isolated individuals in a world of imperfect moral cooperation when a large enough number of obligation-determining situations present themselves, so would overload arise for isolated nation-states in a world of imperfect moral cooperation among states, when a large enough number of obligation-determining situations present themselves (as those obligations would be judged impartially by SIC[18]).

In both cases, individual and social choice, I have assumed some independent moral weight for these two kinds of agent-centred moral claims – the limits on moral demands (such as the cut-off for heroism and the robust sphere of indifference) and special obligations. Both are agent-centred in that, from the perspective of SIC, they appear to give extra weight to the interests of particular persons – the agent who must perform the action or the members of his family or of his country – compared to the interests of everyone considered impartially.

One alternative would be to apply SIC strictly without endowing the factors it leaves out with any independent moral weight at all. At both the individual and social choice levels this would (1) dissolve the ties that define special obligations linking me to my country or to my wife more intimately than to other countries or to strangers, (2) over-run the limits on moral demands that protect us from requiring individual or collective heroism (as in the cut-off for heroism) or moral fanaticism (as in the robust sphere of indifference). Consistent application of such results seems morally unthinkable.

On the other hand, when we attempt to give independent moral weight to these agent-centred claims, we are bringing in a moral factor from outside the SIC paradigm. It is morally incommensurable precisely in the sense that it comes from outside the paradigm. From within the paradigm we cannot rigorously determine how it is to be weighed against the results of SIC because SIC gives it no weight at all. If we balance or 'trade-off' such incommensurable factors, we may arrive at results we find persuasive in individual cases, but we will lack any systematic theory. As Rawls characterises it, intuitionism is 'but half a conception' and in that sense profoundly disappointing to liberal theoretical aspirations.[19]

When the liberal theory of justice was hermetically sealed off from international relations; when it was restricted in its application to members of a given nation-state, the conflicts I am emphasising were obscured. The problem of rationalising special obligations between a state and its citizens, that is, of differentiating those obligations from the claims of non-citizens, did not arise because no non-citizens were considered. Similarly, the problem of somehow limiting the enormous moral demands raised by millions of impoverished non-citizens – once SIC is applied – did not arise when the focus was restricted to citizens. Can liberal theory restrict its application in this way? Perhaps so, but not while offering the fundamental claim that SIC is based on the moral point of view itself. And that, more than anything else, I believe, has provided this paradigm with its basic appeal.

My central point is that crossing national boundaries routinely provides us with cases in which SIC cannot be applied systematically; it can only be applied unsystematically or 'intuitionistically'. We are left to balance morally incommensurable considerations. The result is a kind of non-theory. If such a non-systematic result is inevitable for international relations, should we be disappointed? Table 1 may place it in perspective.

TABLE 1

	I	II	III	IV	V	VI	VII
			Minimal	Subjective			
	Absolutism	Rigourism	objectivism	universalism	Relativism	Personalism	Amoralism
1. The absolutist claim	+	–	–	–	–	–	–
2. The inviolability claim	+	+	–	–	–	–	–
3. The objective validity claim	+	+	+	–	–	–	–
4. The universalis-ability claim	+	+	+	+	–	–	–
5. The interpersonal judgement claim	+	+	+	+	+	–	–
6. The judgement of self claim	+	+	+	+	+	+	–

From James S. Fishkin, *Beyond Subjective Morality: Ethical Reasoning and Political Philosophy.*

Claim 1.   One's judgements are *absolute,* that is, their inviolable character is rationally unquestionable.

Claim 2.   One's judgements are *inviolable,* that is, it would be objectively wrong ever to violate (permit exceptions to) them.

Claim 3.   One's judgements are *objectively valid,* that is, their consistent application to everyone is supported by considerations that anyone should accept, were he to view the problem from what is contended to be the appropriate moral perspective.

Claim 4.   One's judgements apply *universalisably,* that is, they apply consistently to everyone, so that relevantly similar cases are treated similarly.

Claim 5.   One's judgements apply *interpersonally,* that is, to others as well as to one's self.

Claim 6.   One's judgements apply to oneself.

In *Beyond Subjective Morality* I probed the arguments offered by ordinary moral reasoners for subjectivist or relativist moral positions. Note the accompanying chart with its definitions. The six meta-ethical claims listed vertically can consistently be combined into only the seven meta-ethical positions listed horizontally. One of the main findings of the book was that the arguments for subjectivism (positions IV, V, VI or VII) were all arguments based on the *failure* to fulfil absolutist expectations – expectations that unless a moral position held beyond reasonable question or applied without exception (unless it fulfilled positions I or II), it must be merely subjective, a matter of personal taste (as in positions IV, V, VI or VII).

I made a general argument that liberal theory cannot fulfil these absolutist expectations. If my account of the possibilities pictured in Table 1 is correct, this poses, by itself, no difficulty for liberalism, and liberal theory. Even if positions I and II are not available, position III remains as an objective possibility. However, in a culture imbued with absolutist expectations, the vulnerability of liberal theories and principles to moral conflicts and indeterminacies makes them seem subjective, arbitrary, a matter of nothing more than personal taste. Liberal theories and principles that conform to position III in my scheme will undermine their *own* legitimacy in a moral culture imbued with absolutist expectations. Their legitimacy will be undermined because their vulnerability to conflicts and to indeterminacies, when combined with absolutist expectations, supports the conclusion that they are merely subjective – part of an ideology in the pejorative sense, nothing more than an arbitrary mask for power relations.

As we have seen, when the boundaries of the nation-state are crossed, this problem, which was implicit within liberal theory all along, comes into clear relief. If I am correct about the inevitably unsystematic ethics of international relations, then it is in danger of robbing itself of legitimacy – unless we learn to expect less, unless we learn to live with an *unsystematic* ethics and jettison absolutist expectations. The ethics of international relations, more obviously than that of domestic justice, exposes the necessity for moral conflict, for balancing incommensurables and hence the true implausibility of fulfilling absolutist expectations. The middle ground position (III) in my scheme may be disappointingly unrigorous, but it is the only place where a plausible version of liberalism can thrive.

NOTES

1 John Rawls, *A Theory of Justice,* Oxford, 1972.
2 Charles Beitz, *Political Theory and International Relations,* Princeton, N.J., 1979.
3 David Richards, *A Theory of Reasons for Action,* Oxford, 1971.
4 Bruce Ackerman, *Social Justice in the Liberal State,* New Haven, Conn., 1980.
5 Peter Singer, *Practical Ethics,* Cambridge, 1979.
6 *Beyond Subjective Morality: Ethical Reasoning and Political Philosophy,* New Haven, Conn., 1984.
7 Charles Fried, *An Anatomy of Values,* Cambridge, Mass., 1970.
8 Bernard Williams, 'Persons, character and morality' in *Moral Luck,* Cambridge, Mass., 1981.
9 Charles Fried, *Right and Wrong,* Cambridge, Mass., 1978, p. 184.
10 See my *Limits of Obligation,* New Haven, Conn., 1982, Ch. 5 for an attempt to develop this distinction between special and general obligations. The terminology was made familiar by H. L. A. Hart 'Are there any natural rights?' in Anthony Quinton (ed.), *Political Philosophy,* Oxford, 1967.
11 I assume that at certain levels of collective effort, additional small contributions have their advertised likelihood of facilitating the delivery of surplus foodstuffs to starving refugees. One might take a purely cynical attitude toward such claims. To do so consistently, I believe, would be self-serving – although there are clearly some cases that help to justify cynicism.
12 Ackerman, *Social Justice,* p. 93.
13 Peter Singer, 'Famine, affluence and morality' in Peter Laslett and James Fishkin (eds.), *Philosophy, Politics and Society,* Oxford, 1979.
14 As Scheffler notes, 'Having a personal point of view typically involves caring about one's projects and commitments *out of proportion* to their relative weight in the overall sum' (emphasis in original). The general difficulty is that agent-centred claims that give expression to the personal point of view will, from SIC, simply look like unequal counting. See Samuel Scheffler *The Rejection of Consequentialism,* Oxford, 1982, p. 61.
15 We might distinguish a narrow construction of the SIC paradigm in which its application is restricted to distributing the fruits of actual social cooperation. If there is not some actual practice of social cooperation connecting certain persons, then their partial procedure has no jurisdiction over their fruits of social cooperation. This narrow construction can be distinguished from the broader construction in which

the impartial procedure is offered as an embodiment of the moral point of view. On the broad construction even if certain persons are not actually connected by a practice of social cooperation, if justice as conceived by the impartial procedure would require such a practice, then its benefits and burdens would properly be subject to jurisdiction of the procedure. For a spirited defence of the broader view see David A. J. Richards, 'International distributive justice' in J. Roland Pennock and John W. Chapman (eds.), *Ethics, Economics and the Law, Nomos* XXIV.

16 In Rawls's case, the only rationale offered for any other kind of limit comes under the heading of what he calls the 'strains of commitment'. But this factor amounts to what bargains might be entered into in the original position in the good faith expectation that they can be kept. Furthermore, Rawls explicitly excludes the losses of the better-off in an unjust situation as part of the sacrifice to be considered in the strains of commitment. See 'Reply to Alexander and Musgrave', *Quarterly Journal of Economics,* LXXXVIII, 1974, pp. 650–53.

17 See my *Limits of Obligation,* pp. 42–5, for a discussion of 'normal conditions'.

18 Additional recipients for aid who create additional requirements for action can be viewed as defining additional obligation-determining situations.

19 Rawls, *A Theory of Justice,* p. 41. An especially influential statement of intuitionism can be found in Brian Barry, *Political Argument,* London, 1965.

REPLY TO PROFESSOR FISHKIN
Antony Flew, York University, Ontario

In so far as it is the duty of a commentator to be a disagreeing deuteragonist in confrontational conflict with the paper-presenting protagonist, I fear that tonight I shall in large measure fail in my duty. For I can find no fault with what, positively and on his own account, Professor Fishkin has had to say about such things as "the cut off for heroism" and "the robustness of the zone of indifference". Or, rather, I can find no fault here unless it is that he is far too patient with what seems to me the manifest absurdity of suggestions that all of us who are not (yet) poor have an open-ended obligation to support: not only all the people in other countries who, in large part owing to failures to check fertility in those countries, are at present desperately poor and often hungry; but also, presumably, all those further people who will be produced if that fertility is not checked, but instead encouraged by unconditional and indiscriminate charity. If that really is what morality commands, then not only the law but also morality is an ass!

Where I can disagree, and I think usefully, is over Fishkin's again much too generous treatment of such spokespersons of 'systematic impartial consequentialism' as Rawls, Ackerman and Dworkin; most especially Rawls. Spelling out this disagreement should be useful, because my own harsher handling is bound to sharpen the contrast: between, on the one hand, any sort of 'systematic impartial consequentialism'; and, on the other hand, more traditional, unreformed conceptions of the requirements of morality.

1.   Before getting down to matters of philosophical substance, I must mention one source of what may be a purely verbal confusion. For, just as the citizens of Whitman's "athletic democracy" prefer to say 'automobile' or 'elevator' rather than 'car' or 'lift', so they have their own way of employing, or misemploying, the word 'liberal'. I cannot forget that within one week during the academic year 1978–9 I saw the *Los Angeles Times* describing as 'liberals' or 'left liberals': not only J. K. Galbraith; but also Jane Fonda and Bella Abzug. Do I need to remind anyone here that Galbraith is a self-confessed socialist, who in the shadow of the Berlin Wall proclaimed "I am not particular about liberty"; while the other two have for years been reliable supporters of every Marxist-Leninist cause?

So I am quite unsure what I ought to infer: both, in general, when I find Fishkin speaking of "the revival of liberal political philosophy", founded on what he calls "the single basic paradigm" of "systematic impartial consequentialism (or SIC)"; and, particularly when he seems to be employing the expression '*the* liberal theory of justice' (my italics) as a definite description of the work of John Rawls. Certainly what Rawls calls 'justice as fairness' does claim to be neutral as between a private, pluralist economic order and full Clause IV, state monopoly, socialism (p. 66).[1]

This characteristically naïve assertion, however, ignores the original and pervasive assumptions of his entire enterprise. For it is from the beginning assumed that all the wealth either already produced or in the future to be produced within the to them unknown national frontiers of the contracting parties is available for distribution at their absolute discretion, free of all prior claims to individual ownership. (Most remarkably, but it seems never remarked, this collectively owned wealth presumably includes the services which are the actions of individuals.) Consistent with this original and totally socialist assumption, Rawls throughout tacitly takes it for granted that any particular rights or resources enjoyed by any individual either are or ought to be allocated collectively.

Consider, for instance, two statements: first, that "The justice of a social scheme depends on how fundamental rights and duties are assigned" (p. 7); and, second, that "the chief primary goods *at the disposition of society*. . . liberty and opportunity, income and wealth. . . *are to be distributed equally*. . ." (p. 62; my italics) – unless of course, an unequal distribution is positively advantageous (rather than merely not disadvantageous) to the least advantaged group.

2. The first remarkable fact about the form of 'systematic impartial consequentialism' favoured by Rawls is that it is presented as *A Theory of Justice*. For, whereas consequentialism is essentially forward-looking, justice is correspondingly backward-looking. It is, that is to say, concerned with people's retaining or obtaining what they have deserved, or that to which they have otherwise become entitled.

It is a further remarkable fact that what Rawls calls justice is then offered as "an alternative to utilitarian thought generally" (p. 22). It is, therefore, to be an alternative: not, particularly, to an account of justice such as that developed by the younger Mill in chapter V of his *Utilitarianism;* but instead, generally, to any utilitarian form of what Fishkin labels more briefly SIC.

A third remarkable and to us crucially relevant fact is that Rawls, despite an initial insistence that the chief fault of utilitarianism is that "it does not take seriously the distinction between persons" (p. 27), proceeds – as, surely, any SIC person must – to discount as wholly irrelevant every sort of difference upon which any such distinctions might properly be grounded. It is equally remarkable, and equally characteristic, that, although several times saying – in a way which I find sympathetic – that "the most important primary good is self-respect" (p. 440), Rawls never notices that by this discounting he is robbing us of any legitimate claim to the individual differentiating characteristics which alone provide rational bases for our self-respect as different individuals.

To appreciate that and how Rawls rules out from consideration all possible grounds for what Fishkin would call special rights and special obligations, we need to look again at the terms of reference under which the Rawlsian contract is negotiated. Behind 'The Veil of Ignorance' (p. 136) the contractors have to choose "the first principles of a conception of justice which is to regulate all subsequent criticism and reform of institutions" (p. 13). It is well to remind ourselves here, as it were between parentheses, that classical Utilitarianism too was intended to serve this sort of reform purpose; rather than to constitute a contribution to analytical moral philosophy.

In these days, and after the captivating frankness of his confession that "We want to define the original position so that we get the desired solution", it should come as no surprise that his contractors cannot but "acknowledge as the first principle of justice one requiring an equal distribution". Indeed, Rawls adds, "this principle is so obvious that we would expect it to occur to anyone immediately" (pp. 150–1).

To bring out the reason why this became "so obvious" to Rawls we must recognise the stated main purpose of 'The Veil of Ignorance'. It has been usual for commentators to discuss this comprehensive blinkering as having been stipulated in order to secure impartiality; which – as Richard Hare remarked in his Critical Notice[2] – makes the whole exercise a dramatisation of the colourless Humean appeal to the ideally impartial spectator. Certainly Rawls does mention this as one purpose: "We should insure further that particular inclinations and aspirations, and persons' conceptions of their good, do not affect the principles adopted" (p. 18). But the stated primary aim is altogether different, and altogether preposterous: "Once we decide to look for a conception of justice that nullifies the accidents of natural endowment and the contingencies of social circumstances as counters in the quest for political and economic advantage, we are led to these principles. *They express the result of leaving aside those aspects of the social world that seem arbitrary from the moral point of view*" (p. 15: my italics).

In the end it emerges that Rawls will have to include under the rubric 'Things "that seem arbitrary from the moral point of view"' everything which distinguishes one individual from another; everything, that is, which any individual has done or not done, as well as everything which one is and another is not. For only by such wholesale discounting as morally irrelevant of the differentiating characteristics of every individual can he maintain "as the first principle of justice one requiring equal distribution". Without that discounting he would be laying himself open to pressure from those who do indeed "take seriously the distinction between persons". For we want to respect some of the different and hence often – horrid thought – unequal claims urged by and on behalf of different people; claims grounded in differences between what those different people severally have done, or are.

Rawls never spells out in full how much he would have us include under the descriptions "the accidents of natural endowment and the contingencies of social circumstance. . . those aspects of the social world that arbritrary from the moral point of view". Had he done so, even he might have realised the absurdity of offering his version of 'systematic impartial consequentialism', or indeed any other, either as *A Theory of Justice* or as a reform alternative to utilitarianism. For it is he who insists, rightly, that the great fault in utilitarianisms is precisely their failure "to take seriously the distinction between persons".

What Rawls does do is present some unsound argument for the crucial conclusion that these accidents and contingencies are indeed "arbitrary from a moral point of view". He starts from the observation that natural endowments are not themselves deserved. From this innocuous truth he draws two invalid inferences. First, that what these endowments make possible cannot, therefore, be itself a proper basis of desert. Second, because they are not deserved therefore they must be, and in some scandalous way, undeserved.

This second invalid inference is taken to establish the "principle that undeserved inequalities call for redress; and since inequalities of birth and natural endowments are undeserved, these inequalities are to be somehow compensated for" (p. 100). Such compensation is provided by the Difference Principle: this, Rawls tells us, "represents, in effect, an agreement to regard the distribution of natural talents as a common asset and to share in the benefits of this distribution whatever it turns out to be. Those who have been favoured by nature, whoever they are, may gain from their good fortune only on terms that improve the situation of those who have lost out" (p. 101).

As Rawls sees it "the natural distribution of abilities and talents", and also presumably of disabilities and ineptitudes, is "the outcome of a natural lottery". And, furthermore, "Even the willingness to make an effort, to try, and so to be deserving in the ordinary sense is itself dependent upon happy family and social circumstances" (p. 74).

Two further objections against this seductive line have to be raised, however briefly. First, the lottery analogy is applicable only where there are antecedently existing participants hoping to increase their resources by some (for them) lucky spin of the wheel or fall of the die. Something has to be either (part of) me or a legitimate property of mine if I am to be in a position to make acquisitions, whether these are deserved or undeserved or – as Aristotle might have said – not-deserved.

Second, Rawls never explicitly entertains the possibility of not-deserved entitlements. Yet he is no more able than anyone to avoid admitting or affirming the moral legitimacy of some such claims. After all: is he not himself acknowledging what he would have to rate as not-deserved equal entitlements when he "acknowledge[s] as the first principle of justice one requiring equal distribution"? Or suppose we borrow an even more powerful example from Nozick. Suppose half the population was born with two eyes and half with none, would the *aficionados* of 'equality and social justice' want to say that it was an imperative of justice that the two-eyed must be forced to make one of their eyes available for transplanting into the empty sockets of the no-eyed? Even if there are Procrusteans so ruthlessly consistent that they would take this hard line, would they not still have to say that it was justice precisely because the no-eyed have a necessarily not-deserved entitlement to one eye?

3. Fishkin warns of a threatening "legitimacy crisis". But nothing he says has any tendency to show that any such crisis threatens what I should myself describe as 'the revival of liberal political philosophy' – namely, the revival centred on *The Constitution of Liberty* and other works of F. A. Hayek. The legitimacy crisis to which Fishkin's arguments actually point is a crisis for all and only those who want to present (some more or less qualified form of) equality of outcome as the supreme imperative of justice. As I have argued at greater length elsewhere,[3] this is a radically and irredeemably misguided enterprise. What Rawls and all the rest of them ought to do is present their recommendations as determined by a quite different, alternative ideal; and, they might well argue, an alternative ideal which is, because of its systematic impartial consequentialism, both more rational and less disputatious in its applications.

I take it, and, until and unless someone confronts me with some convincing argument to the contrary, shall continue to take it, that the just person is the person who follows the rule: *Honeste vivere, neminem laedere, suum cuique tribuere.* The key clause is the third, which suggests, though it does not strictly entail, that everyone's own – their dues, their deserts and entitlements – are neither the same nor equal. Justice is essentially connected with equality only in as much as any following of rules necessarily requires that all relevantly like cases be treated alike. Equality before the criminal law, for instance, does not mean that there must be no difference between the treatment accorded to the innocent and to the guilty. What it does mean is – say – that if a clergyman in a small and unpopular and rather right-wing sect is prosecuted, convicted, and jailed for an offence, then those clergymen in larger, less unpopular and more left-wing denominations who have committed the same offence must be arraigned and punished similarly. Again, procedures which "grant equal consideration to everyone's interests" do not involve that everyone's interests have to be accorded equal weight: any more than the insistence that everyone is entitled to their day in court commits the courts to handing down the same verdict on every litigant.

Someone may object that Rawls has a different conception of justice. Certainly he has a different conception. But is it a conception of justice? Ignoring the concluding words of Socrates at the end of Book I of *The Republic*, Rawls appears to be indifferent to this question. Indeed, towards the end of his enormous book, he actually claims credit for making an assumption which "allows us to leave questions of meaning and definition aside and to get on with the task of developing a substantive theory of justice" (p. 579).

Mine is, however, no merely verbal question: the difference between us counts as merely a matter of one word only in the silly sense in which the difference between 'Guilty' and 'Not guilty' is a difference of or over only a single word. There are some very solid, though not by the same token respectable, reasons why Rawls – and many others much nastier and more worldly wise than Rawls – want to present their cherished Procrustean norms as the mandates of (social) justice.

In the first place, of course, there is the enormous propaganda advantage of presenting their new and alien SIC wine in old and well-loved bottles. And what Procrustean does not wish to see himself, and to be seen, as a sort of *Shane* figure from a traditional western – doing the justice 'which a man has to do'? Then again, if the Procrustean can get us to accept that his norms are the imperatives of justice, he will have acquired a knock-down answer to an objection which might otherwise be embarrassing: 'By what right are you proposing to employ the machinery of the state to impose on everybody – more often it is everybody else – your own new-adopted personal ideal?' For everyone is ready to allow that what's prescribed by (moral) justice may properly be enforced by (legal) law.

I will end, at deplorably long last, with an observation the pressing home of which provides my sole hope of persuading the Procrusteans to abandon their false claims to be promoting (social) justice. If justice really did require an equal distribution, then everyone would be entitled to no more and no less than an equal share (tautology). But now, all the Procrusteans of my acquaintance are on these assumptions rather conspicuously under-deprived. They are all therefore, to speak less delicately, in possession and enjoyment of considerable amounts both of capital and income over and above the equal shares to which they are justly entitled; and these excesses are, on their own account and in accordance with their stated principles, property stolen (by keeping) from others worse off than themselves.

NOTES

1 This and all other parenthetical page references in the present commentary are to John Rawls, *A Theory of Justice*, Oxford, 1972.

2 R. M. Hare, 'Rawls' *A Theory of Justice*', *Philosophical Quarterly*, XXIII, 1973.

3 See my *The Politics of Procrustes*, London, 1981, chs.3 and 4 ; and compare 'Justice: real or social?', *Social Philosophy and Policy*, I, 1983; and 'Legitimacy and the gadfly challenge', *Philosophical Quarterly*, XXXIII, 1983.

CHAIRMAN'S COMMENTS
Renford Bambrough, St John's College, Cambridge

It seems very likely that Professor Fishkin will wish to reply to Professor Flew, and no doubt they will both wish to contribute to the discussion at appropriate stages, but I propose not to reserve any time for the purpose. I hope that all three of us on this side of the table will take part in the discussion, and I shall not now do more than make the opening remarks of the discussion.

I first saw Professor Fishkin's paper this morning, and I did not see Professor Flew's paper until teatime. In between I met Professor Fishkin and asked him if he were by any chance a convert from the view that he was criticising. He asked why I thought so, and I explained that he seemed to me to be rather tentatively suggesting that we should move in a direction in which I for my part thought that we should march boldly forward. Professor Flew has now diagnosed some of the political and substantively moral presumptions to which Professor Fishkin is inclined to cling, in spite of the general tenor of his criticism. I should like to reinforce what Professor Flew has said about morals and politics by suggesting that there are also some philosophical, some *epistemological* presumptions, which he is also inclined to cling to, which cause the programme of his paper to be, in my submission, unduly tentative. It is as though the little boy in Hans Andersen's fairy tale, instead of coming right out with it, had said, 'The emperor must be feeling rather cold,' or 'Is the emperor trying to save on tailors' bills?' where there is, as the story itself enacts, a more direct way of making the point that needs to be made.

Professor Ian Watt, now a Professor of English at Stanford, used to be a colleague of mine in my college. In the *Eagle,* the college magazine, he wrote a review of a book about Wordsworth that had been published by an American scholar. Wordsworth was an undergraduate at the college, so we hear a good deal about him, and have a substantial collection of Wordsworthiana. Watt reported in his review that the author spoke of his discovery of important Wordsworth material in the Library of St John's College, Cambridge. This discovery, Watt commented, was worthy to set beside that of Christopher Columbus, who also discovered something whose existence had long been known to the natives. *We* have long been aware of some of the paradoxes that Professor Fishkin has noticed in Systematic Impartial Consequentialism. We have long been aware, as natives of the human world, of the falsehood of a great many of the consequences of the view that Professor Fishkin is now tentatively questioning. The unacceptable consequences of such a view seem to me to be of two kinds. One of them is trenchantly expressed by W. H. Auden. "Writers," he says, "can be guilty of every kind of human conceit but one, the conceit of the social worker: 'we are all here on earth to help others; what on earth the others are here for, I don't know.'"

The others were put on earth – if they were put on earth as human beings –

in order to live their independent sovereign lives, in order to enjoy their particularities and individualities, which will often involve them in difficulties and conflicts with other human beings who are also enjoying their particularities and individualities. But if we try to get rid of all these troubles too systematically, as the Systematic Impartial Consequentialist does, we shall be in danger, as Professor Flew has pointed out, of getting rid of far more than those troubles.

But in the few brief remarks I still have time for I should like to concentrate on what I called the epistemological source of the Systematic Impartial Consequentialist view: this preference not only for system and principle, but for a particularly rigid and narrow conception of what it is to be systematic and principled, one that involves the hallowed but hopeless search for a single foundation, or at least for a very small group of fundamental principles for a human understanding which, inside and outside of morality, is of enormous range, complexity, intricacy and subtlety. Professor Fishkin should not be so surprised as he sometimes sounds in his paper that it is not possible to capture in a diagram the full range and substance of what, in being highly trained human beings from our youth upwards, we already understand though we may find it hard to articulate. We need to seek not so much for foundations as for the intricate and elaborate *roots* of our understanding, both in ethics and elsewhere. John Stuart Mill, himself one who has sometimes and reasonably been suspected of over-attachment to system and principle, makes some well judged remarks in the first chapter of *Utilitarianism* about the distinction between the roots picture and the foundations picture of the sources and ground of human knowledge:

> The truths which are ultimately accepted as the first principles of a science, are really the last results of metaphysical analysis, practised on the elementary notions with which the science is conversant; and their relation to the science is not that of foundations to an edifice, but of roots to a tree, which may perform their office equally well though they be never dug down to and exposed to light.

Professor Fishkin is rejoining the natives of the human world when he recognises the complexities that systematic theorists have sometimes obscured. He is welcome – there is more joy over one that repenteth than over ninety and nine that have no need of repentance – and I invite you to continue to explore some of these complexities with him and with us.

DISCUSSION

Professor J. P. Sterba, University of Notre Dame. I have a question for Professor Fishkin concerning the robust sphere of indifference. You mentioned that it was a common assumption of our culture, but it's just not clear to me that people in Third World countries also share this assumption. What argument could you give to such people if they could gather together and launch an attack on people in affluent countries to enable them to take from us the resources that they need?

Professor Fishkin. One way to develop such an argument would be to endow national boundaries with a significance that is ignored by SIC except at some derivative level. Such boundaries generate the sort of special obligations that I have argued are ignored by the SIC paradigm.

Professor Sterba. But people in the Third World countries may not see this rationale. We have to make a special case to them; it's no good saying that we just have special obligations not to cross national boundaries.

Professor Fishkin. Would you try to make the same sort of argument if someone tried to take resources of food away from your family and give them to somebody else? You would appeal to the system of property rights, and various conventions, as generating special obligations.

Professor Sterba. No, I wouldn't. I don't have a good argument against the actions of other people taking what they need from me.

Professor Flew. I can't see why your proposal for a Third World looting party is any sort of challenge to the robustness of the sphere of indifference, because to show that Third Worlders don't accept the idea of the robustness of the zone of indifference, surely, you would have to show that they were all Systematic Impartial Consequentialists, and they didn't recognise a stronger claim to fellow members of the tribe. But my own visit to Malawi suggested that the absolute contrary was the case; indeed it was rather rare to find any Malawian who recognised any sort of obligation outside the tribe! You're not raising a problem about the robustness of the sphere of indifference; you're simply advocating Systematic Impartial Consequentialism independently, aren't you?

Mr Warbrick, University of Durham. Can I put this in terms of a concrete case? Imagine that my father made a million pounds out of illegally peddling drugs. He made sure that I never sullied my hands with it. Am I entitled to say that the special obligations and privileges etc. I have arising out of being brought up as the son of a wealthy drug dealer can be legitimately considered against the general principles that, say, Rawls would propose?

Professor Flew. I don't think it's particularly helpful to introduce a specifically criminal example, and try to suggest that all people who own anything have acquired it either by their own criminal activities or the criminal activities of their parents. Of course, if the money was criminally acquired, your claim to it is very weak, that's for sure!

Mr Warbrick. I think the point of general relevance is this. The way of life, with all of its special obligations, that we have in the Western world, is, in part at least, derived from international relations of trade which are themselves a causative factor in the adverse situation of people in the Third World.

Mr Renford Bambrough. Well, this illustrates the point that no one on this platform is either for or against a redistribution of resources by whatever means. The question is, how is it going to be justified in the particular instance? And it's one thing to offer evidence that these gains were ill-gotten, and another thing to say that the mere fact that there is an inequality is itself a proof that somebody's gains have been ill-gotten. We need evidence, we need to consider the particular instances, and see upon what grounds, if any, it is possible to argue that this person should give up so much to that.

Dr J. Harris, University of Manchester. But surely the moral criticism of the rich man who is indifferent to the plight of the poor man outside his gate does not turn on whether his riches were ill-gotten or not?

Mr Bambrough. Well, you are talking about the poor man outside his gate. You are putting them in some relation. You say 'outside his gate', but I take it that this means 'very near his gate', coming to him to ask for assistance. Now I know that there is scope for argument about whether every poor man in the world is outside my gate; I know that it's not obvious that he's not. But part of what I wanted to indicate by my reference to Auden is what an extemely rigorous Christian commitment is being asked for, and I just wanted to put in a reminder about the alabaster box of ointment. And we also have to consider what life would be like, and whether it would be a human life, if everybody did all that is asked by the sort of morality that Dr Harris proposes. That is, whether there would be any individualities left of families, individuals, communities. The question is whether this would still be the life of human beings, and this is a form of the question whether there is such a thing as a human nature or not. The idea that there is a human nature tends to make people angry for some reason – no doubt because they always suspect that the specification of what it is will come in some extremely brisk form and then a straitjacket will be put on human life. But my purpose in asking this question is quite contrary to that, and therefore it's perhaps better to put the question in the form: what range of possibilities of human life are there? They may be indefinitely wide but they cannot be infinitely wide, because we can identify human beings as distinct from other beings, and we can say quite a lot about what distinguishes them from other beings. Now what distinguishes them needs to be considered in trying to decide what kind of life it is appropriate for them to have. And I am raising the question to Dr Harris and others as to whether they are satisfied that if the rigorous commitment they want to impose on us were carried out, if we even had conditions in which it would be thinkable to carry it out, what would remain would be a human life.

Dr Harris. I don't know whether I can say whether it would be a life appropriate to human beings, but it seems to me plain that the life of most of the human beings suffering in the Third World now is not a life appropriate to human beings; we have to set against a hypothetical problem as to whether or not we would still be happy with ourselves as human beings under much more greatly constrained circumstances, the real and present existence of lives which are palpably not fit for human beings.

Mr Bambrough. Well, I agree that by producing evidence concerning particular people and their situation, it is possible to justify on particular occasions particular actions. But I wasn't raising the question about whether we would be happy in such a kind of life; it's possible that the creatures we would then be would be extremely contented. I'm raising the question whether they would be living a life that could continue to be called a human life.

Mrs Mary Midgley. I like what Mr Bambrough has said very much. But it's a bit odd, isn't it, that we're confronted with three people on the platform, all of whom are worried lest people comply *too much* with the demand to assist others! Of course, it's correct that if everyone complied with this extreme demand, we'd have a world which would not be very satisfactory. But as we have so much the opposite extreme, is it very surprising if this demand is put in just the way that moral demands are usually put to redress the balance? And can I just draw attention to the effect of similar extreme demands in producing reforms in the past that nowadays most of us would accept? When you talk about the robust zone of indifference, I think about the abolition of slavery. Here, of course, was a way of life that was normal to people, and included in the robust zone. The frontiers of the zone shift. Similarly ill-treatment of animals, similarly ill-treatment of women. These are normal things. If one is to shift the zone of the normal, it's almost inevitable, I think, that you'll find yourself shouting these generalisations which, as generalisations aren't really defensible, but are the only way of making the thing skid.

Professor Fishkin. The robust zone of indifference is a limit on how much can be demanded of us. If our lives were taken up totally with the fulfilment of obligations, then we should be saints or heroes, and that cannot be required of us. On the other hand, when you've got concrete injustices like slavery, or discrimination against women, or whatever, there's certainly a demand on each of us to do something, and perhaps collectively we can do a great deal more.

Professor Brian Barry, California Institute of Technology. What counts as heroic depends entirely on the existing power relationships. Giving half your income to people in other countries may seem pretty heroic; well, maybe if it was left to people voluntarily to give half their income to the Government this would seem pretty heroic too, but we all do that. This is not regarded as heroic at all because the taxman is there to collect it. Suppose other countries had the power to collect some of our resources, would you have any better claim against their doing so than you do against the Government collecting some of your income? In other words, this talk of heroism can't establish any fundamental moral principles, because what's heroic moves around in relation to what's enforceable.

The ethics of
international intervention[*]

JEFF McMAHAN
St John's College, Cambridge

In recent years the American government has persistently accused Nicaragua of unwarranted intervention in El Salvador, on the ground that Nicaragua has been supporting insurgents fighting against the Salvadorean government. Yet the US has itself been providing extensive support for guerrillas fighting against the government of Nicaragua. American officials have also complained of Cuban and Soviet intervention on behalf of the government of Nicaragua; yet in every respect in which Cuba and the Soviet Union are supposed to have intervened on behalf of the Nicaraguan government, the US has also intervened, and usually to a greater extent, on behalf of the Salvadorean government. Thus the American charges against Nicaragua, Cuba, and the Soviet Union have been echoed by Nicaraguan charges against the US. And, at the formal level, the charges on each side are identical. Relatively few people believe that none of these interventions is justifiable, and even fewer believe that all of them are. But can one consistently support intervention by one side while objecting to intervention by the other?

Cases such as the American interventions in El Salvador and Nicaragua, and the alleged Nicaraguan intervention in El Salvador, raise fundamental questions about the ethics of international intervention. What counts as intervention? What are the grounds for the common presumption that intervention is always unjustified? Can intervention ever be justified, and if so how and under what conditions? Can one give a plausible account of the ethics of intervention that is politically neutral? These are some of the questions which this paper will address.

Let us begin with the preliminary question of definition. Most accounts agree that intervention involves coercive external interference in the affairs of a population that is organised in the form of a state. Beyond this agreed core, however, there is much dispute concerning the nature of the restrictions which would be imposed in order to narrow the scope of the definition. For there seems to be an assumption, which is seldom explicitly stated, that a broad definition must be unsatisfactory.

[*] I have benefited in writing this paper from discussions with Noam Chomsky and Raymond Geuss, and from comments by Virginia Held.

In most cases this assumption seems to be motivated by a desire to uphold the view that intervention is never morally justified. As we shall see, this view will seem most plausible if one's definition of intervention is highly restrictive. But, in this case as in others, it seems a mistake to tailor our definition of an essentially non-normative concept to fit our moral views.[1] This being the case, there seems to be no obvious objection to allowing the core definition to stand unaltered.

Certainly the various restrictions which have been imposed on the core definition seem not only incompatible with ordinary use but also entirely arbitrary. It is sometimes suggested, for example, that intervention, properly understood, must involve the use of military force. This suggestion would, however, exclude as instances of intervention a great many acts of coercive interference which would ordinarily be identified as intervention – in particular those instances of interference based on the *threatened* uses of force, such as the Soviet Union's efforts to intimidate the Polish government and people in the early 1980s, and the American government's recent use of military exercises in Central America and the Caribbean to intimidate left-wing elements in those areas. For this reason most writers have accepted an expanded definition which allows threatened use of force to count as instances of intervention.[2] But even this leaves us with a definition which is far too narrow, since it excludes other modes of coercion which are commonly recognised as interventionary: for instance, economic pressure such as the US applied to Chile under Allende, and which it is now applying to Nicaragua, and acts of subversion, such as covert interference with elections, the bribing of officials, and the manipulation of the mass media (all of which formed part of the American intervention in Chile which was instrumental in bringing about the overthrow of the Allende government). It would seem reasonable, therefore, in formulating our definition of intervention, to impose no restrictions on the mode of coercion. Among other things, this allows us to consider arms sales and military assistance, as well as financial and other forms of support for military or police operations, as forms of intervention when such aid can be expected to be used for coercive purposes, either by the government against domestic rebels, or by rebels against the government, within the beneficiary's own state.

Many proposed definitions of intervention have stipulated either that the coercive agent must be a state, or that the target of coercion must be a state. Some definitions have insisted on both stipulations.[3] But both are again entirely arbitrary. For what reason is there to exclude, as possible agents of intervention such 'non-state actors' as multinational corporations, military or political organisations of national groups not represented by a state (the PLO, for example), terrorist organisations, regional organisations, international organisations such as the UN, and so on? United Fruit Company played a key role in engineering the overthrow of the Arbenz government in Guatemala, while the American government liked to pretend that the principal agent of intervention during the 'rescue mission' in Grenada in October 1983 was the Organisation of Eastern Caribbean States (OECS). It is hard to think of two more paradigmatic instances of intervention than these.

The requirement that the target or victim of intervention must also be a state is equally without justification. In order to explain why, it will be helpful first to clarify what is meant here by the term 'state'. There is a sense in which states are trans-historical entities, in that they can survive and retain their identities over time through changes of government, population, and borders, and even through changes of institutional and constitutional structures. In this sense the United States now is the same as the United States in 1800. In general when I use the term, however, I shall not be referring to states so conceived. For there is another sense of the term that is more relevant to the question of intervention, according to which a state consists of the union at a particular time of a population and a government, together with a formal or informal political constitution that shapes and determines the structure of the government and its relations with the people. Thus a single state in the first, historical sense can encompass a number of different states in this second sense. For example, while the state of Nicaragua was in the broad sense continuous through the 1970s and early 1980s, there is another sense in which one Nicaraguan state was destroyed and supplanted by another in 1979. It is with states in this second, narrower sense, that I shall be primarily concerned. Understood in this way, the state becomes closely identified with the government, the administrative structures, and with what might be called the state apparatus (that is, the military, the police, etc.). Thus, when a state is internally divided, we tend, without denying that the opposition is in some sense included within the state, to identify the state with the government and its organs and supporters rather than with those fighting against the government. Intervention against the state therefore means intervention against the government, while intervention on behalf of the state means intervention on behalf of the government and against its domestic opponents. (The term 'state' certainly attaches to and follows the government in this way in UN parlance.)

With that much said by way of clarification, we can now explain why the claim that the requirement that the target of intervention must be a state is arbitrary. It is arbitrary because it excludes the possibility of intervention *on behalf of* the state against the state's internal opposition. This requirement would therefore exclude numerous undeniable instances of intervention, including the American intervention in South Vietnam (at least in its initial stages) and the present American intervention in El Salvador (though in each case the US has claimed, falsely, to be defending the state against external aggression).

There are three further commonly proposed restrictions which should be mentioned. Whereas the restrictions we have previously considered have been on either the mode of coercion or the types of agents involved, these final three restrictions limit the aims which a course of action can have in order to qualify as an instance of intervention. The first restriction is that intervention must be directed at the structure of political authority in the target society.[4] There is, however, no reason why an intervening agent's concern should be limited in this way: an intervening agent could just as reasonably be concerned with, for example, the mode of economic organisation in some other country (though of course it would normally be difficult to affect the mode of economic organisation without at the same time affecting the structure of political authority), or even some specific government policy (for example, a policy of torturing political dissidents). The second restriction on an intervener's aims qualifies the first by insisting that the aim should be to *change* the structure of political authority in the target society.[5] This is obviously unacceptable, for, in addition to focussing exclusively on political structures, this restriction excludes an aim which, historically, has been an important motive for intervention: namely, to preserve the structure of political authority (or indeed the mode of economic organisation) from the threat of endogenous change. A third, more generous restriction insists only that intervention must involve interference with the internal affairs of another country. But, in so far as this is not just a restatement of the requirement that the victims of coercion must be members of the state in which the intervention occurs, this final restriction is also arbitrary. For an intervening agent might wish to influence, not the target state's internal affairs, but instead its foreign policy, perhaps in particular the target country's policy towards the intervening agent itself.

Since all of the proposed amendments or qualifications to the core definition seem arbitrary and unduly restrictive, it would appear that this definition should stand unaltered. Intervention, then, is simply coercive external interference in the affairs of a population organised in the form of a state. It will, however, be important to bear in mind as we turn now to the substantive part of our inquiry that this definition is broader than many which have appeared in the literature (though it is narrower than some[6]). Because some of the arguments which have been put forward for or against intervention have presupposed a narrower concept of intervention, they are sometimes inapplicable to various forms of intervention included within the scope of our broader definition. Thus, for example, some of the arguments which conclude that intervention is impermissible are really concerned only with intervention *against* the state, and have nothing to say about the permissibility of intervention on behalf of the state. This reflects the widely accepted view (widely accepted at least at the verbal level) that, while intervention against the state is impermissible, intervention on behalf of the state is perfectly acceptable.

This view is now enshrined in international law. The blanket prohibition on intervention against the state is emphatically stated in the Declaration on Principles of International Law concerning Friendly Relations and Co-operation among States in Accordance with the Charter of the United Nations, which was adopted by the UN General Assembly in 1970:

> No State or group of States has the right to intervene, directly or indirectly, for any reason whatever, in the internal or external affairs of any other State. Consequently, armed intervention and all other forms of interference or attempted threats against the personality of the State or against its political, economic and cultural elements, are in violation of international law.[7]

On the other hand, intervention *on behalf of* the state in order to assist it in combating domestic opponents is held by international law to be permissible – as long, that is, as the rebels or insurgents are not sufficiently strong, or in control of sufficient territory, that the conflict must be considered a civil war (in which case the opposition acquires the rights of a belligerent, and intervention on behalf of the government also becomes impermissible).[8]

The position of international law is among the most stringently anti-interventionist of the major current views on the ethics of international intervention.[9] What is the moral foundation of this view? Its defenders commonly appeal to an argument known in the literature as the anti-paternalist argument. This argument draws on an analogy between persons and states. Just as persons are autonomous agents, and are entitled to determine their own action free from interference as long as the exercise of their autonomy does not involve the transgression of certain moral constraints, so, it is claimed, states are also autonomous agents, whose autonomy is similarly deserving of respect. The implied right of states to freedom from coercion by other states (or by other external agents) is articulated in the doctrine of state sovereignty. According to that doctrine, the state alone has rightful jurisdiction over the conduct of its own affairs, and may not be subject to external coercion as long as it avoids violating the rights and prerogatives of other states. In particular, respect for autonomy implies that states, like persons, may not be coerced in an effort to do them good. Thus all forms of intervention against the state, even what is known as humanitarian intervention, or other forms of intervention deemed to be in the interests of the state itself, are ruled out.[10]

This argument has plausible implications in a great many cases. For example, it rightly condemns the attempt to impose democratic institutions on another country, for this is an objectionable form of paternalism which (paradoxical as it may seem) violates the self-determination of the people. The problem with the argument, however, is that it is not concerned with the autonomy or self-determination of *people*. Its emphasis is instead on the autonomy of the *state*. The argument does not, moreover, require that the autonomy of the state should be in any way derivative from or connected with the autonomy of the people, nor that respect for state autonomy should entail respect for the autonomy or self-determination of the people. Rather, the state's claim to sovereignty is based entirely on the analogy between persons and states. How valid, then, is the analogy?

The analogy between persons and states holds in several important respects. States can be agents, and can have ends. Like persons, they can also have interests. And, just as persons can harm themselves, so states can harm themselves. Just as persons can harm or be harmed by other persons, so states can harm or be harmed by other states. But, unlike most persons, states are not always or even usually integrated agents with unified wills. They can be and often are divided, with the government engaged in the repression of the citizens, and the citizens in revolt against the government. There is no serious analogy to the divided state in the case of an individual person. In this resect, then, the analogy between persons and states breaks down.

When a state turns upon its own citizens, or some group of its citizens, intervention on behalf of the victims is not paternalism. This is especially clear in the case of requested intervention. The intervening agent is not pretending to be acting in the interests of the *state;* rather, the agent is acting to protect the interests of the state's victims. (Of course, intervention on behalf of the victims of state violence or repression may ultimately be in the best interests of the state as a whole, just as preventing a potential murderer from killing his intended victim may be in his own best interests.¹¹ But, as the latter example shows, not all instances of coercion which benefit the person coerced are paternalistic.) In the case in which a government turns upon its own citizens, as in all cases in which one person or group of persons causes unjustifiable harm to others, or violates their rights, the government forfeits its claim to non-interference based on respect for autonomy. Neither personal nor state autonomy entails a right to disregard the rights or interests of others. Indeed, in cases in which the state authority abuses its autonomy by acting against its citizens, respect for autonomy may itself dictate intervention, for it is then the autonomy of the citizens rather than that of the state which may require defence.

One might attempt to rescue the anti-paternalist argument by construing the case in which the state authority acts against its own citizens as simply a case of the state harming itself. After all, it might be argued, the state is a compound of both the government *and* the citizens. On this view, intervention to protect the citizens from the government, even by request, would count as paternalistic intervention. This argument, however, presupposes a view of the essential unity of the state, similar to that held by Hegel, according to which citizens lose their moral claims as individuals and simply disappear into the state – a view which is implausible at both the metaphysical and the moral levels.

This conception of the state contrasts with the more plausible view that states are mere constructions or artefacts which derive whatever moral status they have from their relations to the individuals of which they are composed. According to this latter view, if the state is to enjoy the rights of sovereignty, those rights must be granted to it by the people it represents.

This latter conception of the state underlies a further, though closely related argument for non-intervention against the state which appeals directly to the value of human autonomy (rather than treating states as ends in themselves and basing the prohibition on intervention on an ideal of respect for states *per se,* as the anti-paternalist argument does). This argument begins with the claim that it is valuable for each distinct human community to be autonomous and self-determining (or, as some would perfer to say, that each human community has a right to autonomy or self-determination). Communities organised in the form of states are no exception. Indeed they are the paradigm case, for the citizens of a particular state normally share common interests and aims, and are bound together by shared social, political, and cultural affinities and traditions; and, the more integrated and distinctive a community is, the worse it is that its affairs should be directed from the outside, by persons who neither fully share nor fully understand the values, aspirations, and traditions that bind the community together. Intervention against the state may therefore be presumed to involve an offence against the autonomy of the political community, and to deprive the community, at least in certain respects, of its self-determining character. Correspondingly, the doctrine of state sovereignty, which implies a strong principle of non-intervention against the state, is justified on the ground that the inviolability of the state serves to protect the autonomy of the political community.[12]

This argument, which I shall refer to as the 'communal autonomy argument', raises two groups of questions – the first about the meaning and value of self-determination, and the second about the relation between communal autonomy and state sovereignty. Let us begin with the first set of questions.

First, what exactly is communal self-determination? Like intervention, the notion of self-determination has been variously defined. Perhaps the most common understanding is that a community is self-determining when it has established a state, so that a community's right to self-determination is simply its right to the establishment or maintenance of an independent state.[13] This is a perfectly acceptable use of the term, but it will not do for our purposes. Apart from the fact that groups too small to be eligible for statehood can nevertheless be said to be self-determining in the sense intended in the communal autonomy argument, the idea that self-determination involves statehood is incompatible with the argument's assumption that intervention can interfere with or undermine the self-determination of a political community without actually depriving the community of independent statehood.

Nor is it satisfactory, though some writers have thought that it is, to equate self-determination with self-government, or democracy. While it might be argued that self-government is a sufficient condition of self-determination, it is clearly not a necessary one. For the individuals of a community might be indifferent or even hostile to the idea of democratic self-government, while at the same time being evidently in command of their own collective destiny. This might be the case, for example, in the aftermath of a protracted and destructive popular revolution, when what the people want would not be the formation of political parties and the initiation of election campaigns, but a powerful central authority capable of acting immediately to restore order and economic stability, provide food and employment, organise relief work, and so on.

Communal self-determination has more to do with freedom from external coercion or domination than with the flourishing of democratic institutions; though, contrary to what some writers have claimed, a community cannot be said to be self-determining if its affairs are directed entirely by a domestic tyranny whose decisions take no account of the desires or interests of the larger community.[14] For a community to be self-determining, the people must at some level be responsible for the conduct and direction of their own collective affairs, and the shaping of their collective future; there must be a sense in which decisions concerning the community's affairs are subject to the approval or, in some weak sense of the term, the consent of the community. That is vague, but it is perhaps as much as can be said; for self-determination is not a precisely determinate phenomenon which must be recognisably either present or absent. It is, rather, a matter of degree, and in some cases the question whether a community is self-determining may not be answerable in the terms of a simple 'yes' or 'no'. For this and other reasons, it is not always clear what respect for communal self-determination requires – a problem with important implications, to which we shall return.

Next we must ask why communal self-determination should be thought to be valuable. The short answer is simply that groups of people with a sense of collective identity do actually assign great value to the ability to act and function autonomously. Of course, while most moral theories (the most obvious example being preference utilitarianism) would allow that the fact that communal self-determination is valued provides a moral reason (though not, of course, a decisive one) for respecting it, it is nevertheless true that the mere fact that something is valued is not a sufficient condition of its being valuable. In the present case, however, there is more to be said than simply that self-determination is valued. For political (and other) communities rightly fear that surrendering control of important aspects of their collective lives to outsiders, even ones who are benevolently motivated, would mean that the community's affairs would then be determined by persons with less than complete understanding of and sympathy for the community's values, aims, and traditions, and thus that the community's interests would be likely to suffer.

But the worry about the efficiency or impartiality of outsiders is not all that lies behind the resistance of communities to external control. Just as individuals are loath to relinquish control over decisions of major importance to their lives even if they would fare better by doing so, so individuals in groups feel a fundamental need for the group itself to exercise control over its own destiny, even perhaps if this is riskier than submitting to external direction. In part this can be explained in terms of the fact that people desire that the conduct and development of their community should be an authentic expression of the community's identity and the values that inform it. But the deep-seated desire of persons, both individually and as members of communities, to control their own affairs is itself a fact of fundamental importance, which must be reflected in our morality.

As we noted earlier, the communal autonomy argument raises important questions about the relation between communal autonomy or self-determination and state sovereignty. We can introduce these questions by first noting that there is a problem of determining which groups or types of groups are the ones whose self-determination international actors are required to respect. As it is normally stated, of course, the communal autonomy argument assumes that there is no problem here, for it assumes that states encompass or constitute single political communities, and thus that the boundaries around the relevant groups are already drawn, and, figuratively speaking, coincide with the boundaries of states. But, as our earlier discussion of divided states shows, this assumption is often false. A state may be divided in various ways, with some or all of the political communities within the boundaries of the state being unrepresented by the state and failing to identify themselves with it. In cases in which the state is not representative of *any* major community, it is itself an obstacle to communal self-determination, Hence intervention against the state may not be inimical to communal self-determination, but may on the contrary promote it. And, in cases in which there are two or more political communities, some but not all of which are represented by the state, it may be radically unclear what respect for self-determination requires. For the efforts at self-determination by different communities may be incompatible, and bring the communities into conflict. Intervention against the state may therefore inhibit or be detrimental to the self-determination of the community or communities represented by the state, while promoting the self-determination of the rival community or communities. By the same token, non-intervention (or, alternatively, intervention on behalf of the state), may respect the self-determination of the community or communities represented by the state, but may be inimical to the self-determination of the community or communities which reject the state's authority.

Because there are cases – cases, for example, of colonial rule, revolution, and secession – in which respect for state sovereignty does not necessarily coincide with respect for communal self-determination, the principle of non-intervention implied by the communal autonomy argument will be more limited in scope than that derived from the anti-paternalist argument. To see just how strong a principle of non-intervention the argument is capable of yielding, we need to examine more closely the relation between state sovereignty and communal self-determination.

It is often claimed that the rights of state sovereignty, including the right of non-intervention, are a corollary of the state's *legitimacy* – that is, its right to rule, and to be obeyed – and hence that only legitimate states have a right against intervention.[15] The ground for this assertion is normally that states can have rights only in so far as those rights are voluntarily transferred to them by the people. Hence the state can have the right to govern only if it is granted that right by the consent of the people. If the state is granted the right to govern, then it follows that it also has a right of non-intervention. For the state's right to govern implies a duty on the part of others not to interfere coercively with its exercise of that right. The right against intervention is thus a corollary of the state's domestic legitimacy.

This is a 'rational reconstruction' of an argument that is not uncommon in the literature on intervention. If valid, it shows that the domestic legitimacy of a state is a sufficient condition of the state's having a right of non-intervention. This conclusion suggests further that domestic legitimacy is also a *necessary* condition of the right of non-intervention, for the right of non-intervention, as possessed by states, would seem to be *nothing more than* a corollary of the right to govern. If a state lacked domestic legitimacy – that is, if it had no right to govern – what reason could there be to protect *it* (as distinct from the people) from external coercion?

The problem with this argument is that, in terms of the criterion it proposes, there are no legitimate states, and hence no states which possess the rights of sovereignty. For there are no states which enjoy the consent of their citizens, if consent is understood as the intentional and voluntary transfer of rights, and the acceptance of corresponding obligations.[16] One can, however, derive substantially the same conclusion (viz, that only legitimate states have a right of non-intervention) by first appealing to the claim of the communal autonomy argument that the right of non-intervention is justified in terms of the protection of communal self-determination, and by then showing that the same facts which would show a state is both a vehicle for and an expression of communal self-determination would also show that the state is legitimate. Of course, our criteria of legitimacy must be weaker than those proposed by the consent theorist. Without going too deeply into the matter at this point, we can say that a state enjoys domestic legitimacy if, first, it is representative of the political community or communities within its territorial boundaries, in the sense that it works for and on behalf of those communities; and, second, if it operates with the general approval and acceptance of those communities.[17] It seems clear that any state which is legitimate by these criteria will also be an instrument of communal self-determination, while any state which is illegitimate by these criteria will not. And thus, if the importance of positing a right of non-intervention is to protect communal self-determination, then the only states which will possess the right will be ones which are instruments or expressions of communal self-determination – that is, ones which are legitimate.

With this as background, we are now in a position to present a more exact restatement of the communal autonomy argument. As before, the argument begins with the claim that it is valuable for political communities to be autonomous and self-determining. Next we note, not that states *do,* but that they *can* serve as vehicles or expressions of communal self-determination. They do so when they are representative, impartially working for and serving the interests of their citizens, and when they enjoy the citizens' acceptance and approval – in short, when they are legitimate. Since a legitimate state is thus one which in general protects, promotes, and expresses communal self-determination, intervention against it will normally be detrimental to the community's efforts at self-determination. Respect for communal self-determination therefore requires that there should be a strong presumption against the justifiability of intervention against states which enjoy domestic legitimacy.

As we noted earlier, the conclusion of this version of the communal autonomy argument is considerably weaker and more limited than that of the anti-paternalist argument. While it implies that there is a presumption, based on respect for self-determination, against intervening in the affairs of states which are legitimate, it also implies that there is no such presumption (that is, one based on respect for self-determination) in the case of states which are illegitimate. Hence in order to be able to apply the argument to actual cases, we must be able to distinguish in practice between legitimate and illegitimate states. How can we test for legitimacy?

Before addressing the question, let me be a bit more explicit about what I mean when I speak of a state as 'illegitimate'. Recall that I am using the word 'state' in such a way that the state is closely identified with the government and the particular political and constitutional structures that give it its shape and determine its relations with the citizens. I distinguished this sense of the term from a broader sense in which the state is to a certain extent distinct even from particular institutional and constitutional structures. Thus, when I speak of a state being illegitimate, I do not mean to imply that the state in this broader sense is illegitimate, and in particular I do not mean to imply that there should be no state at all, or that the people have no right to independent statehood. Rather, I mean only that the particular governmental, institutional, and constitutional structures of the state (in the broader sense) are illegitimate, and hence that the state in the narrower sense – that is, the government, its organs, and the constitution in terms of which it operates – lacks the domestic and international rights and privileges which it claims for itself *qua* state.

Let us return now to the question of how legitimacy is to be determined. Various tests have been suggested. Michael Walzer, in his influential book *Just and Unjust Wars,* has proposed two. His first suggestion consists in the familiar claim that legitimacy depends on consent, though the type of "consent" he has in mind is "of a special sort". For Walzer, the "contract" through which consent is expressed "is a metaphor for a process of association and mutuality", of "shared experiences and cooperative activity of many different kinds", through which a community "shape[s] a common life".[18]

The problem with this suggestion, however, is that it describes certain relations among people, but tells us nothing of their relation to the government; hence it does not describe anything that could reasonably be construed as consenting to the state.[19] If consent, even of a special sort, is what confers legitimacy on the state, then the relations among people which Walzer describes cannot be the basis of state legitimacy. Indeed, it is not difficult to imagine a country in which people share the relations Walzer describes, but in which the state is clearly illegitimate. Nicaragua in the years preceding the overthrow of the Somoza dictatorship was presumably such a country.

Walzer's second proposal is that the criterion of legitimacy is "popular support". While this seems plausible (being roughly equivalent to the criterion suggested earlier in this paper), it does not provide the sort of simplified test we need in order to deal with problem cases. Thus Walzer is led to ask, "What is the test of popular support in a country where democracy is unknown and elections are routinely managed?" His answer is that "the test, for government as for insurgents, is self-help". Hence "a legitimate government is one that can fight its own internal wars".[20] (Governmental legitimacy is not always a sufficient condition of state legitimacy, but we may ignore the exceptions here.)

In putting forward this last claim, Walzer has, in effect, replaced popular support as the criterion of legitimacy with an extremely fallible and unreliable *indicator* of popular support. In other words, one form of evidence which would help to establish whether the original criterion was or was not satisfied has taken over as the criterion itself. Of course, if "self-help" really provided a reliable indication of popular support, then its use as the functional criterion for legitimacy would be acceptable. But self-help at best provides a reliable indication of the state's military strength, which, for obvious reasons, is not necessarily correlated with popular support. For a government can over time build up a formidable military machine without the support or approval of the mass of its citizens. It can do so through the assistance of foreign governments. The fact that the government's military strength would not be of its own creation would not, however, compromise its status as a government capable of *self*-help. If the capacity for self-help meant the capacity to maintain power against domestic opponents without external assistance, where external assistance includes weapons and training acquired at some time or other without payment or on specially favourable terms from external sources, then there would be very few governments capable of self-help. (In cases in which arms sales and military assistance constitute a form of intervention – that is, when they are intended to enable a government to defeat its internal opponents – then they compromise the recipient's status as a government capable of self-help. But military sales and assistance are not always interventionary. More often they are used as bribes, payments, or simply as a means of cultivating influence.)

Walzer rejects this objection. He contends that "armies and police forces are social institutions; soldiers and policemen come from families, villages, neighbourhoods, classes. They will not fight cohesively, with discipline, or at length unless the regime for which they are fighting has some degree of social support." Hence, he concludes, even if its military hardware has come from external sources, a government which passes the self-help test will be shown thereby to enjoy popular support.[21]

This reply is inadequate. States which lack legitimacy are often characterised by the fact that the government, the military, and the police are controlled by a wealthy élite, whose interests they serve, while the mass of the population lives in terrible poverty. In these conditions, when people are desperate for employment and the military can offer stable jobs with comfortable wages, it is not difficult for the oligarchs to put together a viable 'security' apparatus. This is the case, for example, in El Salvador today, where the rank and file of the army consist primarily of illiterate and demoralised teenage peasants who have joined the army in order to escape starvation.

Hiring some of the victims of state oppression to fight the others is only one way in which illegitimate governments can maintain themselves in power without external assistance. Some are able to survive even without the direct assistance of their victims. Consider the case of South Africa. There the white minority is sufficiently large, disciplined, and cohesive, as well as sufficiently wealthy and technologically advanced, to be able to maintain its patently illegitmate rule over the black majority without substantial external support of any kind. South Africa, indeed, is a clear case of an illegitimate state whose government is perfectly capable of fighting its own internal wars.

Both Walzer's proposals are, therefore, fundamentally flawed. A seemingly more plausible proposal has been put forward by Alan Goldman. Goldman's argument runs in the reverse direction from the standard arguments in this area. He begins with the assumption that only a state which is legitimate can claim moral immunity from intervention. Next he considers the question: 'What entitles a state to claim moral immunity from intervention?' The answer to this question then furnishes the criterion of legitimacy. His argument may be reconstructed as follows.

Goldman's answer to the question 'When is a state entitled to freedom from intervention?' is based on an appeal to the analogy between persons and states. According to Goldman, paternalistic intervention in the affairs of an individual is ordinarily objectionable because, by overriding the individual's own values and imposing on him the values of the intervening agent, it fails to respect him as an autonomous source of ends and values. Thus paternalistic intervention in an individual's affairs may be justified only if the intervention seeks to advance the individual's own values, rather than those of the intervening agent. Goldman argues that this view is supported by both moral relativism and subjectivism. Subjectivism holds that a person's reasons for action must derive from his own "subjective values, interests, or desires", while relativism claims "that there exists no value-neutral. . . way to prefer one self-consistent value system to another with which it is incompatible". Because, therefore, these theories "view the individual as creator of his own values, they do support a positive valuation of individual freedom and autonomy and of the toleration that allows them to flourish".[22] (There are problems with this view. To mention only one, it is not clear how one could, on this view, justify discriminating between paternalistic intervention and non-paternalistic *moral* intervention in cases in which each would involve overriding an individual's own values. But we need not pursue this problem here.)

Arguing by analogy with this view of intervention at the individual level, Goldman claims that intervention in the affairs of a nation-state can be justified only if it seeks to advance values accepted by the nation state itself. It is a necessary (though not sufficient) condition of intervention being justified that the nation-state which is the target of the intervention should be failing, not in terms of some external standard, but in terms of its own standards and values. Thus, according to Goldman, a nation-state which is "just in its own eyes" has "a right to territorial integrity or self-determination" – that is, a right against intervention. Correspondingly, a state which does not pass this test has no such right. Finally, since all and only those states which are legitimate can have a right against intervention, it follows that the criterion of legitimacy is that a state should be "just in its own eyes".[23] Another way of putting this point would be to say that a state is legitimate if and only if its citizens believe it to be legitimate.

This proposal faces several objections. One is that the citizens' belief in the legitimacy or illegitimacy of their state may be based on false beliefs about the nature of the state, perhaps acquired through indoctrination. But a more fundamental objection is that Goldman's proposal is no more specific, and therefore no more helpful at the practical level, than Walzer's claim that a state is legitimate if it has popular support. How can one determine when a state is held by its citizens to be legitimate? Goldman proposes something approaching a requirement of unanimity. He contends that "the state must pass this test of legitimacy [being "just in its own eyes"] not only in the eyes of its supporters, even if they are a large majority, but from the point of view of its victims".[24]

The obvious objection to this proposal is that, if, as the thrust of Goldman's approach suggests, the "victims" of a state are simply those who identify themselves as such, then there will be no states which are legitimate, and hence no states which have a right against intervention. For all states are to some extent divided, and contain minorities hostile to the state structure. Goldman recognises that there is a problem here, but suggests that it is only that the proposal is liable to yield too permissive a principle of non-intervention. Thus he assumes that the problem can be surmounted by showing that there are further constraints on intervention which would prevent the practice from becoming too common – for example, potential intervening agents must share the perception of injustice of the dissidents within the target state, and the probable costs of the intervention must be proportionate to the probable benefits.

This response may, though I doubt it, be adequate if we assume that the problem is only that the proposal might generate too permissive a principle of non-intervention. But this is not the case. It is a sufficient reason for doubting the proposal's plausibility that it condemns virtually every state in existence as illegitimate. Moreover, the implications of this fact may not be as Goldman supposes. For, if all states are illegitimate, then instances of justified intervention may be difficult to find. It would be odd to suppose that one illegitimate state could have a right to inter-vene in the affairs of another, citing the latter's illegitimacy by way of justification.

While it is not implausible to suppose that the legitimacy of a state is a function of its representativeness, or of the fact that it enjoys popular support, or the consent or approval of the citizens, the latter concepts are such that they do not always have a determinate application. There are clear cases of states which do enjoy popular support and which are clearly legitimate (Sweden), and clear cases of states which do not have popular support and which are clearly illegitimate (Nicaragua under Somoza); but there are also cases of states which are sufficiently divided that it cannot be said either that they enjoy popular support or that they lack it. If popular support (or consent, or whatever) is the criterion of legitimacy, then the question whether the states in this category are legitimate may not have a 'yes' or 'no' answer. We will consider the impli-cations of these facts for the question of intervention nearer the end of the paper.

First we must complete our review of the arguments against interven-tion, beginning with two arguments intended to show that, even in the case of divided states, a strong principle of non-intervention can be sup-ported by appealing to the value of self-determination. In effect, these arguments attempt to buttress the communal autonomy argument in cases in which that argument appears to fail.

The first of these arguments was put forward by John Stuart Mill, and has been developed and defended more recently by Michael Walzer.[25] According to this argument, the requirement of respect for self-determination rules out intervention against the state even if the state is illegitimate, and even if the aim of the intervention would be to promote the self-determination of the state's internal opponents. Mill supports this paradoxical claim by arguing that "it is during an arduous struggle to become free by their own efforts" that people have the best chance of becoming genuinely free and self-determining: "the liberty which is bestowed on them by other hands than their own will have nothing real, nothing permanent".[26] Because intervention, even on behalf of those struggling against an illegitimate state, thus denies people the opportunity to exercise and develop their own capacities, it is ultimately inimical to the development and flourishing of self-determination.

There is certainly something to this argument, but, as Walzer's critics have suggested, it may set the value of self-determination too high relative to other values.[27] For the benefit which people might be deprived of by intervention – namely, the benefit of developing a more robust capacity for self-determination – must be weighed against the harms which they might be spared by intervention. For example, intervention could make the difference between a quick and relatively bloodless campaign against an illegitimate state authority and a protracted struggle involving an enormous number of casualties not only among the combatants on both sides, but also among the civilian population; and it is far from obvious that the loss of these lives is an acceptable price to pay for the enhanced capacity for self-determination that the survivors would enjoy.

It is the internal opponents of the illegitimate state whose capacity for self-determination would supposedly be impaired by the receipt of external assistance in their struggle. It is also they who would suffer more at the hands of the state in the absence of intervention. Why, then, should not *they* be allowed to choose whether to accept or reject external assistance? To refuse them this choice is to fail to respect their autonomy. It is, indeed, an objectionable form of paternalism to refuse people one's assistance, not on the ground that helping them would itself be paternalistic, but on the ground that facing adversity by themselves will be good for them. This insistence on what Walzer calls a "stern doctrine of self-help" is seldom the right position to take towards individuals who are in trouble; it is even less likely to be appropriate when a nation-state comes under *external* attack;[28] and few (not even Walzer) seem to think it an appropriate position to adopt towards governments facing domestic rebellion. If the reason for denying external assistance to the domestic opponents of a doubtfully legitimate or even obviously illegitimate state is that to do so might impair their capacity for self-determination, then the same reasoning should apply in the three other types of case just cited. The fact that this reasoning is seldom decisive in these other types of case suggests that it cannot be very powerful in the present case either.

The second argument designed to butress the communal autonomy argument has also been put forward by Walzer. Walzer distinguishes between the domestic and the international legitimacy of a state, and claims that, at the international level, a state is always presumptively ·legitimate. The reason for drawing this distinction is essentially epistemological. For, according to Walzer, people are always sufficiently distanced from a state which is not their own that they cannot know all that they would need to know in order to make a reliable assessment of its legitimacy.

They don't [he writes] know enough about its history, and they have no
direct experience, and can form no concrete judgements, of the conflicts
and harmonies, the historical choices and cultural affinities, the loyalties
and resentments that underlie it. Hence their conduct, in the first instance
at least, cannot be determined by either knowledge or judgement. It is, or
it ought to be, determined instead by a morally necessary presumption:
that there exists a certain 'fit' between the community and its government
and that the state is 'legitimate'.[29]

Like Mill's argument, this argument overstates a valid point. In so far
as Walzer's point can be interpreted as a counsel of caution, based on the
recognition of the fallibility of an external observer's judgement, then it
is valid. Some presumption against intervention remains even in the case
of doubtfully legitimate states, or even states which seem to outsiders to
be clearly illegitimate. (Since, as we saw earlier, even those immersed in
the culture and traditions of a particular state may be unable to determine whether or not the state is legitimate, a similar counsel of caution
could be usefully addressed to domestic insurgents as well.) But Walzer
intends for the argument to establish more than this. He sees it as a
decisive objection to all but a very limited number of types of intervention. It cannot, however, establish that much. *At best* the argument
shows that all states enjoy a presumptive legitimacy at the international
level, but presumptive legitimacy does not automatically translate into a
virtually non-overridable right of non-intervention. For, as we have
seen, even a state which is clearly legitimate may overstep its mandate,
in which case it may be permissible to bring some pressure to bear on it
in order to coerce it to honour its obligations.[30] Consider, for example, a
case in which a government which enjoys broad popular support
nevertheless persistently persecutes a particular minority group. Here
the imperative to defend this minority might override the moral reason
which foreigners would have to respect the autonomy of the larger community. Here, moreover, there would be no epistemological problems.
Even if they lacked familiarity with the history, traditions, and culture
of the society, foreigners would be unlikely to be so misled by the
society's alien character as to interpret as the systematic violation of a
minority's internationally recognised human rights what was in reality
some innocent and domestically acceptable practice.

Walzer's claims about the fallibility of external judgements are,
moreover, quite exaggerated. What reason is there for supposing that
foreigners are necessarily lacking in historical knowledge, or knowledge
about what is occurring within another country? There are many cases
in which external observers can know *more* about what is happening

within a country than its inhabitants, if the government is particularly efficient at controlling the information which reaches its citizens. There are other cases in which the illegitimacy of a state must be obvious to anyone: even foreigners are entitled to conclude that the near universal revolt of a population against its government and state institutions (as occurred in Nicaragua in 1979) is unlikely to be an alien society's unusual way of expressing consent.

The final argument against intervention which I shall consider applies primarily to intervention against states (as opposed to intervention on behalf of states), and applies almost exclusively to *military* intervention. This argument, which I shall call the 'stability argument', has been succinctly stated by Stanley Hoffman, who writes that even "a state based on morally wrong foundations nevertheless has not only legal rights but moral rights because. . . if its legal rights are not upheld, international society will collapse into a state of war or universal tyranny".[31] Implicit in this quotation there are, in fact, two distinct versions of the stability argument. One maintains that intervention is in general wrong because of its tendency to lead to counter-intervention, escalation, and wider war. The other maintains that it is wrong because it threatens the stability of the system of world order based on the existence of a plurality of sovereign states (and hence threatens to lead to "universal tyranny").

Let us consider the first version first. It is usually articulated by saying that, because a permissive principle of non-intervention would be a threat to peace and stability, a highly restricted principle must be adopted instead. This claim can be interpreted in either of two ways. According to one interpretation, the problem is that a permissible principle is more open to abuse, or more likely to be exploited as a cover for intervention motivated entirely by considerations of self-interest. There are two replies to this claim, so interpreted. One is that the fact that a principle is likely to be abused, and thus is likely to have bad consequences, is not an objection to the principle's *validity,* but only to its *adoption.* It is perfectly possible that the morally correct principle of non-intervention is one which, for consequentialist reasons, we ought not in practice to espouse and adopt. Here, however, our concern is to discover the correct principle or principles, and not (if there is a divergence) the principle or principles which it would be expedient to adopt.

The second reply is that states are unlikely to be significantly influenced by our adoption of one principle of non-intervention rather than another. It is implausible to suppose that our adoption of a permissive principle of intervention would tempt states to intervene when otherwise they would not, or that, if they were tempted to intervene by reasons of self-interest, they might be deterred by our adoption of a more restrictive principle. In short, this interpretation of the argument overestimates the extent to which states are influenced by considerations of principle.

The second interpretation is that any but the most restrictive principle of non-intervention will sanction interventions which carry too high a risk of escalation and war. There is, however, no reason why this should be thought to be true. For the principle can be suitably qualified to take account of the risk of escalation, and yet remain permissive in cases in which this risk is minimal, or in which it seems to be outweighed by other considerations. The suggested alternative – viz., a highly and indiscriminately restrictive principle of non-intervention – would itself serve to sanction the violence of the status quo, which might in many cases be greater than the probable violence resulting from intervention.

Let us now turn to the second version of the stability argument, according to which the practice of intervention threatens the stability of the system of world order based on the existence of separate and sovereign states, and, by doing so, calls "into question the dominant values of [international] society: the survival and independence of the separate political communities".[32] As this quotaton from Walzer suggests, the breakdown of the system of sovereign states is to be feared primarily because it would mean the end of political pluralism: "there will be no place left for political refuge and no examples left of political alternatives".[33]

It is not clear, however, why it should be thought that the practice of intervention will have these consequences. States have regularly intervened in one another's affairs since the doctrine of state sovereignty was first enunciated, yet the system of sovereign states has yet to show any signs of strain. Moreover, even if the practice of intervention were to threaten the system of sovereign states, the breakdown of that system would not necessarily lead to "universal tyranny" and the stifling of pluralism. The breakdown of the system could instead occur through a process whereby states would surrender sovereignty to a world government. And, just as the surrender of sovereignty by individuals to states need not involve the elimination of individuality or the variety of human types within political communities, so the surrender of sovereignty by states to an international authority should be compatible with the maintenance by distinct human communities of political independence and cultural diversity.

Were it to occur in this way, the breakdown of the system of sovereign states would in fact be highly desirable. For the doctrine of state sovereignty serves to sanction and reinforce notions of nationalism, state chauvinism, and the priority of the national interest, all of which, in an era in which states jealously guard their sovereign prerogatives by threatening 'aggressors' with nuclear annihilation, are not only barbarous but profoundly dangerous. If the acceptance of a more permissive principle of non-intervention would, by challenging the doctrine of state sovereignty, facilitate the erosion of support for that doctrine and for the cult of state-worship, then there would be an important consequentialist reason for adopting such a principle.

This completes my review of the major arguments against intervention. I shall now conclude by briefly outlining a proposed account of the ethics of intervention which draws on the results of the previous survey of the arguments.

This account begins by acknowledging the relevance of the question of state legitimacy, where legitimacy indicates that the state is both an instrument and an expression of the self-determination of the community or communities which the state encompasses. Thus the legitimacy of a state entails a presumption against intervention against it. This presumption is grounded on the requirement of respect for communal self-determination. In some cases the presumption is decisive. In general this will be the case where intervention would challenge or destroy those features of the state which contribute to its legitimacy. But, like all presumptions, this one can be overridden, and there are cases in which intervention against a legitimate state might be permissible. One such case might be that of a state which enjoyed popular support but whose foreign policy was extremely aggressive and threatening to other states. And we have already considered another such case – namely, that in which a state which enjoys broad popular support nevertheless persistently persecutes some minority group. Even here, of course, whether or not intervention on behalf of the persecuted minority could be justified will depend in part on the mode of intervention. In general, intervention can be justified only at the lowest effective level – for example, using military means where economic pressures would suffice is nearly always wrong, for military intervention normally has broader coercive effects, has greater costs for both sides, is more likely to seduce the intervening agent to exploit his advantage over the target state for self-interested ends, and carries a greater risk of counter-intervention, escalation, and wider war. (This is not to deny that in some instances economic pressures may result in greater harm to the citizens of the target state than military intervention would, and hence would be a less defensible mode of intervention, other things being equal.)

All the arguments against intervention that we have considered have been either primarily or exclusively concerned with intervention against states. Most writers seem to take it for granted that intervention on behalf of states is in general morally permissible. But it may actually be the case that intervention on behalf of the state is in general less likely to be justified than intervention against the state. The reason for this stems from the fact that, while not all states that can pass the self-help test are legitimate, those that are legitimate can generally pass the test. Thus if a state *requires* intervention on its behalf in order to defeat its domestic opponents, and there has been no significant intervention on the other side, then the state requiring intervention to ensure its survival is unlikely to be legitimate. In short, cases in which intervention is needed by legitimate states will be extremely rare. And cases in which intervention on behalf of an illegitimate state can be justified will be rarer still.

In the case of an illegitimate state, there is no presumption, based on respect for state autonomy, against intervention against the state, except perhaps a weak presumption based on doubts about the veracity of external perceptions of the state's illegitimacy. There may, however, still be a reason to refrain from intervening based on respect for the self-determination of the people, either because they may not welcome external interference (and might indeed resist it), or less plausibly, because of the considerations advanced by Mill. And, of course, another consideration which would militate against intervention even against an illegitimate state is that the potential costs of certain forms of intervention might outweigh the potential benefits – for example, if there were a significant probability of escalation, or a significant probability that the intervention would be ineffective or even counterproductive.

On the other hand, where these countervailing reasons are absent, or only very weak, intervention may be justified. If the moral reasons favouring intervention are very strong, then intervention may even be morally *required*. (This suggestion of course raises questions about how much external agents may be required to do, or how much they may be required to sacrifice. This is an important question, but I must pass over it here.) Cases in which there may be a requirement of intervention include cases of requested intervention on behalf of a population struggling to free itself from colonial rule, cases of requested intervention on behalf of revolutionaries or insurgents fighting against an illegitimate government which is both unjust and oppressive, and cases in which intervention seems the only effective way to stop the persecution or repression of a group or community by their government. In cases where, because intervention is not desired by the intended beneficiaries, or would be too costly, it is *not* justifiable to intervene on behalf of the opponents of an illegitimate state, it would also, of course, be unjustifiable to intervene on behalf of the state against its opponents.

Indeed, in these circumstances, intervention on behalf of the state would be wrong even if it were in response to previous and unjustified intervention on behalf of the state's opponents. This may seem paradoxical, for *unjustified* intervention on one side is normally thought to make counter-intervention on the other permissible. There are two reasons for this, each connected with the grounds for thinking the initial intervention unjustified. One is that the initial intervention may give the advantage to one side in the conflict which does not deserve assistance. The counter-intervention is then justified because it deprives the undeserving side of its advantage. In the case we are considering, however, it is not true that the initial intervention is unjustified because it gives the advantage to the undeserving side. On the contrary, the opponents of the state may merit assistance. The reason why assistance would be unjustified is that it would be unwelcome, or that its costs would outweigh its benefits. Another reason why counter-intervention might be thought to be justified is that it would serve to restore the intitial balance, so that the outcome of the conflict would reflect and be determined by the *internal* balance of forces. This, however, assumes that the balance of forces within a country reflects the popular strengths of the contenders, and, as we saw earlier, this is often false. In the case we are considering, the state is by hypothesis illegitimate, and hence is known to lack popular support (even if it has considerable force at its disposal), so that an outcome determined solely by the internal balance of forces might be undesirable.

Michael Walzer, again following Mill, argues that counter-intervention is always just.[34] It is, however, hard to see how this could be so, unless *all* initial interventions are wrong. For, if, as Walzer concedes, some initial interventions are justified, this would seem to suggest that it is desirable in these cases if the initial balance of forces is shifted. How, then, could it be right to shift the balance back to its original, undesirable position? Walzer replies that our rule of counter-intervention must be neutral; for, as with the rules of war, if our rules were not neutral, "there could be no rules at all but only permissions addressed to the Forces of Good entitling them to do whatever is necessary (though only what is *necessary*) to overcome their enemies".[35] But this reply seems beside the point, for to deny that counter-intervention is always just is not to increase anyone's licence to act, but is instead to impose further *restrictions* on what may be done.

Having now considered the ethics of intervention where legitimate and illegitimate states are concerned, we must turn, finally, to the case of states whose status as legitimate or illegitimate cannot be decisively determined. In these cases, the state will be divided, and the society may. be torn. One must attempt to respect the wishes and the self-determination of the people, but, where the people are divided, both their wishes and their efforts at self-determination will be in conflict. Thus there is no formula for dealing with these cases. Nor is the neutral approach acceptable: we must consult our own values. Would intervention advance the cause of social justice in the target country? Would it increase or decrease the overall level of violence? These and many other questions must be answered before the question of intervention can itself be settled.

Cases of divided states are obviously, therefore, the most difficult. They may also be the most common cases in which the question of intervention arises. While there may be cases of this sort in which it is fairly obvious that some form of intervention would be right, it will in general be best to treat these cases conservatively, and with caution. This is so for a number of reasons, many of which derive from arguments that I have criticised but which nevertheless retain a measure of validity. For example, external assessments of the legitimacy of potential target states are, as Walzer notes, not infallible, and are prone to bias and distortion. Moreover, states are always inclined to exploit any occasion for intervention in order to serve their own ends, even if their initial motivation is not self-interested. Hence there is a general presumption that, even if intervention perhaps *could* advance the self-determination of people in the target state, it probably would not do so, and would more likely be inimical to self-determination. Finally, there is always a chance of escalation and wider war, and the risks which war involves are steadily increasing. So even in cases in which the legitimacy of a potential target state is uncertain, there will still be a strong presumption against intervention.

Because it will have to take account of the distinction between legitimate and illegitimate states, as well as the many other relevant considerations discussed earlier, the correct principle of intervention will obviously be a principle of considerable complexity, hedged about by numerous qualifications. As we noted earlier, however, the correct moral principle is not always the one which we should adopt for declaratory purposes. In the present case, the correct principle of intervention will be too complex to have any chance of actually being accepted and respected as a standard of international conduct. Despite my earlier expressions of scepticism about the role of moral principles in guiding the conduct of states, principles are not entirely without influence, and it is therefore important that we should have a principle closely approximating the correct principle of intervention which is sufficiently simple to be held up as a standard for states to be guided by. Because in the world as it is the dangers of intervention are generally greater than the dangers of nonintervention, this latter principle will presumably be more restrictive than the position for which I have argued.

The position I have defended has definite implications for the cases of El Salvador and Nicaragua to which I referred at the beginning of the paper. What is most clear in my view is that the American intervention in those countries cannot conceivably be justified. In both countries the forces which the US is backing represent the interests and concerns of tiny elites which have sought to maintain their privileged positions at the expense of the mass of people by means of the most bestial and vicious forms of repression. In El Salvador the US has maintained in power a very doubtfully legitimate state which has ruled by terror and intimidation.[36] In so far as Nicaragua has intervened by supplying arms to the domestic opponents of that state, it has been engaged in a morally defensible form of counter-intervention. In Nicaragua the US has been sponsoring the deposed remnants of the illegitimate Somoza regime in their attempts to bring down the Sandinista government. The evidence, which I have reviewed elsewhere,[37] suggests that the present Nicaraguan state is legitimate. The minimal forms of assistance which Cuba and the Soviet Union have provided to help the present regime defend itself against American-sponsored aggression are, when viewed dispassionately, difficult to criticise. In my view, it is the United States interventions in both Nicaragua and El Salvador, that have been inimical to social justice, increased the flow of blood, and violated the will of the people.

NOTES

1   See Charles R. Beitz, *Political Theory and International Relations*, Princeton, NJ, 1979, p. 74.
2   See, for example, Percy H. Winfield, 'Intervention', *Encyclopedia of the Social Sciences*, VIII, New York, 1932, p. 236; and R. J. Vincent, *Nonintervention and International Order*, Princeton, NJ, 1974, p. 8.
3   See, for example, Winfield, 'Intervention', p. 236; Hersch Lauterpacht, *International Law and Human Rights*, London, 1950, p. 167; Ann Van Wynen Thomas and A. J. Thomas, Jr., *Non-intervention: the Law and its Impact in the Americas*, Dallas, 1956, pp. 67–9 and 72; and Mark R. Wicclair, 'Human rights and intervention', in Peter G. Brown and Douglas MacLean, (eds.), *Human Rights and Foreign Policy*, Lexington, Kentucky, 1979, pp. 142–4.
4   James N. Rosenau, 'Intervention as a scientific concept', *Journal of Conflict Resolu-*

tion, XIII, 1969, p. 161.

5 See Beitz, *Political Theory*, p. 72.

6 See Thomas and Thomas, *Non-intervention*, p. 67; and Beitz, *Political Theory*, p. 72.

7 Quoted in Thomas Buergenthal, 'Domestic jurisdiction, intervention, and human rights: the international law perspective', in Brown and MacLean (eds.), *Human Rights*, pp. 112–13.

8 See Richard J. Barnet, *Intervention and Revolution: the United States in the Third World*, New York, 1972, p. 67; and Michael Walzer, *Just and Unjust Wars: A Moral Argument with Historical Illustrations*, Harmondsworth, Middx., 1977, p. 96.

9 This is not to suggest that those who believe that the principle enunciated by the UN is the appropriate principle for international law must also believe that it is the correct *moral* position on the question of intervention. One could consistently believe that, while some other principle is the correct moral principle, the adoption of that principle as an international legal norm would have worse consequences, even perhaps in the principle's own terms, than the adoption of the UN principle. Nevertheless there are a great many people who do believe that the UN principle *is* the correct moral principle.

10 Versions of the anti-paternalist argument have been put forward by S. I. Benn and R. S. Peters, *Social Principles and the Democratic State*, London, 1959, pp. 361–3; Vincent, *Non-Intervention*, p. 345; Walzer, *Just and Unjust Wars*, pp. 58 and 89; and Gerard Elfstrom, 'On dilemmas of intervention', *Ethics*, XCIII, 1983, pp. 712 ff. The argument has been criticised by Beitz, *Political Theory*, pp. 75–81; Wicclair, 'Human rights and intervention', pp. 145–6; and Alan H. Goldman, 'The moral significance of national boundaries', in Peter A. French *et al.* (eds.), *Midwest Studies in Philosophy VII: Social and Political Philosophy*, Minneapolis, Minn., 1982, pp. 438 ff.

11 Here and elsewhere in this paper the words 'he' and 'his' where not used to refer to specific individuals, should be understood to mean 'he or she' and 'his or her'.

12 Variants of this argument are presented and discussed by Benn and Peters, *Social Principles*, pp. 361–3; Walzer, *Just and Unjust Wars*, pp. 87–90; Beitz, *Political Theory*, pp. 77–81; Wicclair, 'Human rights and intervention', and Goldman 'The moral significance of national boundaries', pp. 438 ff.

13 The term is used in this way, by, for example, Beitz, *Political Theory*, pp. 92–3; and by Stanley French and Andres Gutman, 'The principle of national self-determination', in Virginia Held *et al.* (eds.) *Philosophy, Morality, and International Relations*, New York, 1974, p. 138.

14 That self-determination is compatible with domestic tyranny is defended by Walzer, *Just and Unjust Wars*, p. 87. Walzer here follows John Stuart Mill, 'A few words on non-intervention', in *Dissertations and Discussions: Political, Philosophical, and Historical*, vol. III, London, 1875, pp. 153–78.

15 See David Luban, 'Just war and human rights', *Philosophy and Public Affairs*, IX, 1980; and compare Gerald Doppelt, 'Walzer's theory of morality in international relations', *Philosophy and Public Affairs*, VIII, 1978. As both Doppelt and Luban point out, to deny that the *state* has a right against intervention is not to deny that the *people* might.

16 On the consent theory of political obligation and state legitimacy, see A. John Simmons, *Moral Principles and Political Obligations*, Princeton, NJ, 1979, chs. 3 and 4.

17 When this paper was presented to Cambridge University's Moral Sciences Club, it
    was suggested to me by Edward Craig that a state's legitimacy may depend, not only
    on the level of popular support it enjoys, but also on how its popular support arises.
    In support of this suggestion, Craig cited a hypothetical case in which a state
    achieves popular support by simply expelling dissenters. Another case which sup-
    ports Craig's contention is that in which a state achieves and maintains popular
    support through the devious but skilful manipulation and indoctrination of its citi-
    zens.
18 Walzer, *Just and Unjust Wars*, p. 54.
19 Cp. Luban, 'Just war and human rights', p. 169.
20 Walzer, *Just and Unjust Wars*, pp. 98 and 101.
21 Michael Walzer, 'The moral standing of states: a response to four critics', *Philosophy
    and Public Affairs*, IX, 1980, p. 221.
22 Goldman, 'Moral significance', p. 438.
23 *Ibid.*, p. 445.
24 *Ibid.*
25 Mill, 'A few words', and Walzer, *Just and Unjust Wars*, pp. 87–8.
26 Mill, 'A few words', pp, 258–60.
27 See David Luban, 'The romance of the nation-state', *Philosophy and Public Affairs*,
    IX, 1980, p. 396; and Gerald Doppelt, 'Statism without foundations', *Philosophy
    and Public Affairs*, IX, 1980, pp. 402–3.
28 Cp. Stanley Hoffman, *Duties Beyond Borders: On the Limits and Possibilities of
    Ethical International Politics*, Syracuse, NY, 1981, p. 66.
29 Walzer, 'The moral standing of states', p. 212.
30 In fairness to Walzer it should be mentioned that he generally tends to conceive of
    intervention in terms of *military* intervention, and it may seem that his point
    becomes more persuasive when the term is restricted in this way. I am, however,
    inclined to think that it does not. For his argument against intervention is based on
    a claim about the importance of self-determination, and as such should apply equally
    to all forms of intervention, since all forms of intervention interfere with self-deter-
    mination. Hence we might agree with Walzer that military intervention can be jus-
    tified only in the limited range of cases he describes (namely, in support of an
    attempted succession, or in response to a previous intervention, or to prevent the
    wholesale massacre or enslavement of a people), but our reason for restricting per-
    missible military interventions in this way would focus on the undesirability of
    resorting to military force rather than on the undesirability of intervention *per se*.
31 Hoffman, *Duties beyond Borders*, p. 58. It is a mistake to attempt to derive a *right*
    against intervention from considerations of international stability. To attribute a
    right against intervention to an illegitimate state is to imply that intervention would
    be wrong because of the *wrong* it would do to a *state*, whereas the clear thrust of the
    stability argument is to condemn intervention because of the *consequences* it would
    have for *people* everywhere.
32 Walzer, *Just and Unjust Wars*, p. 61.
33 Walzer, 'The moral standing of states', p. 228.
34 Walzer, *Just and Unjust Wars*, pp. 96–101.
35 Walzer, 'The moral standing of states', p. 217.
36 The American intervention in El Salvador, and the character of the regimes it has
    supported, are discussed at length in my *Reagan and the World: Imperial Policy in
    the New Cold War*, Revised and Updated Version, New York, 1985, ch. 5.
37 *Ibid.*, ch 6.

REPLY TO MR McMAHAN
Neil MacCormick, University of Edinburgh

I must thank the St Andrews Centre for inviting me to take part in this conference, and congratulate them on the venture; certainly, Mr McMahan's paper shows the importance of having a Centre for Philosophy and Public Affairs. The doctrine of non-intervention is one of the great sacred cows of the time, and yet Mr McMahan suggests that it is a sacred cow without any clothes (to mix a metaphor).

I don't really want to challenge radically what Mr McMahan has said, but perhaps to try looking at the issue in a slightly different way. Mr McMahan has a wide conception of intervention. First of all, as to what counts as intervention: he includes not only violence, but also other forms of coercion. Secondly, as to who can do it: he holds that not only states can be interveners. And thirdly, as to what can be the target: he pointed out to us that on his conception not only states can be the target of intervention. And his conclusion was that intervention is simply coercive external interference in the affairs of a population organised in the form of a state.

His question about intervention, defined in that way, seemed to me really to be a question about the rights of populations organised in the forms of states. That is to say, he seems to me to be asking whether the target of intervention has on any ground a right not to be the object of intervention, always or sometimes. His answer to that, of course, was that anti-paternalist arguments, communal autonomy arguments, and stability arguments, each and all fail to establish that states always have a right that others refrain from intervening in them. So, as he concluded, there would be at best a non-conclusive presumption against intervention. Sometimes intervention is both justified in itself and justified on consequential grounds, yet, he concedes, in a practical world the UN position is perhaps a good one to adopt for declaratory purposes. (And there, by the way, he introduced again that teasing distinction between principles which are right in themselves and principles which it is wise to adopt. And I think that whether that distinction holds is one that there may be some discussion of later on.)

The position at issue is the UN position. It does seem to me that when we think about the UN position it's making an assertion which is not quite an answer to the type of question that Mr McMahan is raising. For observe: the UN position is actually a prohibition on a certain kind of conduct by states, and as a prohibition ('Oh states, intervene not!') it doesn't depend upon there being some view about the rights of potential targets. And this is despite the language in which it is phrased; it says, if you will recall, "No state has the right to intervene". But of course when we use the formula 'You have no right to do x' what we mean is 'You have a duty not to do x'.

Now I want to ask the question whether there are reasons that back up the UN position about what states shouldn't do which are wholly other than the kinds of consideration which were dismissed in the main paper. (I thought rightly dismissed.) That no state has an absolute right not to be intervened in, if true (and I think it is true), doesn't entail that there would be nothing wrong with a practice of state intervention. May I say that it seems to me that it would be difficult for Mr McMahan to be wrong given his way of arguing the proposition. This doesn't mean of course that his argument is trivial. States are artificial persons, and artificial persons can't have natural rights. Hence non-intervention, if justified, can't be justified by recourse to the natural rights of states. If states have any sort of moral rights, they could have them only derivatively, and, as McMahan's paper shows, the moral rights of states are dependent upon the moral rights of human beings as individuals and as aspirationally autonomous communities. Hence, where the rights of humans, either as individuals or as members of communities, are being set at nought by states, the states can have no moral rights to rest on. And this is, I think, a main point of what Mr McMahan has argued. Still, as I say again, this doesn't constitute a conclusive case against the UN position. The UN position doesn't say that states have a right not to be intervened in; it states that they have a duty not to intervene.

So the question I want to raise (and I want to raise it quickly, since I don't know the answer!) is the question whether there could be reasons for imposing a legal duty not to intervene, or for asserting a moral duty not to intervene, other than the types of rights-based reason which we were given in the main paper. Perhaps there could. If I were to try to do that I would first of all play around a little, I think, with the question 'What is a state?'. Mr McMahan has a definitional section at the beginning of his paper. My own view of this is that the best analytical account of states is the one given by Kelsen in his *General Theory of Law and the State* and *Pure Theory of Law* and other writings, according to which a state is in some sense identical with, or derivative from, a certain kind of legal order. By legal order, we mean precisely not just an abstract set of norms but a set of norms concretely implemented in the life and activities of a population. Where you have a legal order which is relatively centralised and territorially located, then also you have a state. But there is an ambiguity in our usage of the term 'state'; sometimes we use it to refer to the organised agencies of the legal order, that is, the state as a government, and sometimes we use it in a wider sense to allude to the state as organised government plus the citizenry subject to the legal order living in the territory. Now I'm sure there's that ambiguity. Not merely is the state a legal order, it's an order of positive law, understood in the sense of coercively enforced law. And a central characteristic of this idea of the state as a mode of social organisation has been an emphasis on the centralisation and monopolisation of coercive force; states are coercive agencies therefore. This, of course, poses the standard question: how far is it justifiable at all for human beings to tolerate and acknowledge monopolisations of coercion? To which one might say: it is tolerable only upon restrictive conditions. And we might want to say that the tolerability of the existence of states depends upon both internal and external restrictions upon the use of the monopoly of coercion. As to the internal uses of the monopoly of coercion, we might say that this should be subject to the formal constraint that the rule of law be observed. (Due notice of the rules, no punishment save for breach of a rule, and so on.) And substantial, but much more contestable: human rights should be observed and social welfare should be promoted. Why it's worth drawing this distinction between the formal and the substantive requirements of the proper use of coercion is precisely because the substantive ones are contestable in a way that the formal ones are at least less contestable. And externally, we might say that the whole point is that states are tolerable so long as they organise force to that level required for self-defence but no further. Now if that were true, and we could justify this thesis as to the external limits on the rightful use of coercion, then, in a sense, we could establish the principle of non-intervention simply as a corollary of that. If the only thing for which it is legitimate to organise a monopoly of coercion is the internal maintenance of the rule of law and external maintenance of self-defence, then there is just no scope left for legitimate intervention. If one could make up an argument of that kind, it might be suggested that there is a case for a principle of non-intervention which looks upon the matter not in terms of whether there is something in states which makes them never properly targets of intervention, but rather poses the question: Is there something about states which makes them always, in moral terms, inept interveners? And if it is the case that they could always be shown to be morally inept interveners, then the UN position could be defended by a line of argument different from that of Mr McMahan.

That said, however one needs to add a qualification or two. A problem which is posed always is: What if there are states around (Idi Amin's Uganda, for instance) in which the internal restrictions on state force are being manifestly, hugely and awfully overridden? Could it then be morally legitimate for somebody else to come in from the outside and help the population to get rid of the tyranny? I think one has to have a very strong moral stomach indeed to think that there is always something wrong with intervening in a case like that. The trouble, therefore, is that it seems as though even if there are arguments which show that states are in principle inept interveners, yet there are circumstances which might well lead us to believe that there can just occasionally be moral imperatives to intervene. And therefore, even on the view which I have suggested, the UN principle is only a principle and not an absolute rule.

CHAIRMAN'S COMMENTS
Stephen Clark, University of Liverpool

I think what's been said is clear enough to us all. Briefly, Mr McMahan has argued that allowing rather more intervention in the affairs of other states would have the good consequence of eroding a certain amount of state authority. Professor McCormick on the other hand has pointed out that in a sense allowing this intervention in the affairs of another state gives states more authority, because it gives states, who are certainly morally inept actors, rather more range within which to do things. However, both sides appear to be agreed that the usual arguments for saying there is an absolute ban on such intervention really don't work.

Arguments from the supposed autonomy of states as quasi-moral agents have odd consequences. I think myself that Mr McMahan was a bit rapid in saying that because states can be divided against themselves, there is no analogy with individuals. It seems to me that, traditionally, there has been a view that people can be divided against themselves quite easily. And that's usually been part of the state–individual analogy. However, I don't want to present that case now.

Arguments from the autonomy of communities do get some way to providing a reason not to intervene in the affairs of another state, but these are obviously going to be defeasible reasons: there are going to be occasions where the autonomy of the communities which compose it is not at present respected by the existing state.

And the argument from stability of the world order again doesn't provide an absolute argument for non-intervention: it merely provides reasons sometimes for not intervening.

Both sides therefore seem to be agreed that though there is no absolute moral rule saying that we should never intervene in the affairs of another state, there might well be good reasons for advancing this rule as a programme of action for a community of nation-states. I find it slightly odd to suggest that though this is not the correct principle, it is none the less the principle that we ought to adopt now: what *is* a correct principle if it is not one that we ought now to adopt?

DISCUSSION

Professor Thomas Donaldson, Loyola University of Chicago. I find myself in agreement with a great many, if not all, of the arguments in your paper. At the same time, I'd like to press you a bit on what you mean by suggesting that we should have one policy as a declaratory policy, as it were, but accept a rather different set of principles for moral decision-making. One thing one might mean by making that distinction is that when we are promulgating principles in international documents we are necessarily forced to simplify; so, for instance, we simplify what is complex when we generate the UN Declaration of Human Rights. But I take it that's not quite what you mean, because the policy that you want to accept as proper on the declaratory level is considerably less permissive than the one which you think ought to be action-guiding for individual nations.

Mr McMahan. What I did have in mind was what you said I couldn't have in mind! Just that the sort of principles I would like to defend as action-guiding would be too complicated, too detailed, too difficult for declaratory purposes, or formulation in things like the UN Declaration on Human Rights. And when we are formulating simplified principles for declaratory purposes I would hope that they would have a slightly conservative slant to them for the reasons I gave in the paper.

Professor Donaldson. Would you find acceptable an international policy which rejected intervention but added the caveat: except where there are compelling moral reasons otherwise?

Mr McMahan. No; that would be too open-ended. I do think that there is a valid distinction here between the principles that we would hope would be action-guiding and the principles that we have to be satisfied with for declaratory purposes. The latter will have to be the closest approximations to the principles that we hope will actually be action-guiding compatible with being universally recognised, accepted and understood. But I don't attribute any great importance to this distinction, and I would hope that we could bring the two types of principle as close together as possible.

Sir Arthur Hockaday, Commonwealth War Graves Commission. It seemed to me that a thread running right through Jeff McMahan's paper was the associ-ation between the legitimacy of intervention and the legitimacy of the state within which the intervention would take place. There was almost an inverse relation between the legitimacy of the state and the legitimacy of the interven-tion. So the legitimacy of the state becomes absolutely crucial, and then the question arises as to what determines the legitimacy of the state. Jeff McMahan spoke several times of self-determination in this context, and that is certainly one criterion of legitimacy, but only one. There are surely a whole raft of different criteria that might be adopted. These range from, at one end, simply, evidence that the government of the state is clearly in charge and that the state is, at any rate, temporarily a stable community, to the requirement that every member of the population should be able to play a part in the political process, at the other end. And there are many stages in between. But it seems to follow from that that the state contemplating intervention may make any one of a number of judgements along that line. And perhaps it's at least better to have that sort of criterion than simply to decide on intervention on the basis of whether you like the general political attitudes of some government, or whether they are compatible with yours. But I think this really makes it frightfully difficult to lay down a general criterion. And I think Jeff McMahan gave the game away a few moments ago when he said "the sort of principles I would like to defend". Anybody can say that. So I think I would conclude that he was very wise in the end to come down with a pretty conservative conclusion.

Mr McMahan. I do think that the criterion of legitimacy that I would defend, and which I sketched briefly in the paper, at least makes legitimacy not at all relative to the particular political character of a government, state, or regime, but to the extent to which the state enjoys popular support. And that, I take it, is a fairly politically neutral criterion of legitimacy. So there won't be political bias introduced into my account of the ethics of political intervention by the notion of legitimacy.

Sir Arthur Hockaday. But is there not likely to be in real life some political bias in the potential intervener's definition of legitimacy?

Mr McMahan. Well, yes, if the intervener doesn't pay strict attention to the argument! If he adopts some other criterion of legitimacy, never mind that I have given an account of legitimacy in the paper, and then runs the argument on the basis of that, then he may get a quite different conclusion. But that is why I tried to give a neutral account of legitimacy.

Mr John Hall, University of St Andrews. There are two questions, I think, that need to be distinguished. One is about what principles of intervention should be established as part of international law. And the other is what principles should be adopted by individual states. Now, with regard to the latter question, the principle that we hope will ultimately be established is that states abide by international law – whatever international law may be. Now admittedly there is, as yet, no sufficiently powerful international legal order to make such a principle one that can be adopted by individual states in general; but any rival principle to be adopted by individual states that has regard to the merits of the particular case should be regarded as provisional pending the establishment of the international legal order which we hope there will ultimately be. When it comes to the question what principle with regard to intervention should be established as part of international law, the question must surely arise whether any proposed principle is going to be judiciable. And principles that are concerned with such vague questions as whether the government of a state has the support of its people would have to be refined to something very much more precise before it can form a part of international law.

Professor Brian Barry, California Institute of Technology. I'd like to address the comments that Professor MacCormick made. As I understood it, he was suggesting that you derive a principle of non-intervention from the premise that states are entitled only to defend themselves. The trouble with that seems to me that states very often regard the best means of defending themselves as intervening in the affairs of other states, to put in friendly regimes or oust unfriendly ones. So it seems to me that you would have to take the principle of non-intervention as one of the definitions of what is a legitimate means of self-defence. In which case of course you are no longer deriving the principle of intervention from the principle of self-defence.

However, it seems to me that the notion of self-defence, which wasn't mentioned at all by Jeff McMahan as a possible reason for intervention, is not necessarily an absurd one. And quite apart from the fact that it's clearly going to happen anyway, and so it would be more sensible to have principles regulating and limiting it than simply ruling it out altogether, it seems to me fairly clear that if you accept the legitimacy of states at all then you do have to accept the legitimacy of their self-defence and that in some cases is going to involve their not tolerating the presence of outposts of, let's say, hostile superpowers very close to their own borders. (This will depend on the state of weapons technology, and so on.) In that case it seems to me that what you really need to be thinking about is what kind of acceptable ways of arranging things, ways that can be tolerated by superpowers, are most compatible with the autonomy of the people in the small states who have the misfortune to be in the way of these superpowers. And I think that this leads one towards a solution that has often been mentioned, and which seems to me to have great merit, of trying to increase the number of areas of neutralisation. That is to say, you try to arrange things so that some strategically important area is no longer perceived by a superpower as a threat to itself. And I think that guaranteed neutrality is one of the ways of doing that. And I would see this as the only conceivable chance for Eastern Europe, because none of us, if we were responsible for the security of the Soviet Union, would tolerate the prospect of, say, Poland joining NATO.

Mrs Mary Midgley, University of Newcastle. It seems to me that the distinction between principles which we put out for declaratory purposes and principles which we mean to live by is a quite general one about moral principles. The Ten Commandments, and similar very general principles, are always put forward in that general form because you don't want to invite everybody to kill people by saying, 'Don't kill people except with good reason'! The exceptions then have to be dealt with. And they always are dealt with by calling attention to conflicts, aren't they? Now the UN is presumably committed to things like human rights, as another general principle, and the only cases where it's going to be remotely plausible to think that it's right to intervene are ones

where the conflict with human rights is so gross that one says that in this case
the one principle has to prevail over the other. Now of course, the details are
frightfully complicated and we can't deal with them here, but I do think it's
important to be clear that there is no question of hypocrisy about this distinction. It's pretty obvious from which angle, and from which power status,
inteventions are most likely to happen. Therefore, what you need is a general
rule saying, 'Don't do it!' and that doesn't mean that you can't sometimes
produce good reason for doing it. But of course, the fact that we haven't got
a genuinely impartial and infallible authority – and we haven't within states
either; the best existing state, Sweden or what not, isn't always sure whether
some particular case was, say, a justifiable killing – so that what's actually
going to happen will be miles from what the principle is, doesn't stop us
saying in general, since you have to choose the one side or the other, that the
first thing to say is 'Don't intervene'. But that doesn't mean you can stop
thinking there.

Professor MacCormick. The distinction between declaratory principles and the
principles that we think are actually correct is a bit like the problem of such
things as euthanasia. Most people agree that there are some circumstances in
which the terminally ill can properly have their deaths accelerated, and most
people agree that attempts to frame in any sort of legislation exactly when
these cases are will probably do more harm than good, by encouraging hostility and suspicion among members of families and so on. So it would be better
simply to leave the general statement unqualified, but acknowledge that particular cases will arise when particular agents will do something different and
we'll all think they are right. It may seem that it is easier to grasp this distinction in legal terms where we know that whatever the law is there will be some
text of it, and know that it will be an imperfect text. And since there are no
texts of morality but only moral reasons for or against doing things it would
seem that there can never be that gap between the practical and the ideal in
moral matters. But even our moral thoughts have to be framed somehow,
and it may be that it is sometimes wisest – and I think that this may be what
Jeff McMahan is getting at – that we should, even in framing our moral
concepts, frame them in such a way that we acknowledge that there are
unacknowledgeable exceptions.

About the problem that Professor Barry raised for my position, I am not
sure. Certainly, in the international sphere, the problem of what is called in
the criminal law 'excessive self-defence' is a very large problem. But I think
that, rather as in the criminal law, there is here a genuine enough distinction
between excessive self-defence and, so to say, plain wanton aggression or
intrusion. We do indeed need to get better at deciding what are the proper
limits of self-defence – I agree with that. But I think there is a distinction
between the self-defence case, where the objective is to make myself safe not
to make you good, and intervention, which is aimed at making you good and
which, according to Jeff McMahan, is sometimes justified.

Mr McMahan. Let me return to the distinction between principles that we hold for declaratory purposes and principles that we actually guide our actions by. John Hall's comment raised an interesting point here, which is that in setting up a theory of intervention we need to determine what that theory is going to imply for international law. And what I would like to claim is that what our legal theory might say about intervention is not necessarily going to coincide with what our moral theory might say about intervention, just as the law and morality do not always coincide in the domestic case. And it will often be the case that the legal position on a particular moral issue will have to be simplified to some extent, it will have to use concepts that are precisely determinate, it will have to be susceptible of verification in ways that we might not demand for our moral evaluation.

Can states be moral?
International morality and
the compliance problem*

BRIAN BARRY

California Institute of Technology

It is quite a mistake to suppose that real dishonesty is at all common.
The number of rogues is about equal to the number of men who act
honestly, and it is very small. The great majority would sooner behave
honestly than not. The reason why they do not give way to this natural
preference for humanity is that they are afraid that others will not; and
the others do not because they are afraid that *they* will not. Thus it
comes about that, while behaviour which looks dishonest is fairly common, sincere dishonesty is about as rare as the courage to evoke good
faith in your neighbours by showing that you trust them. [F. M.
Cornford, *Microcosmographia Academica.*]

I

I am delighted to have been given the opportunity to give one of the
papers at this meeting. I think it's a great achievement to have started
something new at a time when in British universities things are generally
being closed rather than opened. And I think it's particularly good that
there is a centre of this nature. The application of philosophy to issues
of public policy is important not only as a contribution to public discourse, but also to the way in which it forces ideas in moral and political
philosophy to be revised and refined. This is particularly so in the area
of international affairs.

In the last few years I have read a number of papers on issues of

* I gratefully acknowledge the contributions made to this paper by my commentators at
two meetings at which earlier drafts were read: Robin Lovin at the University of
Chicago, and Robert Fullinwider at the University of St Andrews. On the first occasion
(April 1984), the paper was delivered under the auspices of the Committee on Public
Policy under a grant from the Council on Religion and International Affairs, New York.
On the second occasion (September 1984), it was presented as a part of a Fulbright
Anglo-American Colloquium on Ethics and International Affairs held at the University
of St Andrews to mark the opening of the Centre for Philosophy and Public Affairs. I
am also grateful for the points made by both audiences and for comments from colleagues
at Caltech. I hope that I have been able to improve the paper on the basis of all these.

international morality to various audiences and also conducted several courses, taken by college students and also by people in the professions. It is, I have found by experience, a pretty safe generalisation that the objection will come up in any such context sooner or later – and usually sooner rather that later – that this is merely flailing the air. For, it is said, the conduct of states is not an appropriate subject for moral evaluation or censure. Now of course some people will suggest that there is no point in moral discourse in any sphere of life. This kind of universal moral scepticism raises deep philosophical issues which would be well worth discussing on some other occasion. But for the present purpose I wish to direct my attention to those who do not deny the appropriateness of moral appraisal in ordinary life but who do nevertheless hold that it is inappropriate in the international area.

Why might someone make a distinction along these lines? Two reasons are, I think, most commonly put forward for scepticism specifically about international morality. The first is that governments almost invariably do, and in any case have a duty to their citizens to, pursue the national interest whenever it conflicts with the interests of other countries. And the second has been put as follows by Terry Nardin (though this is not his own view):

> The international system is not to any appreciable extent a society united by common rules, but simply an aggregate of separate societies each pursuing its own purposes, and linked with one another in ways that are essentially *ad hoc*, unstable and transitory. The conduct of each state may in fact be rule-governed, in the sense that each observes rules of its own choosing. But because the decisions of each are governed by different rules, the separate states cannot be said to be members of a single society united by common rules of conduct – rules whose authority is acknowledged by all states.[1]

The reasoning that connects the two is, roughly speaking, that, if each state pursues its own national interest, rules will be complied with by a given state only to the extent that it can be made in the interest of the state to comply. But in the absence of "a common Power to keep them all in awe", as Hobbes put it,[2] there is no way of ensuring that most states most of the time will comply with any set of rules. So there are not, in any real sense, any rules governing international conduct.

Before we go any further, it is worth observing that both of these points have analogues in commonsense morality as it operates within societies. This would cut no ice if we were dealing with a universal moral sceptic. But since we are not this is a potentially significant finding. Thus, in commonsense morality it is generally held that it is acceptable (and indeed in some conditions praiseworthy) for different people to have different "moral aims", as Derek Parfit has put it.[3] That is to say, we do not think that there is a single good that all are equally under a moral obligation to pursue. Rather, we believe that, for example, it is right for a given individual to pay more attention (give more weight, if you like) to the interests of those to whom he or she is related by ties of family or other associations and commitments than to others. (This includes giving more weight to one's own interests than to those of randomly-selected others.)

Again, in commonsense morality it is generally thought that there is a class of social norms adherence to which is morally obligatory only if enough other people adhere to them. Wherever we have a practice that is collectively beneficial provided that it is generally observed (refraining from wearing a path by taking a short cut across a lawn is the standard philosophical example), there is a presumption that fairness requires each to observe it on condition that enough others do to achieve the object served by the norm. If, however, the norm is not efficacious in providing people with a reason that they accept (and act on) for eschewing their private, anti-social interests, then the moral obligation on each one to observe the norm tends to evaporate.

I am being deliberately evasive about the form of the relation between compliance by others and the obligation to conform to it oneself for this reason: I believe that it will vary according to the details of the case. In some instances just one bit of non-compliance releases everyone else from an obligation to refrain from doing what the norm prohibits. Thus, if one neighbour shatters the peace of the neighbourhood by using a power mower early on a Sunday morning, it does not make much difference if others do so too. But in other instances much of the collective benefit may be achieved even if there is a substantial amount of non-compliance.[4] Even if only, say, three-quarters of the householders in a city centre comply with a rule against burning their garden refuse, the air may still be very much less dirty than it would be if there were no restraint, and this might plausibly be thought to generate an obligation of fairness to comply, though a weaker one than it would be if compliance were closer to being universal.

I should emphasise here, since it may not be apparent from these examples, that the structure of commonsense morality is not utilitarian. That is to say, the question is not simply: which act – compliance or non-compliance – would have the most net beneficial consequence, given what all the others are doing? In cases where there is a threshold effect, the dictates of common sense will commonly coincide with those of utilitarianism. Thus, suppose that so many people have already walked across the grass that a path of completely bare earth has been created. Then utilitarianism and common sense would agree that there is no moral obligation on anyone to refrain from taking the short cut. They unite in dissenting from the view held by some philosophers that the right thing to do is unaffected by the absence of beneficial consequences when some threshold has been passed.

Such a view is characteristically arrived at by taking a framework for moral decision-making that is not unreasonable in itself but then applying it too immediately and simplistically, without recognising the need for institutional mediation between the ultimate criterion and the demands of morality in concrete situations. One way in which this happens is that Kant's formulation of the categorical imperative – that one must be able to will the maxim of one's action as a universal law – is misapplied. (One can perfectly consistently will the universal adoption of the maxim that one walks across the grass whenever, because of the actions of others, there is no point in not doing so.) Another route which can lead to the same conclusion is to take ideal rule utilitarianism – the doctrine that the best set of rules is the one which would have the best consequences if it were generally adhered to – and then say that the right thing to do in any actual situation is to act on the rules of ideal morality so understood, whether or not others either recognise or act on these rules.

To common sense it is mere quixotry to feel obliged to do something that is in fact pointless on the ground that in some counterfactual state of the world it would have a point. And I think that the commonsense position on this will withstand any amount of philosophical scrutiny. Those who claim to find an argument against utilitarianism (act utilitarianism, as against the curious form of ideal rule utilitarianism that I just mentioned above) in getting what they regard as the 'wrong answer' in threshold cases are, in my view, kicking the ball through their own goal. What they regard as an argument is actually a *reductio ad absurdum*.

Commonsense morality is thus not unconcerned with beneficial overall consequences in evaluating actions. But where it differs from utilitarianism is that it is not concerned *solely* with the production of beneficial overall consequences. The prescriptions of the two will normally coincide in threshold cases but even then the way in which they get to their shared conclusions is not quite the same. For utilitarianism the decisive point (and the only one that could possibly matter) is simply that, given the actions already taken by others that have worn the path in the grass, there is no collective benefit to which walking round the edge will now contribute to be set against the benefit that the agent himself gains from cutting across. Therefore there is obviously a net overall benefit from cutting across. The line taken by commonsense morality includes all of the above considerations but it does not stop there. It goes on to say that there is no collective benefit that others are helping to provide: if other people go to the trouble of walking round they are not, in the actual circumstances, helping to provide it; they are merely taking gratuitous exercise. Since there is no collective benefit from which one gains as a result of the forbearances of others, there can be no unfairness in not contributing to it oneself, and this is the real reason why it is normally permissible to walk across the garden. One cannot be accused of being a free rider if the train never leaves the station.

Now in a threshold case this extra loop is trivial because there is no way in which one could help provide any of the collective benefit by one's own action even if one chose to. It is precisely because of this that the conclusion of commonsense morality coincides with that of utilitarianism. Fairness does not get a chance to bite because the issue of fairness is pre-empted by the consideration that the 'co-operative' move does not in fact do anybody any good. We might say that here, whereas the utilitarian conclusion is determined by its own single criterion, the more complex common-sense conclusion is overdetermined.

To see that there really is a difference between the practical implications of commonsense and those of utilitarianism, all we have to do is look at a non-threshold case. This does not have to be one where the net benefit from an agent's contributing to a public good is invariant with respect to the number of others who contribute. That is the simplest case but the general form of the relation that we require is just that, even when few other people are contributing, there is still a net benefit to be produced (subtracting the cost to the agent from the increment in the collective benefit enjoyed by all) from any given agent's contributing to it.

Such cases are, I am inclined to believe, quite common in real life, though, in the nature of the case, it will often be hard to establish what the collective gain from a single contribution is so as to compare it with the cost of that contribution to the actor. But it is what Parfit correctly calls a "mistake in moral mathematics" to suppose that a small effect diffused over a large number of people is not a real effect. It may be significant in determining the moral quality of the act that brings it about.[5]

Thus, to return to air pollution, it is quite possible that there is no upper threshold in many such cases. It is quite possible that, even if everyone who lives in the city centre except me is burning soft coal, there is still a net benefit from my refraining from doing so: the overall reduction in air pollution from what it would be if I joined the others outweighs the cost to me of using some alternative means of heating. On the utilitarian criterion, this is enough to generate the conclusion that I have a moral obligation to refrain from adding my mite of smoke to the pall already created by the rest of the city-dwellers. But I believe that I am correctly recording the deliverances of commonsense morality by saying that, according to its dictates, I have no such obligation. The failure of the others to contribute to the collective good of clean air releases me from the moral obligation to do so myself. I cannot reasonably be accused of behaving unfairly if I fail to act on a norm that so many others, situated (let us suppose) symmetrically with myself, are failing to act on.

In terms of the 'free rider' metaphor, the point is not now (as it was before) that there is nothing I can do by myself to make the train go but simply that I am not riding at the expense of others. My fare would suffice to move the train a minute fraction of an inch. But then the others would be free riding at my expense, and I have no obligation to give them a free (even if extremely short) ride.

I should add that commonsense morality is capable of discriminating between different kinds of moral judgement. Thus, although in the conditions stated it would not be morally obligatory to refrain from burning soft coal, it would certainly be admirable to do it. Anyone who did so would be exhibiting the virtue of beneficence. Where commonsense morality differs from utilitarianism is in denying that what does the most good is in general obligatory and in recognising other virtues besides beneficence, such as that of behaving justly towards others.

For utilitarianism, then, the relevance of what other people are doing is purely contingent. We need to know what other people are doing simply because that may make a difference to the net benefit that a single act of contribution would bring about. But once the presence of a net benefit has been established, that determines the obligation to contribute, however few others are contributing. Indeed, we can imagine a case (for example staying off the roads over a holiday weekend and thus reducing traffic congestion) where, the fewer who contribute, the larger the net benefit from a single act of contribution. Then, on the utilitarian criterion, the obligation to contribute becomes more stringent the smaller the number of others who contribute. For commonsense morality, however, the obligation of fair play would always diminish the smaller the proportion of those who were eligible to contribute actually did so. It should, however, be observed that, if a single contribution would do a lot of good, and in particular if it would alleviate suffering or destitution, then it might be required by commonsense morality as an obligation of humanity. Normally, however, the benefits that fit this description are not collective in character.

II

So far, I have been suggesting that the two grounds that are most often advanced for denying that international affairs can be subjected to moral appraisal have clear analogues in what commonsense morality holds about morality within societies. Thus, corresponding to the claim that political leaders have a right, and perhaps a duty, to pursue the national interest is the notion that people have their own legitimately differing 'moral ends', which will permit or, again, possibly even require them to give more weight to the interests of themselves and of others connected to them in various ways than they give to the interests of others. And corresponding to the claim that the lack of assurance that others will comply with international norms releases states from any obligation to observe them there is in commonsense morality a complex connection, which I have just tried to sketch, between the degree of compliance by others and the obligation to conform oneself to a norm.

My purpose in pointing out these connections is simply this. These two features of commonsense morality are not usually thought to cause it to self-destruct as a source of moral obligations and other moral phenomena. And I believe that in fact they do not. Why then should it be supposed that their international analogues must have such devastating implications for the possibility of moral appraisal in international affairs?

Let us take up the two alleged grounds for the amorality of the international order in turn. If we think for a moment about the first we shall be led to realise that the relevant implication for states of the notion of different 'moral ends' is that governments have some duties (which might be quite extensive) towards their own citizens that they do not owe to citizens of other countries. (Those who prefer to formulate issues of political obligation in lateral rather than hierarchical terms could put the same essential point by saying that citizens of a single country owe one another things that they do not owe citizens of other countries.) But this does not entail that anything goes. Generally speaking, my special obligation to my family does not legitimate lying, stealing, cheating or killing on their behalf. The special obligation is set in a context of constraints on the morally acceptable ways of advancing my 'moral ends'.

Now it seems to me that countries are in an exactly analogous position to this. We can easily enough allow that a government has duties to its own citizens that it doesn't owe to people in other countries. But this does not entail that it has a moral licence to do whatever appears to it to advance the national interest, however much that may violate the legitimate interests of others. What, after all, is so magical about one particular group, a nation-state, that can dissolve all wider moral considerations? Why should this one level of association be exempted from the moral constraints that apply to all others?

I believe that, to the extent that we can talk about a common international morality, it does take the form of a belief that there are morally binding constraints on the things governments can do in pursuit of their national interest. But this brings us up against the second question: how can there be morally binding constraints without a centralised agency of enforcement? In the Hobbesian "condition of mere Nature" in which states find themselves in their relations with one another, would not anyone adhering to moral constraints "but betray himself to his enemy"?[6] "For he that would be modest, and tractable, and perform all he promises, in such time, and place, where no man else should do so, should but make himself a prey to others, and secure his own certain ruine."[7] The simple answer, which is not complete but is still worth making, is that the moral norms that govern everyday life in a society are not for the most part backed up by legal sanctions either but are none the less quite broadly effective in restraining conduct.

The response will inevitably be that this is to evade the issue because the security provided by the legal enforcement provides the essential underpinning of the whole system of mutual constraints within a society. This undeniably has an element of truth in it. Of course, international relations are fundamentally conditioned by the absence of an agency capable of enforcing compliance. A state normally demands a monopoly of the use of violence within its territory, whereas international law and morality permit the waging of war under certain conditions. However, the notion that in the absence of a core of centrally enforced norms there can be no others that are effective is simply a crude error. It is belied by the way in which huge numbers of international transactions take place every day on the basis of norms – some codified into international law and others developed through custom – that are the vast amount of the time relied on by the parties and in fact adhered to.

It should be observed that a great deal of compliance with these norms can be accounted for without going beyond the rational pursuit of interest. It is to the advantage of a state not to be excluded from the system of diplomatic relations, to have a reputation as a reliable trading partner, and so on. Hobbes, whose name is often advanced as an authority by the 'realists', deduced from the postulate of survival that one should "seek peace" in the state of nature and drew up a long list of prescriptions – "laws of nature" – that should be acted on so long as doing so is compatible with safety. Immediately following the passage that I quoted above, Hobbes adds that "he that having sufficient Security, that others shall observe the same Lawes towards him, observes them not himself, seeketh not Peace, but War; and consequently the destruction of his Nature by Violence".[8] In practice, states can very often follow the (admittedly quite undemanding) prescriptions of positive international morality without putting their security at risk in the slightest.

However, it is surely equally true to say that there are much of the time self-interested motives for sticking to the prescriptions of common-sense morality in everyday life. At the same time it is surely our ordinary experience that, at any rate to the extent that others are observing the norms, we feel an obligation to do so too. Perhaps the truth of the matter is that the vast majority of the time we don't inquire too minutely into the reasons for doing the thing that's required: we recognise the general advantageousness of the system and accept its authority in guiding our actions. States are, I suggest, not so different in this respect. Their standard operating procedures are to adhere to the appropriate international norms, and it would actually be quite unworkable to make a determination on each occasion of where the exact balance of long-term and all-things-considered interest lay before ever doing anything.

I have conceded, however, that the content of the common international morality is such that it does not in general press very hard the question of reasons for adhering to it because it doesn't ask a lot. Nardin, whom I quoted from earlier, has summed it up as follows:

> The moral element in international law is to be found in those general principles of international association that constitute customary international law, and above all in the most fundamental of those principles, such as the ones specifying the rights of independence, legal equality, and self-defence, and the duties to observe treaties, to respect the immunity of ambassadors, to refrain from aggression, to conduct hostilities in war in accordance with the laws of war, to respect human rights, and to co-operate in the peaceful settlement of disputes.[9]

When we look at economic affairs, what is striking is the absence of any equivalent of the system that is standard within countries of taxing those who can afford it in order to provide assistance to those who would otherwise be destitute. This is not to say that there is no mechanism at all for international redistribution: the World Bank does after all exist and does make loans on favourable terms to poor countries, but these are discretionary and in any case do not represent a sizeable transfer. The domestic analogy would be closer to a system of soft loans from the government to small businesses than to a welfare system. Here, no doubt, the absence of coercion makes itself strongly felt: if contributions to the government coffers had to be raised by voluntary subscription, even tax rates of 10 per cent would no doubt be regarded as quite visionary and utopian, in the same way as they are in the international context. We should hear a great deal about how it would be asking far too much of human nature for the wealthy to tithe themselves for the benefit of the poor. Even the rate of 0.7 per cent of gross national product in official aid to which the affluent countries are in principle committed greatly exceeds the amount provided by almost all countries.

III

But is this an inevitable consequence of the lack of an international sovereign? I think that the best way to approach this question is to adopt an indirect strategy. Let us first ask what the ideal would be if we were entirely to ignore the problem of compliance, and then see what adaptations are required when we take account of it. Unless we know what to aim at, we are in no position to ask how far short of the target we are bound to fall.

Let me be a bit more precise about the nature of the moves to be made. What exactly do we mean by ideal morality? Derek Parfit, who makes heavy use of the notion of ideal morality, defines an "Ideal Act Theory" as one that "says what we should all try to do, simply on the assumption that we all try, and all succeed".[10] This is not quite right because we do not want our ideal morality to include prescriptions to attempt things that we have good reason to suppose people (or collectivities such as states) could not in fact succeed in doing even if they tried. We are interested here in utopian thinking but not in science fiction. When we say that we wish to construct a "full compliance" theory of morality [11] what we should be looking for is, I suggest, one that abstracts from what I have called the "compliance problem". This is the problem that people may not act on the prescriptions embodied in a normative system that covers them, even though they could perfectly well do so if they chose. We normally focus particularly on the prospect that people will fail to comply because the prescriptions of morality ask them to act in some way that runs contrary to (what they perceive as) their self-interest. But we should also allow for the prospect that people may simply not accept the particular set of prescriptions with which we are concerned as being valid.

Since many people are familiar with the concept of 'ideal theory' introduced by John Rawls in A *Theory of Justice*,[12] it may forestall confusion if I take a moment to observe in what ways my notion of ideal theory agrees with his and in what ways it departs from it. The element of similarity is that when Rawls talks about ideal theory he equates it with what he calls "strict compliance theory",[13] and by "strict compliance theory" he means a theory of justice constructed on the assumption that "the parties can depend on one another to conform to them".[14] But there is an important way in which my conception of ideal theory diverges sharply from that of Rawls.

For Rawls, we should take account, when drawing up our ideal theory, of what he calls "the strains of commitment".[15] What this means is that we should take into account that people may find it difficult or impossible to adhere to some sets of principles.[16] This could, of course, be interpreted so that it would simply amount to my demand for utopia rather than science fiction: we certainly don't want principles that require people to do what is impossible or even what is difficult, if this carries the implication that if they try they are liable to fail. But this is not what Rawls has in mind.

What Rawls says is that, even when designing an ideal theory, we should throw out "principles which may have consequences so extreme that [people] could not accept them in practice".[17] And Rawls's example of such an 'extreme' principle is the utilitarian principle that people should act to maximise overall well-being. For it requires some people "to accept lower prospects of life [than what? presumably than their prospects under some alternative principle] for the sake of others".[18] Thus, the utilitarian principle, as a basis for a social ethic, "is threatened with instability unless sympathy and benevolence can be widely and intensively cultivated".[19] Without one word of discussion, Rawls assumes that this cannot be done and moves immediately to the conclusion that we should "reject the principle of utility".[20]

This cavalier way of disposing of an important and difficult psychological question illustrates exactly what is wrong with Rawls's conception of ideal theory. By incorporating the problem of compliance (as I have defined it) into the ideal theory under the description of "the strains of commitment", Rawls moves too fast towards practicality, while at the same time stopping short of it. His "ideal theory" is an unsatisfactory hybrid of ideal and practical considerations. It is neither really ideal nor really practical.

It is hard to know what we are supposed to do with a theory that makes large concessions (perhaps too large concessions) to the fact that people may not be willing to do things that are perfectly within their power but which would require them to make sacrifices, and at the same time assumes that, provided some threshold of non-demandingness is passed – as Rawls supposes his own theory to pass – we are entitled to assume absolute and invariable compliance with the dictates of the theory. It seems to me better to start from an ideal uncontaminated by the compliance problem but then when we move away from that introduce *all* the problems of compliance, in all their grisly variety and complexity.

In thinking about the dimensions of the compliance problem, it may be helpful to observe that there are two ways in which an ideal theory may run into difficulties with compliance. These two ways by no means invariably go together and there is some reason for thinking that they will tend to be inversely related.[21] First, then, an ideal theory of morality may run into practical difficulties because it is excessively *liable* to non-compliance. And second, it may run into difficulties if it is excessively *vulnerable* to non-compliance.

Other things being equal, a rule will be less liable to non-compliance the less that conformity with it entails a conflict with some strong desire, the more readily non-compliance can be monitored by others, and the more incentive others have to react to non-compliance in a way that reduces or eliminates the advantage gained. Other things being equal, a rule will be less vulnerable to non-compliance the less the difference to its value that is made by any level of non-compliance. In particular, it is important that the point of the rule – the ends that justify it – should not be frustrated by a small number of cases of non-compliance.

IV

I shall return to non-compliance later in this paper. For now, let me relax the constraint imposed by the problems of compliance and ask what an ideal set of international norms would look like. I shall focus particularly on the question of international economic distribution.

There is an influential view, put forward among others by Rawls, that distributive justice can be predicated only of relations within a society, where a society is understood as a scheme for mutual advantage through joint participation in cooperative undertakings. The idea is that distributive justice concerns the distribution of gains from social cooperation. This seems to me mistaken, if it is taken as setting the limits of distributive justice.

If one country builds tall smokestacks and pumps sulphur into the atmosphere which descends on another country downwind in the form of acid rain, then it has injured the other and should either clean up its act or compensate, as a matter of justice. There need be no reciprocal advantage or even any other form of relation between the two. Again, not all economic value is created by the cooperative effort that goes into it. Production requires land to take place in, and usually will use some raw materials. It will also be more effective in proportion to the capital that the current generation inherited. The notion that claims of justice can arise only among those engaging in a cooperative enterprise gets things back to front. Before the cooperation can occur some answer, good or bad, must already have been given to the distributive questions I have raised about the assignment of rights over land, resources, and other advantages that the would-be cooperators did not themselves create. As a matter of ideal morality, I think that the answer currently in vogue among the international community – that each state has an absolute right to everything in, under, over and extending two hundred miles beyond its national territory – is a rotten one. But the present point is simply that an answer has to be given and that it will establish a global distribution of some kind among countries that need have no cooperative relations at all.

The insistence on cooperation as a condition of morality stems from a conception of morality as a scheme of mutual advantage from mutual restraint. This, however, introduces the compliance issue too soon and too strongly – it provides a self-interested motive for compliance with moral norms by making the content of moral norms entirely coincident with what a sophisticated calculation of self-interest would require.

There is, however, an alternative conception of morality that can be found in Rawls (sitting very uneasily alongside the other one) and that has been put forward most clearly by Thomas Scanlon,[22] though we can find anticipations in, for example, David Hume and Adam Smith. According to this tradition of thought, there is a strong connection between morality and impartiality. A moral position is one that can be accepted from any viewpoint. If I claim to be talking morality, it is not enough for me to say, 'This arrangement suits me'. It must be capable of being defended to all those affected by it. If I could not reasonably be expected to accept it in the absence of coercion if I were in the position of any of the other people affected, then the arrangement cannot be morally justified. On this view the primary motive for behaving morally for its own sake (I have already pointed out that much of the time there are good self-interested reasons for doing what the moral norms of one's society require) is simply "the desire to be able to justify one's actions to others on grounds they could not reasonably reject", where the basis for the others' reasonably rejecting one's actions is given by *their* "desire to find principles which others similarly motivated could not reasonably reject".[23]

It may be complained that this is circular as a way of defining morality and the moral motive because the notion of reasonableness already presupposes that people have some moral ideas. I am not sure what Scanlon would say about this charge but for my part I think it ought to be admitted. We can in fact avoid giving 'reasonableness' a moral tinge here in two ways, but both of them, while tidying up the theory, lose its central idea in the process.

One possibility is to impute to the parties purely self-interested motivations, so that each will agree only to whatever will best serve his interests. 'Reasonableness' is thus construed as if it corresponded to the 'rationality' of game theorists and decision theorists, and, indeed, the whole theory is propelled by this interpretation of 'reasonableness' into making morality a subject for one or other of those disciplines.

If we set things up so that the parties have (as they usually have in real life) conflicting ends – what is optimal for me is rarely optimal for everybody else – we get a problem in game theory. Assuming, as seems plausible, that there must be some agreement that is better for everybody than a free-for-all, the problem is to identify the payoffs from a free-for-all and then devise some rule for distributing the gains that can be achieved by moving from that to an agreement. We thus arrive at a theory like that of David Gauthier,[24] behind whom stands the sardonic figure of Hobbes.

If, on the other hand, we eliminate confliciting interests by introducing constraints on the information about their own particular characteristics and position that is available to the parties, we get a decison-theoretic problem. Since the 'veil of ignorance', whatever the precise details of its construction (thick or thin, etc.), gives each party identical information to work with – information laundered of any clues that would enable them to differentiate themselves – they are all faced with the same set of calculations. Hence, we can represent the problem as one presented to a single decision-maker. We thus get theories such as Harsanyi's derivation of utilitarianism[25] or (one strand of) Rawls's theory of justice, where a maximum decision rule for choice under uncertainty is seen as leading to the difference principle which prescribes that the worst off should be raised to as high a level as possible.[26]

The other direction in which we could go in order to purge the notion of 'reasonableness' of any moral content would be to take Scanlon's formula literally and suppose the parties to be *solely* motivated by the desire to reach agreement. On this version we would not impute to them any substantive views at all about the acceptability of one outcome rather than any other. This line of thought would bring the problem of the terms of agreement under yet a third branch of formal theory. It is no game theory because there are no conflicting interests and it is not individual decision theory because it requires the parties to make estimates about each others' decisions. It is the study pioneered by Thomas Schelling in *The Strategy of Conflict*[27] of pure co-ordination problems: the sort of problem that arises when two people want to meet in a town without having made prior arrangements about a rendezvous and where each tries to decide where to go with the best chance of meeting the other, given the knowledge that the other is trying to make the same decision. The moral theory that will arise from this is conventionalism: the content of morality is arbitrary but it is still binding because it matters that we all act on the same rules, whatever they may be. Morality, on this view, becomes the search for "prominent solutions" (or 'Schelling points' as they have come to be known) in situations where some rule is needed.[28]

The youthful David Hume, ever on the look-out for paradoxes with which to jolt the world of polite learning into paying him some attention, came close to maintaining in the *Treatise* that the rules governing property are conventional in this way. The operations of 'fancy' – the disposition of the human mind to make associations between different ideas where there is no connection in reality – were invoked heavily to explain why the details of the rules about property took the form they did.[29] But by the time he came to write the *Enquiry* he had modified his position and now maintained only that fanciful analogues or associations of ideas might come in to settle the issue between two or more alternative rules which were equally beneficial. This is surely more plausible. The rule, for example, that assigns the lambs to the owner of the ewe stems not merely from a tendency for the fancy to run from the one to the other but from the rule's convenience and its avoiding the creation of perverse incentives.[30] The rule of the road is scarcely a paradigm of a moral rule. Usually it does make a difference what the content of the rule is.

I have spoken of two ways in which the notion of reasonableness could be construed so as to purge it of distinctively moral content. If we assimilate it to the rational pursuit of self-interest we get (depending what we do about information conditions) a problem in game theory or a problem in decision theory. And if we press to the limit the idea of seeking an agreement with others who are also seeking one we get a problem about the co-ordination of expectations. I have not indicated what I think is wrong with the first approach, though I have mentioned in passing the massive implausibility of the second. All I want to say here about the first is this: in seeking to transform what was intended as a guide to thinking about morality into a calculus capable of deriving moral conclusions from premises devoid of any moral content, it seems to me to miss the original point.

The notion of reasonableness is admittedly indefinite but it is not devoid of content. What we need to do to build up the theory is to specify it further, not substitute some simpler and more tractable notion. Thus, if we say that somebody has made a reasonable offer we mean, roughly speaking, that it is an offer that it would be reasonable for the other party to accept. And a reasonable person is one who (among other things) has a tendency to make – and accept – reasonable offers. We certainly will have to tighten this up if we want to characterise further the range (and it is likely to be a range rather than a unique point) of reasonable offers in some specific situation. But even without doing any of that further work we can be quite sure that a reasonable offer will not be identified with a rationally maximising offer (either with full information or behind some kind of veil of ignorance) and that a reasonable person will not turn out to be a rational maximiser.

I do not have the further development of the theory in hand, though I hope to do so in a few years' time, and even if I did this would hardly be the occasion on which to lay it out. I must press on with the problem to which this paper is addressed, while admitting that at this crucial point I have no more than gestured at the way in which one might understand morality as what it would be reasonable for all to accept.

Let me, however, suggest (without filling in all the steps) how we might bring evidence from the real world to bear in order to establish what, on this conception of morality, its dictates are for international distribution. As it stands, it sets up an ideal decision-making context of uncoerced agreement that is rarely found anywhere and, it seems safe to say, never in large groups such as states.[31] Nevertheless, societies approach the ideal more or less closely, and I do not think it is mere sentimentalism or unreflective submission to the local ideology to suggest that the modern Western liberal-democratic states are, by comparative and historical standards, relatively high on the criterion of unforced agreement. With obvious exceptions such as Northern Ireland, the jails do not contain many political prisoners and there is no sizeable section of the population that is thoroughly alienated from the society's major institutions. Suppose, then, that we look for invariant features of these societies. If we find them, cannot we at least say that we have a presumption in favour of these features being ones that arise in conditions of uncoerced agreement? Such, at any rate, is going to be my claim.

There are, I suggest, two features that are common to all the liberal-democratic societies. I do not indeed maintain that they are equally well-developed in all of those societies. But this actually strengthens my case if, as I believe, there is a positive correlation between the degree to which these features are present and the extent of universal uncoerced consent.

The first feature is this. Wherever the operations of the market (and these are all more or less market societies) have the consequence that people's incomes will vary enormously from year to year due to factors outside their control, the market will be suppressed or intervened in heavily by the state in order to mitigate or eliminate these effects. The obvious and striking illustration is, of course, the agricultural sector. The USA, that bastion of the free market, no less than the countries of the EEC, has an elaborate system of quotas, subsidies, and price supports to cushion farmers from the rigours of the market.

The second invarient feature that we find in all these countries is some kind of system for the relief of indigence caused by illness or injury, unemployment, age or youth. The well-being of those who, for some reason beyond their control, are unable to maintain themselves at a certain minumum standard is regarded as being the responsibility of the society, with the state acting to raise the taxes necessary to make the required payments. That a mechanism of this kind is crucial for the uncoerced acceptance of the basic social institutions is evidenced by the way in which such schemes have typically expanded as the suffrage has been extended to new groups further down the social hierarchy. It is particularly impressive that in some cases – Bismarck's Germany being the famous example – welfare legislation was introduced by a conservative government as a concomitant of the extension of the franchise precisely in order to forestall destabilising demands on the system.

When we turn from this history of domestic intervention and redistribution to that of the world economy, we are immediately struck by the absence of anything remotely comparable to either feature. With only very spotty exceptions (for example the STABEX scheme for certain primary commodities operated by the EEC countries and their former colonial dependencies), countries with one-crop or one-mineral economies are at the mercy of the ups and downs of an international market. And, as I have already observed, there is no scheme for the systematic transfer of funds from affluent countries to poor ones. The demands of the Third World countries for a 'New International Economic Order' centre around the attempt to bring commodity markets under some kind of international control, and proposals for the continuous creation under the International Monetary Fund of Special Drawing Rights for poor countries might be seen as an admittedly imperfect way of easing the constraints on their economies.

Both lines of initiative have foundered on the unwillingness of rich countries, led by the USA, with Japan, Germany and latterly Britain in support, to countenance any steps towards a new deal for the poor countries. Yet it seems clear that this refusal sticks only because the rich countries have the power to make it stick. The poor countries do not accept the reasonableness of the status quo and nor, if we were in their position, would we. It is, I have argued, a basic presupposition of the domestic politics of all countries in which the basic institutions achieve a fair level of consent from the population that people should not face ruin and destitution as a result of circumstances over which they have no control such as market forces or personal misfortunes. I think that this presupposition should carry over to international situations, where people's life chances are set primarily by their being born in a certain social position in a certain country and where no plausible personal exertion can raise the mass of people in a desperately poor country above poverty.

For the present purpose, I don't think it is necessary to argue about the precise implications of these ideas for the amount and nature of international redistribution that is called for, as a matter of ideal morality. It is enough if I am allowed to assume that it is very much larger than the current level of transfers, and also a good deal more for all relatively wealthy countries than the one per cent of gross national product that is the most given in aid by any country now. There are, we must suppose, practical limits on what the poorer countries could absorb, and these might well limit transfers. The point is that there is no need to settle any of these questions to know the direction in which things ought to go.

V

Let us now bring in the problem of compliance. The immediate question that we should confront here is: wherein does the compliance problem actually reside? It is easy to fall into the assumption that we have to come up with some scheme that will make it appear to all actors – in this case states – that it is in their interest to comply. But recall that that was not how we approached it in the earlier discussion of compliance in every day life.

There, the issue was presented as being that the system of obligations should not be too prone to subversion by non-compliance. This was analysed into two components. The first was liability to non-compliance, which I suggested was a function of the sacrifice demanded and the degree to which non-compliance could be monitored and sanctioned by others. The second was vulnerability to non-compliance, which I treated as in particular a matter of how serious a threat to the achievement of one's 'moral ends' was posed by non-compliance on the part of others.

If we turn this apparatus onto international affairs, I believe that we get the perhaps surprising conclusion that the problem of compliance is not a serious impediment to a move towards a much greater degree of international cooperation on economic matters and a great deal more international redistribution of income. Take vulnerability first. It seems reasonably clear that no government's 'moral ends' would be gravely jeopardised if it were to cooperate in an international scheme (say that proposed for the Law of the Sea) and there were some non-compliance. At a pinch, it can pull out or cease to comply if enough do so, and in the meantime the relative disadvantage from complying where others do not is scarcely likely to be of disastrous proportions. Similarly, it is irritating rather than a major setback to the interests of those countries that pay their share in some redistributive arrangement (say a certain proportion of gross national product to be paid into some fund) if some countries pay less than their share. We might say that the self-sufficiency of states, in comparison with individuals, has the implication that norms for states are in general less vulnerable to non-compliance than norms for individuals.

Of course, it may be thought that the other side of this is that international norms are particularly liable to non-compliance: just because states are less dependent on the cooperation of others to achieve their 'moral ends', they have less of a self-interested motive to play their part in observing any set of international norms. Now, I have already given full weight to the obvious point that legal sanctions of the centralised kind available within countries do not exist internationally. But we should not let that blind us to the way in which states already feel constrained, not by fear of military force directed against them, but simply by the anticipated consequences of violating international norms. The stock case is the extreme reluctance of governments to repudiate loans, even where the regime has changed and (as in Nicaragua) the proceeds of the loans taken out under the previous regime were misappropriated. A more complex example is that of the European Common Market, which succeeds in running a system of taxation of its member countries and a great mass of economic regulation with no sanction except the disadvantages to any country of withdrawing or being expelled. I do not want to overstate the general relevance of this example, but the point to be made is that, to the extent interdependence exists, it tends to make compliance with the norms defining that interdependence more reliable.

The number of states in the world, unlike the number of people in a country, is small enough that – provided the obligations are defined as those of states – there is some real chance of monitoring compliance with some scheme and making its continuation dependent on the achievement of some level of compliance. Thus, there is nothing in the problem of compliance to prevent governments from looking for ways of implementing the requirements of ideal justice by setting up international schemes. The great difficulty facing such moves is not compliance but motivation, and one of my major aims in this paper has been to try to avoid the confounding of the two. The problem of compliance, as I have presented it, presupposes some willingness to act morally simply for the sake of acting morally but allows for legitimate concern about the performance of others. The structure is, in terms of game theory, an assurance game rather than a prisoner's dilemma.

F. M. Cornford, in his classic analysis of academic politics *Microcosmographia Academica*, remarked that there is only one argument for doing something – that it is the right thing to do – and all the rest are arguments for doing nothing.[32] It sounds much more portentous to say that some admittedly desirable change is infeasible because it depends on too many other people doing the right thing than to confess simply that you choose not to make the change because, although it's the right thing to do, doing it would result in you incurring some cost.

In the current celebration of selfishness at home and chauvinism abroad that is apparently electorally popular in both Britain and the USA, it may indeed be that hypocrisy – the tribute paid by vice to virtue – is no longer in fashion. The pure assertion of naked national self-interest may not raise a blush. Unfortunately, on the account of morality that I have relied on here there is no way of making logically coercive arguments to get people to behave morally. I cannot, for example, maintain that those who violate the requirements of morality are engaged in some kind of self-contradiction.

In the view I have advanced, people have to want to behave in a way that can be defended impartially – in a way that has a chance of being accepted by others without coercion – for moral motivation to take hold. We are dealing with a psychological phenomenon rather than a logical one. If people once have moral motivation, rational argument has its place in helping to determine what concretely the requirements of morality are. But I do not think that people can be argued into having moral motivation if they lack it. Psychopaths are not necessarily lacking in ratiocinative capacity.

If this is correct, then it is natural to ask what are the conditions that predispose people to acquire moral motivation. I speculate that at any rate a part of the answer is going to be that the experience of dependence on others is an important predisposing factor. Those who are in a position to control the lives of others commonly become tyrannical. They behave in ways that they certainly would not voluntarily put up with if they were on the receiving end. There is nothing like constantly finding oneself in situations where one has to gain the cooperation of others in order to achieve one's own ends for encouraging one to cultivate the habit of looking at things from the other person's view and asking oneself what kind of conduct he might reasonably find acceptable.

I should emphasise that what I am here talking about is the conditions under which the moral motive may be aroused. As a proposition of speculative moral psychology, the suggestion is that – roughly speaking – equality of power, or at least not a too extreme inequality of power, is what is conducive to formation and elicitation of moral motivation. It is important to recognise that I am not reinstating the Hobbes/Gauthier conception of morality through the back door. In other words, I am not saying that the *reason* for acting morally is that, under conditions of approximately equal power, it is necessary for the pursuit of one's own advantage to cooperate with others on terms that can be mutually accepted as reasonable. The motive for acting morally remains what I said it was: the desire to be able to justify our conduct. My point is simply that that desire is more likely to come to the fore in conditions of approximately equal power than in conditions of radical inequality.

If there is anything in all of this, then the application at the international level is fairly apparent. The world is a place in which states are

very unequal indeed in power. The question is whether to follow Robert
Tucker (one of President Reagan's advisers in the 1980 election campaign)[33] in rejoicing in this fact, as he did in his book *The Inequality of
Nations*,[34] or whether to regard it as regrettable. Clearly, for anyone who
would like to see more moral motivation in the conduct of international
relations the current degree of inequality must be seen as a great misfortune. The problem is not only one of global inequalities of power,
though that is obvious enough, but one of extreme regional imbalances
of power as well. The Soviet Union's invasion of Afghanistan and the
USA's invasion of Grenada are paralleled by Israel's invasion of Lebanon
and South Africa's invasion of Angola, all carried out in the teeth of
virtually unanimous hostility from the rest of the world. There could be
no better illustration of Lord Acton's dictum that all power tends to
corrupt than the arrogant reaction of the governments of all our countries
to international criticism, typified by Reagan's reaction to the UN vote of
108 to 9 condemning the invasion of Grenada (apart from the six Caribbean countries that took part in the invasion only Israel and El Salvador
could be found to cast a vote in favour): "It didn't upset my breakfast at
all."[35]

The best prospect for the future that we can hope for is the reduction
of the present obscene inequalities of power among nations. In the long
run, there is some hope. The period since the Second World War has
seen massive decolonisation and the creation of new states that, though
individually weak, are certainly better placed to defend their interests
than before independence. It has also seen the end of the American
hegemony that was inevitable for a time in the aftermath of the Second
World War but was bound to disappear once recovery set in. The long-
term trend is, it seems to me, towards a more interdependent world.

Unhappily, however, it looks as if this evolution will be opposed by
the superpowers with all the forces at their command: covert 'destabilising' operations, military aid to regional surrogates, and, if all else fails,
direct intervention. In the long run it seems doubtful that this will prevent the equalisation of power from working itself out. But in a world
teeming with nuclear weapons it poses the danger that, to adapt Keynes's
famous remark, in the medium run we shall be dead. Ultimately we shall
be saved, if we are, by political action rather than political philosophy.

NOTES

1   Terry Nardin, *Law, Morality, and the Relations of States*, Princeton, N.J., 1983, p. 36.

2   Thomas Hobbes, *Leviathan*, ed. C. B. Macpherson, Harmondsworth, Middx., 1981, ch. 13, p. 185.

3   Derek Parfit, *Reasons and Persons*, Oxford, 1984, p. 99. An earlier, simpler, and clearer exposition is 'Prudence, morality, and the prisoner's dilemma', *Proceedings of the British Academy*, LXV, 1979, pp. 539–64; see esp. p. 559.

4   See Brian Barry and Russell Hardin (eds.), *Rational Man and Irrational Society?*, Beverly Hills, Calif., 1982, p. 108.

5   Parfit, *Reasons and Persons*, pp. 78–82.

6   Hobbes, *Leviathan*, ch. 14 (p. 196 in Macpherson).

7   *Ibid.*, ch. 15 (p. 215 in Macpherson).

8   *Ibid.*

9   Nardin, *Law, Morality, and the Relations of States*, p. 233.

10   Parfit, *Reasons and Persons*, p.99.

11   *Ibid.*

12   John Rawls, *A Theory of Justice*, Oxford, 1972, p. 9.

13   *Ibid.*, pp. 8–9.

14   *Ibid.*, p. 145.

15   *Ibid.*

16   *Ibid.*

17   *Ibid.*, p. 178.

18   *Ibid.*

19   *Ibid.*

20   *Ibid.*

21   I am indebted to Robert Goodin for pointing this out to me.

22   T. M. Scanlon, 'Contractualism and utilitarianism', in Amartya Sen and Bernard Williams (eds.), *Utilitarianism and Beyond*, Cambridge, 1982, pp. 103–28.

23   *Ibid.*, p. 116 and p. 116 n. 12.

24   David Gauthier, *Morals by Agreement*, Oxford, 1986.

25   John C. Harsanyi, 'Cardinal welfare, individualist ethics, and interpersonal comparisons of utility', *Journal of Political Economy* LXIII, 1955, pp. 309–21.

26   See Brian Barry, *The Liberal Theory of Justice*, Oxford, 1973, ch. 9, pp. 87–107; Rolf E. Sartorius, *Individual Conduct and Social Norms*, Encino, N. Mex., 1975, pp. 122–9.

27   Thomas C. Schelling, *The Strategy of Conflict*, Cambridge, Mass., 1960, ch. 4, pp. 83–118. See also David Lewis, *Convention*, Cambridge, Mass., 1969.

28   See for a discussion of this idea Karol Soltan, *Moral Reasoning and the Justification of Inequality*, unpublished Ph. D. dissertation, Department of Sociology, University of Chicago, 1982.

29   David Hume, *A Treatise of Human Nature*, ed. L. A. Selby-Bigge, 2nd edition by P. H. Nidditch, Oxford, 1978, Bk. III, Sec. III, pp. 501–13.

30   David Hume, *An Enquiry concerning the Principles of Morals* in *Enquiries*, ed. L. A. Selby-Bigge, 3rd edition by P. H. Nidditch, Oxford, 1975, pp. 195–6.

31   It is commonplace in the literature that Rawls's "original position" has some

similarities to Habermas's 'ideal speech situation'. What is more interesting is that they are not the same, and the spirit of the present enterprise is, I believe, closer to Habermas. Thus, Habermas writes that "it is a question of finding arrangements which can ground the presumption that the basic institutions of the society and the basic political decisions would meet with the unforced agreement of all those involved, if they could participate, as free and equal, in discursive will-formation", Jürgen Habermas, 'Legitimation problems in the modern state', in *Communication and the Evolution of Society*, trans. Thomas McCarthy, Boston, Mass., 1979, pp. 178–205, (quotation from p. 186). See also Joshua Cohen and Joel Rogers, *On Democracy*, Harmondsworth, Middx., 1983, ch. 6, pp. 146–83.

32 F. M. Cornford, *Microcosmographia Academica*, London, sixth edition, 1964, p. 22.
33 See Jeff McMahan, *Reagan and the World*, London, 1985, p. 11.
34 Robert Tucker, *The Inequality of Nations*, New York, 1977.
35 McMahan, *Reagan and the World*, p. 166.

REPLY TO PROFESSOR BARRY
Robert Fullinwider, University of Maryland

Professor Barry's paper is rich and complex, and there is much in it from which I would not dissent. I will restrict my comments to two facets of the paper – its discussion of compliance with rules and its description of a point of view from which to make judgements about international duties.

The object of Professor Barry's attack is someone he terms the *Realist*. Barry, like many others, wants to claim extensive and strong duties of nations towards each other, in particular duties of redistribution of wealth or resources. The Realist has a counter that allegedly undermines such claims: he raises the problem of compliance.

One problem of compliance is practical: how to get people or nations to abide by the rules they ought to. The second problem of compliance is the one raised by the Realist. I will call it the normative problem of compliance. It is that the failure of others to comply with a rule can nullify my duty to comply with it. Or, more strongly, that if I have no reason to believe others will comply with a rule, this may void any duty I might have had to act on it.

Let me give an example. I may believe I ought to act on the rule 'Take up arms to defend my country from unjust aggression'. But I need assurance that others will likewise take up arms: otherwise I have no duty of armed defence. This assurance might be provided by public manifestations of support for resisting the invader and other evidence of widespread volunteering, or it might be provided by a coercively enforced military draft.

How much of a problem *in general* is the normative compliance problem? I think it is plain that non-compliance by others does *not* threaten to undermine many of my moral duties. Consider standard duties of forbearance, such as duties not to murder or rape. These duties don't disappear if others are not complying. It is still morally incumbent on me not to do these things.

The same is true for many standard positive duties of aid. If I travel the road to Jericho, I should stop to bind the wounds of the robber's victim even if the priest and the Levite have passed by on the other side.

Non-compliance undermines duties only in special cases, namely where a good can be accomplished only by substantial joint action. A rule aiming for such a good, is, in Professor Barry's words, "vulnerable" to non-compliance. That is to say, the non-compliance by others threatens to destroy the very point or value of the rule. On the other hand, non-compliance does not undermine duty where the end of a rule is accomplished by my adherence no matter what others do. When a rule is vulnerable, let us say that the problem of compliance *applies*. When the problem of compliance does not apply, let's say the rule is *immune*.

To illustrate: the end of the rule against murder is to avoid wanton killing, and by adhering to the rule even when others do not, I avoid such killing and fulfil the end of the rule *for my part*. The end of the rule of aid is to improve another's needful condition, and by adhering to the rule even when others add nothing, I improve another's condition at least a bit, and fulful the end of the rule *for my part*.

On the other hand, an enterprise such as armed defence has an end that requires joint and co-ordinated action; if enough others do not comply, my isolated compliance does *not* accomplish the end *for my part*. The end of armed defence is not the killing of individual enemy soldiers but the blunting and repelling of the enemy attack. Isolated action cannot count as even trying to gain *this* end.

The rules against murder and for aid are *immune*. The problem of complance *applies to* armed defence, but may be *avoided* if assurance can be had.

How does the normative problem of compliance enter into the Realist's argument about the extent of a nation's duties to others? The Realist argues that states are justified in following their self-interest in international conduct. Because there is no central agency of enforcement among them, states can have no assurances of compliance to rules by other states. Thus, many rules which would otherwise be ideal impose no actual duties on nations. The thoughtful Realist, of course, acknowledges that states are bound by some moral duties, but he sees these as limited to duties against aggression and for humanitarian relief of distress.

Let us suppose with Professor Barry that ideal moral rules of international conduct call for extensive redistribution of wealth and resources. What are the *actual* redistributive duties of states? The answer to this will depend on the nature of the ideal rules – whether they are vulnerable or immune to non-compliance.

One possibility is that ideal rules are vulnerable to non-compliance and hence the problem of compliance applies. Moreover, it is *not avoided*, because assurances of compliance are not to be had. This is the Realist view sketched above. On this view, the actual redistributive duties of states will be very much less demanding than the ideal rules (perhaps limited only to humanitarian aid).

A second possibility is that the ideal redistributive rules are vulnerable to non-compliance but that the normative problem of non-compliance is *avoided* because assurances are to be had. There are reasons to expect compliance from other states. On this view, the actual redistributive duties of states will approach more closely the ideal duties. This second view is, I believe, Professor Barry's.

His rebuttal of the Realist relies upon showing that states do now commonly comply with rules of international behaviour and live up to their contractual and treaty obligations. That there is no international agency of enforcement does not mean that compliance with rules cannot be expected. For one thing, states often have much to gain through compliance. For another, because they are more or less self-sufficient, they don't risk great harm to themselves if they start acting on ideal rules and others don't reciprocate.

There is yet a third possibility. The ideal rules of redistribution may be immune to non-compliance. If this is so, the actual redistributive duties of states will be the same as their ideal duties.

Thus there are two ways to answer the Realist. The first concedes that ideal rules are vulnerable, but argues that assurances are available. The second denies that the ideal rules are vulnerable. Suppose we think ideal morality requires each nation to give a tenth of its income to improve the conditions of poorer nations. If most nations acted on such a rule, the result would be considerable international redistribution. But even if other nations ignored the rule, our own nation ought to give a tenth anyway. Non-compliance does not appear to nullify the duty.

Since Professor Barry does not specify the ideal redistributive rules he prefers, we cannot say whether they are immune or vulnerable. He hints at an international tax and distribution system modelled on the welfare state. Whether a taxation scheme is immune or vulnerable depends on its ends. If the end is to raise as much money for good use as can be done, then the non-compliance of others would not undermine our nation's duty to contribute or to self-tax; by doing so it would be contributing some money for good use and thus carrying out the end of the scheme *for its part*. On the other hand, if the end of the taxation scheme is to support some fixed level of entitlement or public accomplishment then the normative problem of compliance applies to the scheme and in circumstances where it cannot be enforced nor other assurances of compliance given, no one may have an obligation to contribute.

What if the ideal redistributive rules are vulnerable? In that case, I do not believe Professor Barry's answer to the Realist is fully persuasive. First, evidence of substantial state compliance with current rules of international conduct is not probative. The current system is, in Barry's judgement, undemanding. The ideal rules he favours would be very demanding. Second, it seems likely that a genuine international taxation system, as opposed to a voluntary contribution system, would require erosion or elimination of state sovereignty. In that case, one of the main reasons for pointing to the self-sufficiency of states and the minimal risk they incur in adhering to the ideal rule(s) is undercut. Consequently, Barry has failed to show that although ideal international redistributive rules are *vulnerable*, the normative problem of non-compliance can be *avoided* because excessive non-compliance is not as likely as the Realist predicts.

Now, I want briefly to turn to Professor Barry's comments about the moral foundations that would yield his strongly redistributive ideal rules, whatever they are. The foundations lie, he claims, in the operations of a principle of *impartiality*. Here is what Barry has to say about impartiality: "A moral position is one that can be accepted from any viewpoint." And again he says: "People have to want to behave in a way that can be defended impartially – in a way that has a chance of being accepted by others without coercion." "If," he goes on, "people in rich countries were in the same boat as those in poor ones they too would demand a new deal." Now this last claim is almost certainly true. But why should the demand count for anything?

Professor Barry implies a strategy here: put ourselves in the shoes of others. But this strategy cannot tell us anything about what ought to be done; so it cannot tell us whether there should be international redistribution or not. If the rich person puts himself in the place of the poor person he wants a new deal. But if the poor person puts himself in the place of the rich person, he *doesn't* want a new deal! All that Barry's statergy yields is *information*. When I apply it, it tells me I want one thing from one point of view and another thing from a second point of view. It doesn't tell me which point of view is authoritative, or how to amalgamate the two points of view into one, or how to transcend the two points of view with a better one.

Moreover, Professor Barry's implicit solution – i.e., to make it a condition of moral acceptability that a position can be consented to from any point of view – is surely unsound. From the point of view of the convicted criminal facing sentencing, that is, from the point of view of a person facing extreme deprivation, incarceration is not consented to without coercion. This does not make the judge's sentencing the criminal to imprisonment wrong. In fact, morality requires of the criminal that he take up a point of view different from his own for evaluating and understanding what is happening to him. Morality requires impartiality as disinterestedness, not as acceptability from all viewpoints.

Professor Barry needs to say a great deal more about the principle of impartiality and how it might generate the richly redistributive results he desires.

There *is* a viewpoint which produces richly redistributive implications, and is also one which has very much to do with the terms in which we think it acceptable to justify ourselves to others. It is a point of view in which I am unwilling to benefit unless you benefit as well. I am unwilling to say to you that you must be content with the cards fortune has dealt you: it was none of my doing that you stand still while I prosper. This is the point of view of *fraternal relations*.

There are yet other similar points of view. When Jesus told the parable of the Samaritan, which I made use of earlier, he was not urging his listeners to remember their natural duty to relieve distress. He was proposing something more radical – that one view the victim beside the road to Jericho as a *neighbour*. A neighbour, too, is someone with whom we have a greater urge to share our own good fortune.

I believe, in fact, that the richly distributive policies Professor Barry desires are to be founded on such relationships as these and not on a virtually empty principle of impartiality. As evidence for his argument about the implications of impartiality, Barry adduces domestic policies that dampen the ill-effects of market and political processes by providing an economic minimum, unemployment insurance, and other protections. I am inclined to view these policies less as reflecting a growing capability toward impartiality and consent from any point of view than as reflecting a growing capacity for citizens to view each other as interconnected the way neighbours and brothers (sisters) are and thus unwilling to advance in fortune, unconcerned about those left behind.

Thus, I am brought in the end to agree with Professor Barry's final point: what is needed for creating a world honouring the ideal rules of redistribution he desires is not political theory but political action. If such a rich conception of international justice requires bringing persons to see other nationals as brothers (sisters) and neighbours, this can happen only through a transformation of consciousness, not a tutoring in philosophy.

DISCUSSION

Professor Stephen Clark, University of Liverpool. I would like to raise two points, one practical and one theoretical, though they are connected. The practical point is this: attempts to give large percentages of national income to other countries, particularly when that is by state action, don't have such a wildly successful record that it's altogether reasonable to say that one has to do it or one is immoral. What can very often happen is that certain bureaucrats in the recipient country get extremely rich, large numbers of business men and farmers go out of business, and the mass of people remain exactly as impoverished as they were before. And the record of Western state giving is perhaps not as good in this respect as giving through various voluntary charitable organisations with some experience of these matters. That is the practical point. The theoretical point behind it is this: there is at least some suspicion that historical conceptions of justice – historical in two senses: first, they are the conceptions of justice that people have usually had in the past, and historical in a second sense in that they make some reference to what has happened in the past – these conceptions of justice do as a matter of fact make it clear that our sending acid rain across to other nations is aggression and we owe reparation for it, that much of our wealth in the West is founded upon theft of resources and people, and we owe reparation for that. In other words a strongly natural-rights-based libertarianism with an historical conception of justice already says a great deal about the matter of what is owed in reparations, not in terms of what we ought to give people because they are worse off than we would like them to be, but just as a matter of justice, ordinary historical justice. And I think you will find this said quite often in the political tradition to which Professor Barry rather scathingly refers at times.

Professor Barry. Yes, there is certainly some truth in the theoretical point and a certain amount of play can be made of that. But the trouble is, as far as its implications are concerned, that it is very often the very poorest countries for whom it's most implausible to say that their current poverty is the result of exploitation by Western countries. Generally speaking, you've got to have some resources to begin with in order to be exploited, and I think the worse-off countries are precisely those that haven't been thought worth exploiting! So although argument could be made on the lines that Clark mentions, I think it would be unlikely to finish up with the results that I at any rate would favour, namely that the strength of the case for some kind of transfer to the worse-off countries is a matter of how badly off they are. And this should not depend upon some sort of historical enquiry into how things got like this, which seems to me to be morally irrelevant. As far as the practical problem is concerned, this is obviously an enormous problem, and one that I am trying to address elsewhere – but that's no help here. I think a lot of the problems come about as a result of the form that aid has taken. And I would like to see a greater element of automaticity coming into this. That is to say, if you just look at countries that have had an increase in income without any strings attached (the obvious example is that of some country that discovers oil) generally speaking such countries have had a boost to their economic development from having access to this income. And generally speaking, simply making more resources available, so that countries can simply import more without having to export more, is the way to go. Of course a lot of this is going to happen anyway simply because of the huge levels of debt that a lot of Third World countries have already accrued. That is to say, there is already a systematic transfer going on; it is just that it is being covered by an increasingly crazy system of paper debt which nobody expects is ever going to be repaid. You wouldn't actually have to change anything very much to simply arrange a system whereby Third World countries were allowed in effect to write off a certain amount of debt each year and contract new debts on the same basis.

Dr J. A. Carty, University of Glasgow. I'd like to turn to the last thing Professor Fullinwider said, which I found very depressing, since I am not optimistic about such transformations of consciousness occurring. So I would like to see if reasoning can in fact get us a bit further. It is a familiar point in the literature that one could adopt policies which would be substantially beneficial to developing countries which would be nothing more than a consistent carrying out of ideological positions which are very firmly held by Western countries. Examples are very well known. The protectionism of developed countries towards the products coming from developing countries is so serious that it has been interpreted by some economists as meaning that the developed countries prefer to lend money to developing countries whch they cannot pay back rather than allow developing countries to pay for imports from developed countries by exporting to them. That is one example. It would be easy to produce other examples of such irrationality. The European Economic Community's Common Agricultural Policy affords quite a few!

Professor Fullinwider. It seems to me that the problem with that is that national leaders are not deeply stupid people! So that is not the reason why we persist in these apparently stupid policies. Once you begin to ask why we do pursue such policies, you find stories being told that are shot through with references to values or to traditions to which we are deeply attached. So I don't think this is a result of stupidity.

Professor Barry. Whether or not national leaders are stupid, there remains the point that they are being inconsistent. I take it that Carty's point, which I think is a good one, is that the line that I am taking requires an extension to the international order of the sort of reasoning which would lead to the welfare state on the domestic front. And that in some quarters is still controversial. Carty's point is that all the Western governments mouth these things about anti-protectionism and so on, and that at least from the point of view of consistency there are some premises here which they at any rate officially accept. And that seems to me to be right.

Mr John Hall, University of St. Andrews. I'd like to return to the idea that we are bound *in justice* to assist Third World countries. It should be borne in mind that where there is a duty of justice it is irrelevant what the recipient of the benefit awarded then does with what is awarded to him. So if we really believe that poor countries have a claim in justice to certain transfers from the rich countries, then they have this claim even if we know that the governments to whom these transfers are made are going to spend them on golden thrones. I doubt if in fact we do believe that when the question arises whether there should be transfers made by rich nations to poor nations it is in fact irrelevant what the governments to whom the transfers are made will actually do with the resources so transferred. And therefore I don't believe that if we think clearly we believe that justice comes into question. We should regard this issue as entirely a matter of benevolence.

The logic and ethics of nuclear deterrence[*]

ANTHONY KENNY
Balliol College, Oxford

The 1981 statement on the Defence Estimates says that deterrence "rests, like a chess master's strategy on blocking off in advance a variety of possible moves in an opponent's mind". If one understands this, we are told, one will see how shallow are many of the criticisms made of Western security policy. The analogy of the game of chess has clearly caught hold on the imagination of some of those at the Ministry: the leaflet widely distributed by the Ministry of Defence public relations department is covered with pictures of chessmen interspersed between the paragraphs it reprints from the 1981 Estimates.

The analogy deserves to be looked at closely, because I think it is true that Western strategists see their task as being to discover and maintain operational plans that will resemble a winning strategy in chess. But there is a point at which the analogy ceases to work; and the point of its failure reveals the weakness of the deterrent theory. In terms of the analogy, annihilation by nuclear weapons corresponds, obviously enough, to checkmate. Just as the chess master tries to block off possible moves of his opponent by adopting a position in which such moves will lead to the opponent being mated, so the nuclear strategist tries to block off possible options of an enemy by putting the enemy in a position where those options will lead to his nuclear annihilation. Thus far, the analogy holds. But there is this big difference between chess and nuclear warfare: in chess you can only mate once, and only one side can be checkmated, whereas in nuclear war there can be more than one completely devastating stroke, and both sides may be annihilated in the exchange.

It would, in chess, be enough to rule out a move if it could be shown to lead to being checkmated; because, once checkmated, there is nothing more that a player can do; and a player who, at a given move of the game, has it in his power to checkmate has, within the game, nothing to lose by checkmating. But it is not enough to rule out a strike by nuclear power A that it could be shown that it would lead to a retaliatory nuclear strike by power B; for power B, by carrying out that strike, would be

* This paper has appeared previously in my *The Ivory Tower*, Oxford, 1985, and, in a revised form, in my *The Logic of Deterrence*, London, 1985.

risking a counter-retaliatory strike by A. We claim to be able to rule out of consideration, in the mind of Soviet planners, a conventional invasion of Western Europe, on the grounds that this will lead to a NATO first-use of nuclear weapons. But do not whatever considerations rule out the conventional invasion in the Soviet planners' minds equally argue for the ruling out of the first nuclear use in the minds of NATO planners? If they would be mad to trigger off our nuclear strike, would not we be equally mad to trigger off theirs? If it would be rational for them to desist from their conventional invasion because of fear of our nuclear first-use, would it not be equally rational for us to desist from our first-use because of fear of their nuclear retaliation? Thus the logic of deterrence seems self-defeating.

The logic only appears to work, perhaps, because those who believe in it either fail to take the game of threat and counterthreat beyond the first move, or because they think that rationality works in two different ways on the two different sides of the Iron Curtain. If there is any difference, the MOD is anxious to overcome it: they say "planning deterrence means thinking through the possible reasoning of an adversary and the way in which alternative courses of action might appear to him in advance. It also means doing this in his terms, not in ours." It is hard to see how someone who does this can reach the conclusion that there are circumstances in which it would not be rational for an adversary to attack us, for fear of our nuclear retaliation, but would be rational for us to retaliate on him, despite the fear of his nuclear counter-retaliation. At any point where we are deterring him, he must be deterring us from carrying out our deterrent threat.

If there is any difference between the rationality of a Soviet conventional attack under the threat of NATO first use, and the rationality of NATO first-use under the threat of Soviet nuclear counterattack, the advantage is surely with the former. It seems marginally more likely that NATO would at the last minute draw back from its threatened first-use after a Soviet invasion, than that the Soviets would fail to retaliate after an initial nuclear attack from the West. The extra odium which attaches to the initiation rather than the continuation of nuclear hostilities, and the enormous riskiness of the first crossing of the nuclear threshold, make the NATO threat less credible than the Soviet one, to the extent that either is credible at all as an expression of a rationally devised strategy. To the extent to which we may believe that the West is more likely than the East to be deterred from nuclear escalation by moral scruples, the effectiveness of our policy in blocking off options in the Soviet perspective is further diminished.

It may be countered that I have only succeeded in arguing that the deterrent is self-defeating by committing an error parallel to that to which I am drawing attention: having complained that others have not thought past the first threat to a counterthreat, I myself have ended the story with the counterthreat, and have not taken into account the counter-counterthreat, the NATO strategic deterrent, which will prevent the Russian counterthreat from being put into effect. Did not the whole doctrine of flexible response depend on there being a large number of steps up the escalatory ladder? At each point on this ladder, escalation can be undertaken by one side only under the threat of further escalation by the other. So NATO's first-use threat may after all be credible, because though it could be neutralised by a Russian threat to retaliate, that threat is itself rendered impotent because of our ability to retaliate upon the retaliator.

But why should we stop at move three, or four, or five? Should not we be held back from using our ability to counter-retaliate by the Russians' residual ability to strike back in retaliation upon the counter-retaliator? It would only be when one side had exhausted its arsenal, so that the other could use its remaining missiles without fear of drawing a response in kind, that there would exist the conditions for a threat which was not rendered impotent by a counterthreat. But this fact can hardly be relied on by an alliance considering the first use of nuclear weapons; for neither side could be sure in advance of being the one which ended up with the last glorious remaining weapons; and both sides know in advance that before that final state is reached more than enough warheads will have been exploded to destroy many times the civilisations and populations that each side claims to be defending.

To say that deterrence is based on muddled logic is not, however, to say that it does not work. After all we are each afraid, very much, of the other's deterrent, whether this is or is not a rational fear, whether this is a fear of a rational stategy or a fear of an enemy's possible suicidal madness. What I want to argue is that even if deterrence does, in some mysterious and irrational way, work to instil fear, it is still immoral to rely on it for our defence, as the current strategy of the Western alliance is committed to doing.

From the moral point of view there are three things wrong with the current strategy of the Western alliance. There are three main ways in which it can be criticised on ethical grounds. It is wasteful, it is dangerous, and it is murderous. It is wasteful: the current arms race involves an extravagant build-up of armaments which can serve no military purpose. It is dangerous: it enhances the risk of confrontations likely to lead to an outbreak of nuclear war. It is murderous: it involves plans which call for the wiping out in certain circumstances of large centres of civilian population. Because it is wasteful, dangerous, and murderous the current policy of NATO is morally unacceptable.

The three kinds of moral objection are not all of equal weight, and I have listed them in order of increasing importance. Current policy is extravagant, but large military budgets are not inherently evil, and the arms industry is a great provider of employment and a fertile soil for technological innovation. It is the pressure of other claims on the world's resources, when much of the human race goes in need, which makes the extravagance of the arms race an immoral, as well as an imprudent, use of economic power. Current policy is dangerous, but in a world in which nuclear weapons have been invented and cannot be disinvented, no defence policy is going to be free from danger. The objection to current policies is that rather than limiting this danger, as their proponents claim, they actually increase it. This objection needs careful argument which takes account of the probabilities of different outcomes, and the magnitude of the catastrophes involved in each probable outcome. In this paper, I will concentrate on the objection that Western policies are murderous: for this is the most fundamental and most serious of the objections.

Moreover, this is the issue on which a philosophical consideration of the ethical issues has most to contribute. In assessing whether a defence policy is criminally extravagant or unacceptably dangerous it is necessary to bring to bear technical information and to make necessarily conjectural estimates of the costs and consequences of alternatives. But though moral judgements can never be altogether separated from issues of fact, detailed factual information is less important when one is trying to settle whether current defence policies are murderous. When supporters and opponents of NATO nuclear policies argue whether they are or are not murderous, they are usually in agreement about the relevant facts, namely the nature of the proclaimed stategy. Their disagreement is a moral one about the wrongs and rights of the deliberate killing of civilian populations. What is most needed, in order to resolve this disagreement, is a clarification of the moral concepts and principles involved. So in what I have to say I will concentrate on the issue of murder, both because it is the most important of the three moral issues raised by our policies, and because it is the issue where ethical clarification has most to offer.

My main concern will be to bring out what is wrong with current policies: I shall not be considering alternative policies. It is sometimes said, in criticism for instance of some members of CND, that it is wrong to condemn the nuclear deterrent if one has no alternative to put in its place. I do not think this is correct: one may be quite clear that something is the wrong answer to a problem without knowing what is the right one. If someone comes to me for advice and says, 'Please tell me what I should do; my marriage is intolerable; the only thing I can do to bring this mess to an end is to kill my husband', I may perfectly well reply: 'I don't know what you *should* do, but I know you shouldn't do *that*'.

In this paper I am addressing myself to those who agree that nuclear war waged on populations or causing disproportionate numbers of civilian deaths is morally unacceptable, but who accept with various qualifications the policy of possessing and deploying nuclear weapons as a deterrent.

Those who, while renouncing full-scale nuclear war, defend nuclear deterrence fall into two classes: there are those who justify possession of nuclear weapons as a deterrent on the grounds that some uses of those weapons may be legitimate; and there are those who defend the possession of nuclear weapons as a deterrent while agreeing that the use of them in all circumstances must be wrong.

It is possible to imagine uses for at least some nuclear weapons which would be legitimate. Considered in themselves, none of the traditional criteria for the conduct of just war would rule out the interception of ballistic missiles, the use of nuclear depth-charges on submarines, or the explosion of a nuclear weapon as a demonstration shot in an uninhabited area. In concrete circumstances, of course, such activities might be intolerably provocative or dangerous, and might well be intended as an expression of a resolve to proceed to more nefarious uses of nuclear weapons; but in the abstract they are morally defensible. But it would be folly to conclude that because some uses of some nuclear weapons are legitimate, that makes all possession of any nuclear weapons legitimate. The legitimacy of the possession of nuclear weapons depends on the purposes for which they are kept and the likely ways in which they would be used. The defenders of deterrence do not claim that deterrence can be maintained by the threat of these marginal uses alone.

The crucial question is this. Is there any use of nuclear weapons which is both ethically justified and sufficiently extensive to underpin the deterrent threat? Can a potential aggressor be deterred by a threat to do anything less than launch a murderous attack? Or must it be the case that any threat which is sufficient to act as a deterrent to our potential enemies be a threat whose execution would be immoral?

Before discussing this question we may begin by agreeing readily that the nuclear powers are in a position to inflict intolerable damage on an adversary without making use of all the capacity they possess: in order to deter they do not need to threaten to wage war to the limit of their strength. The super powers could execute a deterrent threat with only a fraction of their present arsenals: this is one of the most frequent complaints of critics of the arms race. Even a minor nuclear power like the United Kingdom has the physical power to cause, with a single one of its Polaris submarines, damage on a scale which no Soviet government is likely to think tolerable.

But to say that the damage which a deterrent threatens is less than a deterrer, if unrestrained, could inflict does not settle the question whether such a threat of damage is justified. The Polaris warheads, for instance, in order to carry out a threat adequate to deter the Soviet Union would have to be targeted on cities or military targets in densely populated areas. The defenders of the deterrent whom I am addressing in this paper agree that the execution of such a threat could never be justified.

They argue, however, that a targeting strategy sufficient to deter need not involve any massive attacks on cities as such. An attack aimed at wrecking economic effort, transport systems and structures of command, in conjunction with a discriminating bombardment of forces in the field, could well cripple an aggressive regime in wartime and sap its will for military adventure while leaving the great majority of its population intact. Even such an attack would, beyond doubt, cause a large number of non-combatant deaths; but these would neither be the purpose of the attack nor out of proportion to the presumed goal of warding off totalitarian conquest with the slavery and deaths which this would bring in its train. In absolute terms, the number of deaths could well be substantially less than the number thought tolerable in the war against Hitler.

Hence, it is argued, there could be a scale of strike large enough to rob an aggressor of the will to continue a war, and yet limited enough so that the expected harm to civilians is less than the evil expected if the aggression is successful. It is no doubt difficult to decide in advance, and in ignorance of the exact nature of the aggressor and scale of the aggression, the precise target-plan and mix of weapons of different yields required for such a judicious onslaught. But its possibility is sufficient to justify the maintenance of the deterrent capability to administer such a blow should the occasion arise.

Such an argument, in my view, is the most powerful form that an ethical defence of the deterrent can take. But though powerful, it turns out on examination to be quite inadequate for its purpose.

Whether an attack of the form described would be possible on Warsaw Pact targets in practice is something which is difficult to decide without knowing a considerable amount about the economic geography and military dispositions in the Soviet Union and its satellites. But we do know enough to show that no such attack on Great Britain would be possible. In Operation Square Leg, a Government simulation of a Soviet attack on this country, no bombs were assumed to have fallen on inner London; it was assumed that five targets, such as Heathrow, were hit around the periphery. None the less the consequences, which are described in *London after the Bomb*[1] include five million dead in the London area within two months of the attack. Even allowing for the lesser density of the population in many parts of Eastern Europe, the result of an attack on military and economic targets in Warsaw Pact countries is likely to be tens of millions dead. And of course many of the targets presented by the Warsaw Pact armed forces, on the hypothesis of an invasion of the West, would be in friendly NATO nations.

But suppose even twenty million Russians, Poles, Czechs and their allies are killed in such an attack. Is that not better than that the West should succumb to totalitarian domination? Is it not a lesser number of deaths than were thought tolerable in the war against Hitler?

There is something grotesque in the idea that because the allies were justified in going to war against Hitler, then any war against a totalitarian enemy is justified if it causes fewer deaths than were caused in Hitler's war. First of all, the great majority of deaths in Hitler's war were caused not by the allies, but by Hitler's armies, Hitler's police, and Hitler's gaolers: it is absurd to suggest that because we were justified in going to war against Hitler we would be justified in any future war in causing as many deaths as he did. Secondly, few would now claim that even all the deaths inflicted by the Allied side were justified: the lives lost in the bombing of Hamburg, Dresden, Hiroshima and Nagasaki by the Western allies, the lives taken by the vengeful Russian troops in their victorious advance to the west: these hardly provide a paradigm for the measurement of proportionality in future wars. Can we be certain that the war did more good than harm, in the sense that the world was a better place in 1946 than it was in 1938, or even than it would have been in 1946 had there been no war? Even if we can, that does not mean that we can lump together all the deaths caused in the war and say that the good it did was worth the loss of all those lives.

But even if we waive these difficulties, the comparison with the Second World War leaves out of account the most important thing: that the Third World War would be fought, as the Second was not, against an enemy who is himself armed with nuclear weapons. Even if a damage-plan could be devised which would satisfy the strictest scrutiny in accordance with the principles of non-combatant immunity and proportionality, putting it into action against an enemy prepared and willing to launch massive retaliation would be an act of reckless folly. The criteria for just warmaking include, it must be remembered, not only proportionality and non-combatant immunity, but also the hope of victory.

Defenders of the deterrent, faced with this objection, make two responses. First, they say that a victim of aggression cannot necessarily be held responsible for the response of the aggressor to the victim's self-defence: a woman has no absolute duty to submit to rape, for instance, even if she believes that resistance will lead to further violence. Hence, any Russian retaliation to a limited Western attack would be their responsibility and not ours. Secondly, we have no reason to assume that Western resistance on these lines would inevitably lead to an unlimited counterattack on our cities. In a nuclear war neither side would want escalation; both would be looking for ways to end the struggle; the Soviets would be no less anxious than the NATO allies not to put the cities of their homelands at further risk.

The first response commits an error opposite to that committed in the value-judgement about the death toll in the Second World War. It is a mistake to lump together all the deaths in a war and regard both sides as equally responsible for them: there is a difference between the lives a nation takes and the lives it loses. But it is an equally distorting error to suggest that a government can entirely escape responsibility for the loss of lives which it brings upon its own side by its attacks on an enemy. The major responsibility for such deaths does, of course, rest on the aggressor who causes them; but responsibility also rests on the side which, foreseeing the possibility of such retaliation, goes ahead with its own attack.

It is correct, as the second response reminds us, that there would be no certainty of a massive Soviet response to a limited Western attack: in matters involving human choices and decisions, in times of passion and confusion, there can be no scientific prediction or justified certainty in advance of the outcome. But in order for it to be rational to desist from a course of action, it is not needed that it should be certain to have a catastrophic result; it is sufficient that catastrophe should be a consequence that is more or less likely. After all, the main reason for saying that it is not certain that the Soviets would opt for massive retaliation is that *they* would fear a Western response in kind. But that in turn is uncertain. The mere risk of such a response on our side is supposed to be sufficient to make them, as rational human beings, think twice about launching their attack; but should not the risk of their attack, at the earlier stage, provide an equally strong reason for refraining from the limited attack? Moreover, if the Soviets are deterred from a counter-city counterattack it is because they are afraid of an all-out assault on their population. But this, according to the defender of the deterrent, is something that would be immoral in itself, and the threat of which plays no part in the deterrent strategy.

It seems, then, impossible to defend the view that there can be a use of nuclear weapons sufficiently devastating to underpin the deterrent threat, while sufficiently discriminating to be capable of non-murderous execution. What of those who defend the deterrent while agreeing that no actual use of nuclear weapons is defensible? There are those who are resolved never actually to press the nuclear button, and who yet wish to retain nuclear weapons as a deterrent. This seems to be the policy recommended by the US Catholic bishops, and in the UK by Cardinal Hume: use is forbidden, deterrence is permissible.

The qualified approval given by these authorities to deterrence was no doubt influenced by the statement of Pope John Paul II to the UN special session in 1982. "In current conditions, 'deterrence' based on balance, certainly not as an end in itself, but as a step on the way toward a progressive disarmament, may still be judged morally acceptable." The US bishops, in spite of their profound scepticism about the moral acceptibility of any use of nuclear weapons, stopped short of an unequivocal condemnation of deterrence, though they rejected any quest for nuclear superiority or plans for prolonged periods of repeated nuclear strikes, and they insisted that deterrence must be a step on the way to disarmament, towards which they recommend a number of specific proposals.

Cardinal Hume, in an article in *The Times* on 17 November 1983, wrote that: "The acceptance of deterrence on strict conditions and as a temporary expedient leading to progressive disarmament is emerging as the most widely accepted view of the Roman Catholic Church". It would be wrong, the Cardinal says, to apply to the policy of deterrence the same moral condemnation that would be given to the actual use of nuclear weapons against civilian targets, which was something that nothing could ever justify. Since the purpose of deterrence was to avoid war, servicemen could be commended, and not blamed, for taking their part in maintaining it. But the condition that deterrence should be a stage towards disarmament was crucial: a government which failed to reduce its weapons and limit their employment could expect its citizens to be alienated from its defence policies. And finally, deterrence had to be seen as a means of preventing, not waging, war. "If it fails and the missiles are launched, then we shall have moved into a new situation. And those concerned will have to bear a heavy responsibility." How they should carry out this responsibility, the Cardinal did not say; presumably, whatever they do, they must not use nuclear weapons in the way he has already condemned, "as weapons of massive and indiscriminate slaughter".

The Cardinal admits that his position is a strange one: "There is a tension, then, between the moral imperative not to use such inhuman weapons and a policy of nuclear deterrence with its declared willingness to use them if attacked. To condemn all use and yet to accept deterrence places us in a seemingly contradictory position." Many, even among the Catholic church, are yet to be convinced that if all use is wrong, deterrence is still permissible. Some, convinced of the wrongness of the use of the weapons, deplore the lack of an authoritative and unequivocal condemnation of deterrence; others, accepting the Pope's judgement that deterrence, as things are, is tolerable, take issue with the US bishops' outspoken 'no' to nuclear warfare.

Is the position represented by Cardinal Hume in fact self-contradictory? Would a deterrent operated by people who believed that nuclear weapons must never be used be either credible or ethical? Would there be any point in retaining bombs that one was resolved never to drop and missiles one was determined never to launch?

It can, I think, be argued that such a policy is perfectly consistent with deterrent theory, as well as in accord with the demands of proportionality and non-combatant immunity. The point of deterrence is to provide an input to the practical reasoning of a potential adversary; if an adversary proves to be undeterred, then the deterrent has failed to be effective at the time when it was purported to be effective; it cannot, as it were, be made retrospectively effective by a retaliatory strike. The point of using it therefore disappears. Thus far, then, deterrence without use seems possible.

The difficulty in a deterrent policy of this sort is that if it is announced to the enemy in advance, it is not obvious that the possession of nuclear weapons would continue to deter. The proponents of deterrence normally regard it as essential that the possession of the weapons should be accompanied by the threat, explicit or implicit, to use them if need arise. Those who wish to defend deterrence while opposing use therefore have to be prepared to maintain that it can be legitimate to threaten what it would not be legitimate to do. Is this a defensible ethical position?

It may be argued that the threat to use nuclear weapons cannot be justified: for if it is insincere it involves deception, and if it is not insincere it involves the intention to do what we have agreed it would be wrong to do. This argument moves a little too fast, and it is worthwhile to take it to pieces to see how far it works and how far it does not.

It must, I think, be conceded to defenders of the deterrence strategy that it is misleading for the arguments for and against the morality of the policy to be framed in terms of the intentions of the deterrer. It must be agreed that something less than an intention to use the weapons may be sufficient to deter a potential attacker. A mere willingness to use the weapons will suffice, a willingness which consists in preserving their use as a genuine option.

It is correct to make a distinction between intention and willingness: there can be a great difference between the two states of mind in degree of certainty and resolve implied. But making the distinction does not have a great effect on the course of the moral argument. If it is true that it is wrong to intend to do what it is wrong to do, it is equally true that it is wrong to be willing or ready to do what it is wrong to do. Any argument for the one proposition is an equally good argument for the other. If the wrong in question is an absolute wrong, then it is absolutely wrong to be ready to commit it, just as it is absolutely wrong to intend to commit it. To say that something is absolutely wrong is precisely to say that it is not a permissible option.

To reach a final assessment of the morality of the deterrent we have to ask: what exactly is it that does the deterring? As things are the deterrent has two elements. One is the physical element, the nuclear hardware and the power that gives to each side to destroy the other: this is what has been dubbed by McGeorge Bundy "The existential deterrent". The other is the political element, the declared intention or readiness of the two sides to use the hardware to destroy the enemy society in certain circumstances.

But does this mean that one must unilaterally disarm? Not necessarily: that depends on whether the political and the physical element of the deterrent can be separated from each other. And whether this is possible depends on how the mechanism of deterrence operates.

Now if it could be severed from the *willingness* to destroy an enemy population, would the mere maintenance of the *power* to do so necessarily be wrong? That must depend, in part, on how the power is maintained. As things are, everyone involved in the military chain of command, from the top downwards, must be prepared to give or execute the order to massacre millions of non-combatants if ever the government

decides that this is what is to be done. And this is one of the things most
wrong with our deterrent strategy.

But must it necessarily be so, and is the only alternative total unilateral
disarmament? Suppose that the Western powers announced a decision
of policy that nuclear weapons would never be used in an attack on soft
targets, and that this decision was a serious and carefully thought out
one. Suppose that all who were trained in the operation of nuclear
weapons systems were given standing orders that it was strictly forbidden to take orders from anyone to employ them on soft or unknown
targets. Would it not then be possible, without incurring the guilt of our
present murderous policies, to retain sufficient nuclear hardware to
enforce the best disarmament bargain that we can with the Warsaw Pact
powers?

Objections to this will take the form that such a policy is impossible,
or that it is immoral. It is surely not impossible. A number of former US
Secretaries of State have suggested that the West should renounce the
first-use of nuclear weapons. Such a renunciation would be compatible
with continuing to train servicemen in the use of nuclear weapons; no
one has suggested otherwise. Equally it would be possible for the West
to renounce a second strike, while continuing to maintain, as a bargaining counter, some of the existing systems. But if both first and second
use were abandoned, as a matter of genuine policy and not just as a
propaganda declaration, then there would be no motive for any further
build-up of nuclear arms, nor for the retention of present systems except
for bargaining purposes.

Such a proposal would be quite different from the maintaining of a
deterrent on the basis of bluff. I agree with those who say that you cannot maintain a deterrent by bluff: if bluff is to succeed then you must
deceive the enemy; but you can only deceive the enemy by also deceiving
those on your side who maintain the deterrent; and if you do that it is
highly likely that the bluff will turn into reality. What I am talking about
is not bluff and involves no deception; you tell both the enemy, and your
own forces, that you will *never* use the weapons; and you mean what
you say.

But if theoretically possible, would such a policy avoid the moral
objections? Surely there would be a risk that even if there is an official
renunciation of the use of nuclear weapons this will be insincere: and that
even if sincere it may be reversed by later governments. The risk is
genuine; but it is only a risk that our governments will do secretly or
later what they do now cheerfully and continuously. It is a risk which
has to be weighed against other risks; it is not an intention to do some-

thing absolutely immoral. Thus it avoids the objection to the murderous aspect of our present policies: it preserves the physical elements of the deterrent, *ad interim* and as a bargaining counter, but without the adoption of plans for murder as official strategy, and without demanding readiness to massacre from servicemen involved in its maintenance.

It may seem absurd to concentrate so much attention on the present intentions, attitudes, and options of those responsible for the operation of the deterrent. Surely there is a huge gap between mental states of this kind and actual deeds in warfare: is it not infantile idealism to insist so heavily on purity of intention in policy-makers and strategists? After all, even Christians do not seem to take very literally the saying of Jesus that he who lusts after another woman is an adulterer, or St John's teaching that he who hates his brother is a murderer. Surely it is elsewhere that we should be looking for the morally relevant features of our nuclear policies: we should be weighing up the risks of deterrence against the risks of disarmament.

We shall come to weigh up the risks in a moment; but we must first insist that it is not, in this case, unpractical idealism to focus attention on the peacetime attitudes of those in power and those who serve in the armed forces. In an old-fashioned war there was much time for reflection, for changes of mind, for cabinet discussion, for weighing the pros and cons of strategies, for investigating and evaluating alternative options and battle plans. The actual decisions of the war cabinet of the UK in World War II were very different from anything that the members of the cabinet would have foreseen or planned before the war. (Not, of course, that the changes of mind were always an improvement from the ethical point of view!) But in World War III all will be different: the speed with which decisions will have to be taken will mean that the peacetime attitudes and planning of those involved will play the decisive role.

If a nuclear exchange should ever take place, then the key links in the causal chain which will have led up to it will be the options drawn up in peacetime, and the pre-war intentions, attitudes and mental sets of those who take the eleventh-hour decisions which ignite the holocaust. This fact was well dramatised in a sequence in the film *The Day After*. The American personnel who have, in a matter of moments, launched the ICBM for which they are responsible discuss whether they are obliged to remain at their post by the empty silo. They are persuaded to go home and await there the incoming Soviet missiles. "After all," they say, "the war is over now; we have done our duty."

There will, however, one hopes, be a moment for change of heart or last-minute repentance on the part of those who now proclaim that if it comes to the clinch they will launch a nuclear attack rather than surrender. This, indeed, is the key issue at the heart of the ethical debate about deterrence: the question 'what do you do if the deterrent fails?'. This is the question which Cardinal Hume declined to answer: but it is the one question which separates the sheep from the goats. In argument with defenders of the deterrent, there always comes a point where one wishes to put this question to one's interlocutor: 'Suppose that deterrence breaks down: suppose, that is, that you are faced with a choice of carrying out the deterrent threat, or of forfeiting the good things which the deterrent was meant to protect. What do you do then? I accept that the whole point of having a deterrent is to prevent being faced with the choice of using it and surrendering; but one can have no certainty that this choice will never have to be faced. Suppose that it fails, and you are faced with the choice: what, in your heart, do you think you should do?' If my friend says that if, God forbid, it ever did come to such a point, then obviously the only thing to do is to surrender – if he says that, then I know that fundamentally we are morally at one, and we can settle down in a comparatively relaxed way to discuss questions of risk and danger and expense. But if he says, 'Well, I hate to have to say it, but if you are committed to the deterrent, you have to stick to what you believe in and you must go right on and use it if it ever comes to the crunch' – if he says that and means it, then I can only tell him, quite soberly and literally, that he is a man with murder in his heart.

NOTES

1   Owen Greene, Barry Robin, Neil Turok, Philip Webber and Graeme Wilkinson, *London after the Bomb: what a Nuclear Attack really Means,* Oxford, 1982.

REPLY TO DR KENNY
Sir Arthur Hockaday

There are several substantial points on which I am in agreement with Dr Kenny, and I will begin by setting out this common ground.

First, and let me say in passing that in my own contribution to *Ethics and Nuclear Deterrence*[1] I too questioned the analogy between nuclear strategy and a game of chess, I share Dr Kenny's doubts whether nuclear weapons can any longer, in conditions of broad nuclear parity between

NATO and the Warsaw Pact, be regarded as a valid deterrent to conventional attack. He is right to say that even if this form of deterrence is irrational it may nevertheless still work; Robert S. McNamara carried rationality too far when he said that one cannot fashion a credible deterrent out of an incredible action.[2] Yet it is a shaky foundation on which to rest.

The logic of Dr Kenny's criticism stems from the very validity of nuclear weapons as a deterrent to the use of nuclear weapons by others. If, as I believe, the West's nuclear weapons are a valid deterrent to the use by the Russians of their nuclear weapons, it is reasonable to see their weapons as a deterrent to ours, thus putting both sides in a *de facto* 'no first-use' position. But I wish that Dr Kenny had carried this logic further. In his forceful criticism of nuclear deterrence of conventional aggression he does not explicitly discuss nuclear deterrence of nuclear warfare, which I see as the real essence of nuclear deterrence and which I shall therefore be addressing. Since his prime objection to a strategy involving nuclear deterrence is that it is murderous, he would probably have rejected this second category of deterrence also; but he would have had to deal with a rather different set of arguments.

Secondly, I agree with Dr Kenny in rejecting the proposition that the use of nuclear weapons can be justified simply by saying that they are targeted not against civilian populations *per se* but against military or industrial targets. In a recent Adelphi Paper[3] we can read that the 40,000 or more potential targets in the United States Single Integrated Operational Plan fell into four principal groups – Soviet nuclear forces, general purpose forces, military and political leadership centres, and the economic and industrial base. Likewise the British Government has stated that its concept of deterrence "is concerned essentially with posing a potential threat to key aspects of Soviet state power".[4] But even so, or even on the smaller scale generally assumed for a nuclear response to conventional attack – and I agree with Dr Kenny that special cases of use at sea or in unpopulated regions are morally as well as militarily vacuous – the use of nuclear weapons would infringe the Just War criteria, certainly of discrimination and probably of proportion, to an extent that would make a decision on their use little different, as a matter of practical ethics, from a decision to target them directly at cities.

My third point of agreement with Dr Kenny is in his dismissal of the view that the possession of nuclear weapons for deterrence is all right provided that there is no intention of actually using them. Basing deterrence on bluff would call its effectiveness as deterrence into question, and since there was no intention of using the weapons there would be no moral problem to discuss. The defects of the position taken by the American Roman Catholic bishops were magisterially exposed last year by Albert Wohlstetter.[5]

But Dr Kenny over-simplifies when he asks those who hold this view whether they are prepared to maintain that it can be legitimate to threaten what it would not be legitimate to do. What they are threatening is something which they have no intention of doing; whether this is legitimate is a different question from whether it can ever be legitimate to threaten, and moreover intend to do, something which it would not be legitimate actually to do. This brings us to the really tough question: given that the use of nuclear weapons, even though not directed against populations as such, is virtually certain to involve destruction of non-combatants to an extent that violates the Just War criteria of discrimination and proportion, and given that nuclear deterrence must, if it is serious, involve an intention, however conditional, so to use them, can such deterrence nevertheless be justified?

Dr Kenny seems to accept as a moral principle that if it is wrong to do x it is wrong to intend to do x, and wrong also to be willing to do x. But the discussion of the morality of deterrence is about the morality of conditional intention; and we can distinguish between two quite different sorts of conditional intention – 'if he does not hand over his money I will beat him up' and 'if he attacks me I will beat him up'.

The difference lies in the overall moral context in which these intentions are formulated. In real life we usually do consider actions or intentions in their total moral contexts. We seldom judge an action solely with regard to its consequences with no concern for its nature, or absolutely with regard to its nature with no concern for its consequences – indeed if we say that actions of a certain category are by their nature immoral in any circumstances we are probably impelled to that judgement in part by our knowledge of their consequences. In considering these various conditional intentions in their overall moral contexts I want to concentrate on the *objective* towards which each of them is formulated and the corresponding threat expressed.

I have chosen the word 'objective' with some care. It will not do to say that, when I tell somebody that if he attacks me I will beat him up, I am doing so with the *intention* of not beating him up. I cannot at the same time intend, even conditionally, to do something and not to do it; nor is it in the last resort within my power to ensure that he will not attack me despite my threat and that I shall not have to beat him up.

The precise alignment of the morality of the intention with that of the act no doubt holds good in a situation where the objectives of the intention and the act are the same. Thus the objective of saying 'if you do not hand over your money I will beat you up' is the same as that of beating the man up, namely to relieve him of his money. But the objective of saying 'if you attack me I will beat you up' is exactly the reverse of beating the man up: it is to ensure, so far as lies within my power, that he does not attack me and that I do not beat him up. So it is with nuclear deterrence; the conditional intention that in certain circumstances we will use nuclear weapons is formulated, and conveyed to the potential adversary, with the objective of securing that he will not commit the actions postulated in the condition and that consequently the intention will not be activated. I suggest that a conditional intention formulated with an objective the opposite of that of the act itself is quite different in its overall moral context both from the act and from a conditional intention whose objective is identical with that of the act.

It may be suggested that, even if the kind of conditional intention involved in nuclear deterrence is different morally from a simple intention to use nuclear weapons, it retains some elements of evil since whatever its objective it remains, even if only conditionally, an intention to commit an act which will inevitably destroy large numbers of non-combatants. I would not necessarily dispute this, but would rather point out that real life is not just a matter of doing good and eschewing evil. There are times when we are confronted with a range of possible good actions or dispositions, only one of which is right in the particular circumstances; at other times we are confronted only with a range of possible evil courses or dispositions, one of which will be right in the circumstances.

To sum up my argument so far, the use of nuclear weapons is almost certain to infringe the Just War criteria of discrimination and proportion; nuclear deterrence necessarily involves a conditional intention to use nuclear weapons in certain circumstances; as Dr Kenny points out, this must be a firm intention at least on the part of the submarine commander, if not that of the President or Prime Minister; nevertheless, since it is formulated with the objective of securing that the condition shall not be fulfilled and thus that nuclear weapons shall not be used either by our adversary or by ourselves, it is different in its overall moral context from a simple intention to use nuclear weapons; and even though it may still retain elements of evil the strategy which it underlies may nevertheless be right if we judge it to be the most promising way open to us, so long as nuclear weapons are around in the world, of ensuring that they are not used. Michael Walzer summed it up much more crisply when he wrote,[6] "We threaten evil in order not to do it, and the doing of it would be so terrible that the threat seems in comparison to be morally defensible."

In conclusion I must ask Dr Kenny exactly what he would *do* to follow up the conclusions to which his paper points. He made one passing reference to unilateral nuclear disarmament, and I think I have to assume that, since he appears to be condemning any form of nuclear deterrence, and not simply deterrence of conventional aggression, he is advocating complete nuclear disarmament on the part of the West irrespective of whether the Warsaw Pact retains nuclear weapons.

I cannot see any justification for the levels of nuclear forces maintained by the two superpowers, and I would like to see one or other of them (I rather hope it would be the Americans) stop talking about reductions and actually make a first move more substantial and more far-reaching than what NATO has already done to withdraw obsolescent battlefield systems from Central Europe. I believe that this could be done without significantly affecting security, and I would be very happy to see the moral onus of a corresponding response placed fairly and squarely on the other side. But those who advocate complete unilateral nuclear disarmament must weigh the implications of a one-sided situation so totally different from the approximate balance which at present obtains. We are fortunate that in East–West relations there appears to be, in substance despite occasional bursts of rhetoric, little of what Michael Howard[7] has called the "bellicism" that preceded each of the two World Wars. How far this may be due to the possession of nuclear weapons by both sides is not proven, but if there were to be a resurgence of 'bellicism' with only one side in possession of nuclear weapons I see nothing other than moral scruples to inhibit their limited use either on the battlefield as a means of overcoming unexpectedly tough resistance or against homeland targets to induce a quick surrender as in 1945, or their deployment simply as a threat to compel compliance with a political objective. Such limited use would not carry with it the risk of the 'nuclear winter' which, if confirmed by further studies, offers the most promising deterrent yet to any substantial use of nuclear weapons and the most promising incentive to serious multilateral nuclear disarmament.

In his concluding remarks Dr Kenny painted a picture of me sitting here with murder in my heart. Perhaps Shelley should have written:

> I met Murder in the way,
> He had a mask like Hockaday.

Dr Kenny was able to say what he did because my philosophical position requires me to be prepared, in certain improbable but conceivable circumstances, to commit an act which will inevitably destroy large num-

bers of non-combatants. But I hope I have shown that it is far from
being as simple as that. I hope too that I may equally legitimately, and
with no more and no less over-simplification or caricature, suggest that
in another set of improbable but conceivable circumstances, when the
absence of a Western nuclear deterrent is bringing upon the city of
Oxford the effects of a nuclear attack upon Fairford or Brize Norton, my
friend will at least be able to say that his hands were clean.

NOTES

1   G. Goodwin (ed.), *Ethics and Nuclear Deterrence,* London, 1982.
2   Quoted by Lawrence Freedman in *The Evolution of Nuclear Strategy,* London, 1981,
    p. 298, from Alain C. Enthoven and K. Wayne Smith, *How Much is Enough?,* New
    York, 1971, ch. 4.
3   Desmond Ball, *Targeting for Strategic Deterrence, Adelphi Paper No. 185,* London,
    1983, p. 23.
4   *The Future United Kingdom Strategic Nuclear Deterrent Force,* Defence Open
    Government Document 80/23, Ministry of Defence, London, 1980.
5   Albert Wohlstetter, 'Bishops, statesmen, and other strategists on the bombing of
    innocents', in *Commentary,* 1983, pp. 15–35.
6   Michael Walzer, *Just and Unjust Wars,* London, 1978, p. 274.
7   Michael Howard, *Weapons and Peace,* David Davies Memorial Institute of Interna-
    tional Studies Annual Lecture, London, 1983.

DISCUSSION

Mrs G. Garthwaite. Mightn't it be more effective in preventing nuclear war to
   try to look for arguments in terms of national self-interest rather than arguments in terms of morality? We are more likely to disagree about morals.
   And in any case, we can't be trusted to be sufficiently moral – think, for
   instance, of the case you reminded us of, the allied bombing of German cities
   in World War II.
Dr Kenny. I think you're right that if you want to persuade governments to give
   up nuclear weapons, then probably arguments from self-interest will be more
   effective than moral arguments. But in order for *us* to know what arguments
   we want to use, and for what conclusion, surely we need to know in our own
   minds what we think is the right and wrong of the matter? And only when
   we know, or think we know, what is the right thing to do, do we then turn
   to the secondary question of what are the best methods to achieve our aim.
   It may be that the best method is producing arguments from moral
   philosophy, it may be that the best method is producing arguments from
   self-interest, it may be that the best method is camping outside Greenham
   Common.
Dr John Haldane, University of St. Andrews. You hold that what is wrong with

deterrence is that it involves the preparedness to commit murder. But surely a central feature of the defence of deterrence is the thought that what one is doing is not simply preparing to wage war, but trying to *prevent* war by preparing for it. The defender of deterrence might say that deterrence as such is morally neutral; it's a matter of what other action types it falls under. And in this particular case, it may fall under the action type 'preparing to commit murder', but it also falls under the action type 'trying to save the world', let us say. Now suppose that he could show that in these circumstances there is no other way of achieving this end, and claims that this end is obligatory, just in the way that you want to claim that murder is absolutely prohibited. The policy of deterrence may thus itself be an absolute requirement, and we would then have a conflict between absolute requirements. This sort of moral dilemma is not uncommon.

Dr Kenny. If you take an absolutist position on a certain action then no matter what the further intention is with which you enter upon this action it remains wrong. If murder, say, is always wrong then it doesn't matter what other descriptions your action falls under; provided only that it falls under *that* description, then it's out. Now of course, a lot of people are not absolutists, and nothing in my argument was directed against them. My argument was directed to those who accept the absolutist position of the Just War Doctrine, but from the background of that doctrine wish to defend the policy of deterrence.

Let me also point out something else that seems to me to be wrong with what you said. People talk as if deterrence was the only way to save world from nuclear war. Of course, there is another way of saving the world from nuclear war, and that is to give in to any demands which are made to you by those who have the capacity for making nuclear war. Now I am not recommending that one should do that; I am just saying that the discussion should be conducted in realistic terms where this is one of the options.

Mr David Midgley, University of York. In your paper you hold that it would be morally permissible to hold on to some of our nuclear weapons as bargaining counters if a genuine, public decision were taken not to use them, and all authorisation to use them were explicitly withdrawn. This is obviously attractive to someone who is sympathetic to unilateralism, but also thinks that this policy is impracticable and risky – perhaps immorally risky. But it seems to me that there are only two reasons why these weapons could be effective bargaining counters in these circumstances. Either you would be retaining the conditional intention to restore your original conditional intention to use the weapons if the policy seemed to be failing, or you would be relying on the uncertainty which these weapons would still be able to generate. If the former then your moral stance has obviously been eroded. But if you are relying on the uncertainty that, say, some future government may not reverse your policy, then this seems to me to be bad faith. It's bad faith because you haven't really committed yourself totally to the idea that these weapons must never be used; you are just washing your own hands and, in effect, allowing someone else to do the dirty work for you.

Dr Kenny. I agree that if you are reserving the right to restore the authorisation to use the weapons, then that is bad faith. But if it is just that there remains an uncertainty, and a risk that somebody else will do it, then I think that this is within the area of risks which are not your responsibility, and where you may permissibly weigh off risk against risk. Suppose that I am a citizen who will never ever vote for a president who will reintroduce the authorisation, and will do all I can politically to keep such a president from coming to power. Then I think there is no bad faith involved. If I am myself the president, then I know that I may be succeeded by another president who may reintroduce the authorisation to use the weapons. There remains this risk; but if it is a risk which I do all that I legitimately can to avert, then it is the risk of a third-party kind. It is not a risk that somebody authorised by me, or in power as a result of my actions, is going to do something. So, I may then legitimately weigh that risk, the risk that the succeeding president will reintroduce the authorisation, against the risks of immediate unilateral disarmament.

The self, morality
and the nation-state

BRIAN BAXTER
University of Dundee

I

The moral theories which have attracted greatest support among philosophers in the Anglo-Saxon tradition are cosmpolitan in import. That is, they provide reason for supposing that moral obligations obtain between all the human beings on this planet, irrespective of nationality. For many moral thinkers it is essential to take this cosmpolitan implication seriously if we are to grapple adequately with those global problems of famine and absolute poverty whose existence poses our severest moral challenge.

In this perspective, nation-states have a purely instrumental importance. Their governments are best, or even uniquely, placed to implement on the basis of international agreement such important practical measures towards the solution of global moral problems as transfer of funds, trade reform, regulation of commercial activity and so on. It seems entirely likely that the serious attempt to implement such measures will involve quite substantial alterations in national ways of life, particularly in the affluent West. The assumption that this is so forms one of the starting points of this paper.

Since, from the universalist standpoint of traditional moral theory, nation-states are merely mechanisms whose own interests must be strictly subordinated to those of individual human beings, whatever their nationality, appeal by a state to its 'national interest' as a way of resisting the requisite alterations in its activities and institutions is permissible only when it concerns what is needed to preserve the lives of its citizens. The survival merely of forms of cultural or national life is not allowed as a satisfactory basis on which to reject prima-facie moral obligations *vis-à-vis* humanity at large.

Yet, clearly, most people are *not* cosmopolitan in outlook even when they recognise the force of the arguments presented by moral theorists. As Henry Sidgwick suggested,[1] the common-sense view of global concerns rests on 'the national ideal'. This gives some weight to the interests of foreigners, but adheres to what Henry Shue[2] has called "the priority thesis", namely that when human interests are being considered, one's compatriots should take priority. Charles Beitz, in a recent discussion of the issue,[3] allows the priority thesis to have some plausibility and thus to be capable of limiting the scope of the demands of morality on national governments, although to nothing like the extent envisaged by common-sense morality. Briefly, he takes the best moral argument in defence of the thesis to derive from a limited permission, obtaining in the area of private morality,[4] for the individual to aim at results which are less good, according to the impersonal standard of universal morality, than other results he is in a position to produce.[5] This permission rests on the view that it is important for us to have sufficient freedom to seek the fulfilment of "projects and commitments that express our separate identities as autonomous persons",[6] without our being hampered by impersonal moral considerations.

This permission, Beitz argues, is not limitless,[7] but from it one can derive an upper limit to the burden which morality can legitimately require states to bear in the pursuit of cosmopolitan (or other) ends. For, since individuals possess the right to reject at least some of the sacrifices imposed on them by impersonal morality so as to pursue their own commitments, it is clear that their governments have no right to impose such sacrifices on them. In so far as such commitments are essentially involved in the national way of life, the permission in question presumably justifies individuals, and thus their governments, in resisting alterations in that way of life which would abort these commitments.

I agree with Beitz that this kind of argument, centring on the legitimate interests of the individual, is the most promising kind for producing a principled resistance by individuals and, derivatively, by their governments to the claims of universal morality.[8] What I attempt in the rest of this paper is an investigation of the above-mentioned "projects and commitments that express our separate identities as autonomous beings" in order to ascertain how strong the argument is which appeals to them as a means of resisting cosmopolitan ideals.

I suggest that we can distinguish three kinds of projects and commitments which are relevant in this connection:

(a) Deep personal relationships to other persons
(b) Projects, plans, ambitions and ideals for oneself and one's loved ones
(c) Loyalty to one's nation state and compatriots.[9]

Of these, I suggest that (a) is the strongest source of the possible counter to the claims of universal morality; (b) and (c) are very much weaker, although not entirely negligible.

In the next section I consider (a), and try to elucidate why appeal to what is needed to preserve one's deep personal relationships against the claims of morality is not just special pleading. In the third section I trace a connection between (a) and (b) and consider an argument of Mac-Intyre's which can be used to suggest that an individual's commitment to (b) gives him good reason to resist attempts to alter drastically the customs, traditions and institutions of his nation-state. This is an argument whose weaknesses I try to expose. In the final section I consider (c) and try to show how what is morally acceptable about patriotism need not lead to its trumping the cosmopolitan claims made by universal morality.

II

Let us begin, then, with personal relations. A quotation from a well known paper by Williams[10] takes us to the heart of the matter. He has been arguing that intrinsic to one's having a character, as opposed to one's being the abstract moral agent of traditional moral theory, is the phenomenon of one's having what Williams calls "ground projects". That is, one is involved with other individuals in deep personal relationships and has plans, ambitions and ideals for oneself and one's loved ones. He then says in connection with deep personal relationships:

> But the point is that somewhere. . . one reaches the necessity that such things as deep attachments to other persons will express themselves in the world in ways which cannot at the same time embody the impartial (moral) view, and that they also run the risk of offending against it.
>
> They run that risk if they exist at all, yet unless such things exist there will not be enough substance or conviction in a man's life *to compel his allegiance to life itself.* ·
>
> Life has to have substance if anything is to have sense, including adherence to the impartial system; but if it has substance, then it cannot grant importance to the impartial system, and that system's hold on it will be, at the limit, insecure.[11] [my emphasis]

Thus, for example, in deciding whom to save in some dire situation in which I cannot save everyone, it is reasonable for me to give preference to saving a loved one, even though some impartial utilitarian or Kantian calculation of my moral obligation would counsel me to set aside such claims of personal loyalty. In such situations, one's according absolute paramountcy to the claims of morality would probably involve, as a result of the loss of the loved one, the loss of that interest in continuing to live which is necessary for moral claims to have any force for one at all. In some situations, therefore, the claims of morality cannot reasonably be accorded such absolute paramountcy.

The adoption of such a standpoint is not an endorsement of egoism for, as Williams correctly argues, the loyalty to others which is envisaged as the motive of one's action may well demand, and receive, sacrifices of an individual's self-interest and perhaps even of his life.

MacIntyre has recently suggested,[12] in connection with Williams's argument, that it is not clear whether the 'deep attachments' which it appeals to are meant to be psychological bonds or bonds embodied in social roles. Taken in the latter sense, the kind of action cited, such as giving priority to one's spouse over others, may be viewed as *required* by morality as applied to, for example, the institution of marriage, instead of being taken to involve the setting aside of moral claims completely. For, in our culture, marriage as traditionally understood cannot flourish without justice in the relations between the people involved in it. Only if we prescind from all forms of social particularity and conceive of justice in some totally non-social way can we set up the opposition between morality and personal relations which Williams espouses.

The embedding of personal relations in social structures may well justify this kind of point, but it clearly misses the challenge of Williams's argument. For that, surely, retains its force even when the personal relations involved are *not* bound up with some social practice. The examples we are to consider are ones in which A saves X in preference to Y just because A so deeply cares about X that loss of X would make A's continuing with life seem pointless to A. The kind of thought with which MacIntyre's argument provides A to justify his action, such as 'the social institution of marriage, if it is to thrive, requires (occasionally self-sacrificing) justice between family members' is, to echo Williams's own words, one thought too many for A to have.

The whole point here is that the motivation in question needs to be conceived of as the love and caring of one particular individual for another. So conceived, the 'deep attachments' involved do not provide scope for moral concerns to enter as elements within the motivation of the agent.[13] Is it, however, reasonable to give priority to the demands of personal relations over those of morality in such cases? The clue to a satisfactory answer to this question is provided by the italicised passage in the quotation from Williams. Deep attachment to at least some individuals is essential if one is to be compelled to have allegiance to life itself. The notion of one's having 'allegiance to life itself' may appear strained or at best rhetorical, but it does contain an important insight which becomes apparent when one considers the crucial role which loyalties play in the structure of human motivation.

As Oldenquist[14] has argued, loyalty to various objects is the mainspring of most people's morally praiseworthy activities. Human self-sacrifice and exercise of virtue is most often to be found among people seeking to preserve and foster the objects of their strongest loyalties in any situation, whether it be spouse, family, country or whatever. Let us now suppose that at the lowest limit the most basic object of one's loyalty is not one's self (for, given that loyalty to x involves putting x's interests first, loyalty to one's self would mean putting one's own interests first, which offends against a requirement which Oldenquist cogently argues for, namely that loyalties are not egoistic) but life itself. This phrase has to be taken to mean, I suggest, one's *own* life, not life in the abstract, otherwise its role in Williams's argument becomes puzzling. Taking it in this way also meets another of Oldenquist's requirements, namely that the object of one's loyalty is always described self-referentially as 'my/our x'.

What, then, can be involved in giving allegiance or loyalty to one's life? Clearly, as is the case with all loyalties, it involves granting some kind of priority to one's life. But, since one's life is not something which can meaningfully be said to have interests, this cannot be a matter of giving an individual's *interests* priority. It can only mean, I suggest, acting so as to ensure that one's life continues to have a certain valued character, such as precisely that of exhibiting loyalty to other individuals with whom one has deep personal relations

The notion of loyalty to one's own life usefully imports into our conception of individual action the motivational force that loyalties in general possess. Further, if substance can be given to the claim that the desired character of this object of loyalty just is its manifestation of other loyalties, then it can be seen in what way this loyalty *grounds* all others. But, why should the desired character be the manifestation of loyalties at all? In particular, why should the important loyalties be to other individuals in deep personal relationships, and not to much wider groups, such as the human species, or to abstractions such as the impersonal system of morality itself? In a nutshell, why should it be insufficient, as Williams clearly hints that it is, for an individual's life to 'have substance' that it be devoted to *impersonal* objects of allegiance?

If we can explain the importance for individuals of deep attachments to other individuals, we will be able to vindicate the claim that loyalties to such *individals* are the crucial aspects of the life of the individual and thus will provide the answer to the general question of why it should be *loyalties* that are important. There are, I suggest, at least the following two, related, reasons why deep attachments to particular individuals[15] may be deemed important:

1. We each need to have some others whom we care about and who care for us, for unless we count for someone and make a difference to their lives we might as well not exist. A life which we can see has the character that it might as well not have occurred is a life which cannot reasonably compel one's loyalty. But, to count for others we have to be known by, and to know, them in a deep, not a superficial way. Hence, the personal attachments in question need to be *deep* ones.[16]

2. Our self-image and self-esteem usually are dependent on the views of others whose opinion counts for us. Those whose opinion counts are those whose opinion we value. Hence, the individual needs to be able to evaluate those others and can only do this if he knows them intimately enough. This, then, requires personal relations of a nature sufficiently deep to stand a chance of producing mutual understanding and respect. A life devoid of that which is necessary for the development of one's self-esteem is, again, a life devoid of a character sufficient to compel allegiance.[17]

If such deep attachments to particular individuals have this crucial role to play in the life of each of us, then, since they involve putting those individuals first (for that is what their 'counting for us' in the relevant way amounts to) they will have the character of loyalties. Hence, a life having the substance which can reasonably compel our allegiance needs to be a life embodying loyalties to those individuals to whom we are deeply attached.

As we noted above, the view of deep personal relations needed to sustain Williams's argument is one which prescinds from moral considerations altogether. This is what accounts for the starkness of the contrast between the demands of one's personal relations and the demands of morality in the examples considered. This means viewing such deep personal relations and morality as incommensurable sources of demands on the individual

MacIntyre claims to see a difficulty, centring on this point, in Williams's argument.[18] For, if the two sources of demands are incommensurable, MacIntyre asks, what can be *meant* by saying that one may be *justified* sometimes in acceding to the demands involved in personal relationships as against those involved in morality?

In reply, I tentatively suggest that the considerations adduced in (1) above are conceptual, not empirical in nature. That is, it is part of the concept of one's life having meaning that one's existence makes a difference of the right kind to at least one other person. 'The right kind' means that that person cares about one's happiness and welfare, and the person in question is someone whom one cares about also in that kind of way.

Thus, it does make sense to say that, on occasion, someone's acceding to the demands of deep personal relations, as against those of impersonal morality, is justified, just because all beings like us can see the crucial part such personal relationships play in the meaningfulness of our lives. This is the reason why such preferences and justifications do not involve special pleading, but have perfectly general force.

Are there any reasonable hedgings to the claim that such loyalties as we have been discussing can trump the restrictions laid on the individual by the demands of impersonal morality? I suspect that there is nothing general that can usefully be said with respect to the question of how to balance claims based on loyalty to one's intimates *vis-à-vis* claims based on the interests of wider groups, or on the impersonal system of morality, save the point, similar to that cited earlier from Beitz's discussion, that a trivial advantage to one's intimates is not sufficient to outweigh an important advantage to strangers. The most important qualification apart from that is, I suggest, that the nature of one's deep personal attachments must not itself be morally exceptionable. Thus, if allegiance to one's life depends on its providing one with the opportunity to degrade, hurt or humiliate others in personal relationships then *that* condition of meaningfulness could not count as a reasonable block to the demands of impersonal morality.[19]

III

Turning now to the second set of elements characteristic of individuals' ground projects – plans and projects for oneself and for those for whom one cares – we need to consider whether these have the same capacity to underpin the blocking move as deep personal relations appear to have.

Note, first, the kind of connection which often exists between the individual's need for deep personal relations and his commitment to such projects and plans. As we saw in the previous section, deep personal relations are of importance in the generation of one's self-image and self-esteem. There is usually agreement between the self and those others to whom one is attached on the topic of what is valuable in human life – what standards of worth, success and failure are. Hence, one normally, and probably always initially, derives an estimable sense of self from the attempt to implement those standards in one's own life.

However, mutual caring can survive the development of disagreement over values. Personal attachments of the kind discussed above are primarily to persons, not to systems of value, although clearly if the disagreement is of a sufficiently strong nature such attachments can be broken. But the looseness of connection between the two usually means that a failure to bring mutually cherished projects to fruition, or disagreement over what projects are worth pursuing, can leave the personal relationships intact. This point, then, weakens any argument which seeks to portray the individual's plans and projects as being every bit as weighty blocks to the claims of morality as are his personal relations, by seeking to establish an intrinsic connection between the two.

Still, there remains the possibility that the disruption of an individual's projects and plans is sometimes, in its own right, of sufficient import to make reasonable the view that his resistance to such disruption, even when the latter is required by morality, is justifiable. *A priori* this possibility does not look terribly convincing, given the point just made about the looseness of connection between personal relations, self-esteem and plans and projects. One is strongly tempted to suggest that, for most people at any rate, as long as they believe there are others who care for them, and for whom they care, they can usually find something to make up the substance of their lives if their projects and plans come to grief.

However, MacIntyre,[20] in his discussion of Williams's views on ground projects, has given reasons for supposing that, at least with respect to some ground projects, this riposte is inadequate. To grasp these reasons we need to refer to a distinction MacIntyre draws between two viewpoints it is possible to adopt towards one's ground projects:

(a) *External*. What matters fundamentally about my ground projects is that they are *mine*. Hence, it will always be possible to trace back the reason for my involvement to some desire or motivation of mine. The self to which the projects are related is thus one which exists independently of, and antecedently to, the project in which it is involved, and identifies itself as continuing so to exist.

(b) *Internal*. What matters fundamentally about my ground projects is the character of the projects themselves, a character which I appreciate because I understand myself in terms of my role in the project, and not vice versa. Thus, the self to which the projects are related cannot be defined, and its continuing commitments cannot be understood, except in terms of the role to which the project has assigned the self, and the impersonal goals and requirements which that role imposes upon the self.

MacIntyre then comments that the distinction between (a) and (b) corresponds to a distinction between types of project. Firstly, there are ground projects such that an individual might relate to them in either way. Secondly, there are ground projects which *require* the internal viewpoint. That is, they require the kind of transcending of self that relegates to a position of unimportance the fact that this project happens to be mine.

It is this second type of project that we need to concentrate on; firstly because the individual's sense of self is defined in terms of it, so that whatever threatens it appears to threaten the very self involved. Hence our initial reaction above to attacks on ground projects appears too shallow. Secondly, MacIntyre's interpretation of this type of project involves viewing it as part of a social practice existing outside the individual. Such practices are presumably part of the customs, traditions and institutions (CTIs) of the individual's society. Thus, the intrinsic connection between this kind of project and CTIs is such, one may argue, that an attack on the CTIs of a nation-state based on the requirements of impartial, cosmopolitan morality, would so undermine the basis on which individuals develop a sense of self, and of the worthwhileness of their existence, as to make their resistance to such an attack as reasonable as it appeared to be when it was the lives and important interests of their intimates which was in question.[21]

This argument, however, is, I suggest, an implausible one. To show this, I need to show that the concept of the internal viewpoint as MacIntyre specifies it does not really stand up to scrutiny. The relation between self and project, adumbrated under the 'external viewpoint' *does* make sense. One can see how it is possible for an individual to have a conception of himself independent of (although perhaps not antecedent to) his ground projects in terms of his general capacities, aptitudes, character traits, and so on. These provide scope for the individual to view himself as undertaking new ground projects if he is forced to, projects in which his sense of self may find an alternative outlet. Thus, if all ground projects were such that only the external viewpoint were possible with respect to them, then clearly an estimable sense of self could well survive a disruption or cessation of those ground projects, for whatever reason.

The puzzle is why this possibility should ever be regarded as *not* available for the individual. Consider some hypothetical person whose ground projects are those towards which it is only possible to adopt the internal attitude. Imagine that all those ground projects are nullified for some reason. Clearly, one would expect that person to undergo a period of disorientation, of grievous sense of loss, and so forth. Yet, surely his ground projects, as with the individual who adopts only the external viewpoint, will have required the development within him of talents, capacities and traits of character sufficient to provide him with a sense of self independent of those ground projects which he has seen come to nought? It is very difficult to see why this should not happen, which is, of course, tantamount to denying the validity of the hypothesis that there could be a person all of whose attitudes were internal, and that in turn is because the notion of the internal attitude itself does not make sense.

However, there is something to the argument we are considering, although its validity depends, not on the existence of the internal viewpoint, but rather on the empirical fact that some, perhaps many, people would find it difficult to set themselves to undertake new, or radically transformed, ground projects, perhaps for reasons of age or limited development of their capacities. What this point underlines, however, is the need to make the requisite alterations in CTIs, or other elements affecting people's ground projects, with sympathetic regard to such people's predicament. It would not, however, justify a government in refusing to alter CTIs, and so forth, at all on the basis that the affected individuals are rightfully availing themselves of the permission to reject moral demands in the name of what is crucial for their lives to have substance.

The greatest risk of failure to fulfil a ground project is run by someone whose ground project is absolutely specific – such as that of being the first being on the moon. It is not unintelligible to suggest that the removal of the possibility of completing such a project, around which someone's life has been organised, should lead to a sense on his part that his whole life has thereby been rendered pointless. Such an individual has, of course, engaged in a very imprudent life-plan, and as most people are not imprudent in this way, it is reasonable to suggest, this is going to be a rare case. The wise individual, even if striving for such goals, will not allow everything to hang on their attainment. One strategy employable here is to conceptualise one's ground projects in terms which avoid the achievement of specific goals by, for example, aiming to develop capacities, virtues and attitudes for their own sake, and not for the indefinitely many particular goals they may enable one to achieve.

Clearly, as the example just given indicates, any long-term intention is subject to vicissitudes which have nothing to do with changes in any CTIs. Hence, practical wisdom enjoins us to find plenty of short-term, relatively shallow desires which can be satisfied as well as keeping our long-term deep desires and intentions reasonably indeterminate and flexible. This implies, of course, that one does not allow one's 'sense of self' to become too fixed – though one does not need to go the whole hog with the existentialists on this point.

Two further considerations may be adduced at this point. The first is that challenges to one's existing sense of self can be exhilarating and beneficial. A new national dispensation may give scope for the development of a new sense of self which is experienced as being as valid as the old one, or perhaps even preferable. This kind of experience befalls people who, for whatever reason, move into alien societies as exiles, colonists, long-term visitors or immigrants and discover possibilities within the CTIs of the new society which permit the development of aspects of themselves which they had not previously been aware of and which come to seem to them to be estimable.

Indeed, it is arguable that this, often freely and deliberately chosen, route to personal development provides more of an experience of change in CTIs than any changes that are ever feasible *within* the CTI's of a national culture. This leads to the second point, namely that it is notoriously much harder to engineer completely radical changes in a community's CTIs than, for example, revolutionaries are given to believe. It is now, after all, a commonplace of political science that the character of pre-revolutionary political culture strongly influences that of post-revolutionary institutions. Plainly, in the economy of human action we get most of our ideas of how to cope with new situations on the basis of awareness of past successful practice, whether we are aware of this or not. Hence, it is likely that 'new' CTIs will not be so alien to the societies in which they occur that a plausible case can be made by individuals for saying that they have lost what they needed to give their lives meaning and substance.

IV

I turn finally to consider one other way in which individuals' attachment to their nation-states and the CTIs thereof might be thought so to enter their ground projects as to sustain a defence of the priority thesis. This is the straightforward case in which one of the objects to which individuals give their loyalty just is their nation-state and its way of life. This is, of course, the phenomenon of patriotism.

Clearly, patriotism can inform the most cherished ground projects of many people. They pursue careers in the armed forces or government in which the idea of loyalty and service to their nation-state is central to the intelligibility of their endeavours. For such professional patriots, so to speak, the priority thesis must seem unquestionable.

How well, then, does the citation of the individual's patriotic commitment fare when offered as a consideration weighty enough to counter the
cosmopolitan claims of universal morality? Not very well, I suggest.
Surely it can plausibly be urged that patriotic commitment is much less
obviously central to the substance of people's lives, even people who
proclaim themselves patriots, than is the commitment to others in deep
personal relationships? To suggest, for example, that if one were to be
required to cease implementation of the priority thesis in one's life one
would thereby lose what was needed to give one's life substance is going
to be implausible in the extreme. For, quite clearly, the vast majority of
one's compatriots are complete strangers to one, so that it would be
something of a mystery as to why they would count for one in the way
that one's nearest and dearest do. There remains, of course, loyalty to
the national way of life as such, irrespective of its connection with the
lives of particular individuals. A consideration of this goes beyond the
scope of this paper, but as I indicated in the first section I doubt whether
the value of ways of life can weigh significantly in the balance against the
claims of real human individuals.

Still, patriotism cannot be dismissed as having no moral weight at all.
From the standpoint of universal morality a case can be made for regard-
ing the patriotic attitude as having at least some, and on occasion great,
instrumental value. The existence of nation-states defended by patriots
has often been a good thing, for successful resistance to highly immoral
forces has often depended on it. As long as people are compartmentalised
into nation-states, and as long as sufficient of them are, or have the
capacity quickly to become, committed to their defence to the extent of
sacrificing their lives, then mankind has a chance of surviving a large-
scale disruption of morality in one part of the world.

This concession by universal morality to the claims of patriotism has
to be partial, however. Some kind of balance needs to be struck between
the justifiable claims of patriotic feeling and the justifiable claims of
moral concern which transcends national allegiance.

However, for at least some nation-states it is possible that there is a
way of reconciling the two. There are nation-states in which a key
element in the national way of life, which patriots presumably wish to
defend, just is the cosmopolitan outlook. Provided that the cosmopolitan
outlook is one of the desirable characteristics which make loyalty to one's
community appear reasonable, loyalty to that community involves
loyalty to that ideal.

May we not, then, simply argue that only that patriotism should,
morally speaking, be encouraged which in this way encapsulates a moral

concern? Unfortunately not, for the 'compartmentalisation' argument just given retains its force even when no nation-state is committed to morality. Each nation-state represents a separate plot in which the flower of morality may bloom even where it does not yet do so. Once it has developed, the existence of nation-states may hinder its spread, but they may also prevent its extinction should propitious conditions start to disappear again.

The best hope of reconciling patriotism and cosmopolitanism is to foster concern within nation-states for cosmopolitan ideals so that patriotism, in encapsulating such concern as part of national consciousness, becomes subordinated to it. When that occurs, patriotism will involve commitment to a transformed priority thesis. For, loyalty to one's compatriots, involving the defence of what they care about, will involve putting first at least some of the important material interests of non-compatriots.

NOTES

1 H. Sidgwick, *The Elements of Politics*, 4th edition, London, 1919, p. 309.

2 H. Shue, *Basic Rights: Subsistence, Affluence and American Foreign Policy*, Princeton, N.J., 1980, p. 132.

3 C.R. Beitz, 'Cosmopolitan ideals and national sentiment', *Journal of Philosophy*, LXXX, 1983, pp. 591–600. The argument noted below occurs on pp. 597–9 of this article.

4 C.R. Beitz remarks that there is room for dispute whether this permission is properly conceived as internal to private morality or as an external motivational constraint. As will emerge in due course, I think the correct view is the latter one.

5 This idea, Beitz notes, derives from Samuel Scheffler's *The Rejection of Consequentialism*, Oxford, 1982, pp. 61–2.

6 Beitz, *Basic Rights*, p. 598.

7 Beitz suggests two limitations. Firstly, that the underlying permission does not license individuals to avoid conferring a great benefit on others when this imposes an insignificant burden on themselves, and that this carries over to the national level. Secondly, that governments by fairly distributing sacrifices among citizens, may get over one element in the excessiveness that may be thought to attach to some sacrifices, namely that they put individuals in a disadvantageous position with respect to their fellow citizens. Hence, governments may impose greater burdens on their citizens in the name of morality than those citizens need impose on themselves as individuals.

8 One might attempt to defend national ways of life directly against the demands of cosmopolitan morality. I agree with Beitz as to the inadequacy of such attempted defences, although to demonstrate that inadequacy goes beyond the scope of this paper. I concentrate instead on arguments seeking to show that limits to cosmopolitan claims can be drawn on the basis of what is important for *individuals* with respect to their national ways of life.

9   It might well be claimed that (c) is just a special case of (b), but for my purposes it is worth separating it out.

10   B. Williams, 'Persons, character and morality', in *Moral Luck*, Cambridge, 1981.

11   *Ibid.* p. 18.

12   A. C. MacIntyre, 'The magic in the pronoun "My"', *Ethics*, XCIV, 1983, pp. 113–25.

13   Of course, the actions so motivated may well exemplify moral virtues, and it remains appropriate, as emerges below, to judge the actions morally.

14   A. Oldenquist, 'Loyalties', *Journal of Philosophy*, LXXIX, 1982, pp. 173–93. I make use of various points from Oldenquist's valuable discussion, though I disagree with some of his claims, such as that loyalties always have particulars as objects. As I suggest below, one can surely be loyal to ideals which may well be individuals, but do not seem to be particulars.

15   For some people, the relevant person is God. My remarks are not intended to rule this out as a possibility. Rather they suggest that the requisite relationship with God has to be construed by the individual as a deep, personal one.

16   For some people, their mattering for other people in the appropriate way results from their achieving public status of a kind such that large numbers of people with whom they are not personally acquainted, are known to care about their personal well-being. A religious or political leader may be a case in point. Such cases are naturally very infrequent, and it is doubtful whether even such individuals could sustain the effort needed to achieve that kind of status unless they had, at an earlier stage of their lives, *personal* relations of the right kind.

17   Some individuals may, of course, pursue values *not* shared with their intimates on the basis of the belief, or hope, that others exist who *do* endorse those values. This possibility is parasitic on the 'normal' case cited in (b).

18   A. MacIntyre, 'The magic in the pronoun "My"'.

19   This also covers the case where one's putting the interests of one's intimates first involves one's seeking to acquire for them advantages which cannot be justified on the basis of impersonal morality.

20   A. MacIntyre, 'The magic in the pronoun "My"'.

21   Another recent statement of the view that the individual's sense of self is intrinsically connected with the CTIs of his society can be found in R. Scruton, 'Freedom and custom', in A. P. Griffiths (ed.), *Of Liberty*, Cambridge, 1983.

22   Earlier drafts of this paper were seen by Professor Charles Beitz to whom I am grateful for helpful comments and criticisms, of some of which I have endeavoured to take account.

Multinational decision-making: reconciling international norms

THOMAS DONALDSON
Loyola University of Chicago

I. INTRODUCTION

Jurisprudence theorists are often puzzled when, having thoroughly analysed an issue within the boundaries of a legal system, they must confront it again outside those boundaries. For international issues, trusted axioms often fail as the secure grounds of legal tradition and national consensus erode. Much the same happens when one moves from viewing a problem of corporate ethics against a backdrop of national moral consensus to the morally inconsistent backdrop of international opinion. Is the worker who appeals to extra-national opinion while complaining about a corporate practice accepted within his or her country analogous to an ordinary whistle-blower? Is a factory worker in Mexico justified in complaining about being paid three dollars an hour for the same work for which a US factory worker, employed by the same company, is paid eight dollars?[1] Is he justified when in Mexico the practice of paying workers three dollars an hour – and even much less – is widely accepted? Is an asbestos worker in India justified in criticising the lower standards of in-plant asbestos pollution maintained by a British multinational relative to standards in Britain, when the standards in question fall within Indian government guidelines and, indeed, are stricter than the standards maintained by other Indian asbestos manufacturers?

What distinguishes these issues from standard ones about corporate practices is that they involve reference to a conflict of norms, either moral or legal, between home and host country. This paper examines the subclass of conflicts in which host country norms appear substandard from the perspective of the home country, and evaluates the claim often made by multinational executives that the prevalence of seemingly lower standards in a host country warrants the adoption by multinationals of the lower standards. It is concerned with cases of the following form:

A multinational company (C) adopts a corporate practice (P) which is morally and/or legally permitted in C's host country (B), but not in C's home country (A).

The paper argues that the presence of lower standards in B justifies C's adopting the lower standards, but only in certain well defined contexts. It proposes a conceptual test, or ethical algorithm, for multinationals to use in distinguishing justified from unjustified applications of standards.

If C is a non-national, that is to say a multinational, corporation, then one may wonder why home country opinion should be a factor in C's decision-making. One reason is that although global companies are multinational in doing business in more than one country, they are uninational in composition and character. They are chartered in a single country, typically have over ninety-five per cent of their stock owned by citizens of their home country, and have managements dominated by citizens of their home country. Thus, in an important sense the term 'multinational' is a misnomer. Moreover, for our purposes it is crucial to acknowledge that the moral presuppositions of a multinational, i.e. the underlying assumptions of its managers infusing corporate policies with a basic sense of right and wrong, is inextricably linked to the laws and mores of the home country.

Modern textbooks dealing with international business consider cultural relativity to be a powerful factor in executive decision-making. Indeed they often use it to justify practices abroad which, although enhancing corporate profits, would be questionable in the multinational's home country. One prominent text, for example, remarks that "In situations where patterns of dominance–subordination are socially determined, and not a function of demonstrated ability, management should be cautioned about promoting those of inferior social status to positions in which they are expected to supervise those of higher social status".[2] Later, referring to multiracial societies such as South Africa, the same text offers managers some practical advice: ". . . the problem of the multiracial society manifests itself particularly in reference to promotion and pay. An equal pay for equal work policy may not be acceptable to the politically dominant but racial minority group. . .".[3] Consider two actual instances of the problem at issue.

In 1966 Charles Pettis, employee of an American multinational, became resident engineer for one of the company's projects in Peru: a 146 mile, $46 million project to build a highway across the Andes. Pettis soon discovered that Peruvian safety standards were far below those in the United States. The highway design called for cutting through mountains in areas where rock formations were unstable. Unless special precautions were taken, slides could occur. Pettis blew the whistle, complaining first to Peruvian government officials and later to US officials. No special precautions were taken, with the result that thirty-one men were killed by landslides during the construction of the road. Pettis was fired for his trouble and had difficulty finding a job with another company.[4]

A new American bank in Italy was advised by its Italian attorneys to file a tax return that misstated income and expenses and consequently grossly underestimated actual taxes due. The bank learned, however, that most other Italian companies regarded the practice as standard operating procedure and merely the first move in a complex negotiating process with the Italian internal revenue service. The bank initially refused to file a fallacious return on moral grounds and submitted an 'American-style' return instead. But because the resulting tax bill was many times higher than what comparable Italian companies were asked to pay, the bank changed policy in later years to agree with 'Italian style'.[5]

II. THE MORAL POINT OF VIEW

One may well decide that home country standards were mandatory in one of the above cases, but not in the other. One may decide that despite conforming to Peruvian standards, Peruvian safety precautions were unacceptable, while at the same time acknowledging that however inequitable and inefficient Italian tax mores may be, a decision to file 'Italian style' is permissible.

Thus, despite claims to the contrary, one must reject the simple dictum that whenever P violates a moral standand of country A, it is impermissible for C. Now, Arnold Berleant *has* argued that the principle of equal treatment endorsed by most US citizens requires that US corporations pay workers in less developed countries exactly the same wages paid to US workers in comparable jobs (after appropriate adjustments are made for cost of living levels in the relevant areas).[6] But most observers, including those from the less developed countries, believe this stretches the doctrine of equality too far in a way detrimental to host countries. By arbitrarily establishing US wage levels as the benchmark for fairness one eliminates the role of the international market in establishing salary levels, and this in turn eliminates the incentive US corporations have to hire foreign workers. If US companies felt morally bound to pay Korean workers exactly the wages US workers receive for comparable work, they would not locate in Korea. Perhaps US firms should exceed market rate for foreign labour as a matter of moral principle, but to pay strictly equal rates would freeze less developed countries out of the international labour market.[7] Lacking, then, a simple formula of the sort 'P is wrong when P violates A's norms', one seems driven to undertake a more complex analysis of the types and degrees of responsibilities multinationals possess.

The first task is to distinguish between responsibilities that hold as minimum conditions, and ones that exceed the minimum. We are reminded of the distinction, eloquently articulated by Kant, between perfect and imperfect duties. Perfect duties are owed to a specific class of persons under specified conditions, such as the duty to honour promises. They differ from imperfect duties, such as the duty of charity, which although mandatory, allow considerable discretion as to when, how, and to whom they are fulfilled. The perfect–imperfect distinction, however, is not appropriate for corporations since it is doubtful whether economic entities such as corporations must assume the same imperfect burdens, e.g. of charity, as individual persons.

For purposes of discussing multinationals, then, it is best to recast the distinction into one between 'minimal' and 'enlightened' duties, where a minimal duty is one the persistent failure of which to observe would deprive the corporation of its moral right to exist; i.e. a strictly mandatory duty, and an enlightened duty is one whose fulfilment would be praiseworthy but not mandatory in any sense. In the present context, it is the determination of minimal duties that has priority since in attempting to answer whether P is permissible for C in B, the notion of permissibility must eventually be cashed in terms of minimal standards. Thus, P is not permissible for C simply because C fails to achieve an ideal vision of corporate conduct; and C's failure to contribute generously to the United Nations is a permissible, if regettable, act.

Because minimal duties are our target, it is appropriate next to invoke the language of rights, for rights are entitlements that impose minimum demands on the behaviour of others.

III. THE APPEAL TO RIGHTS

Theorists commonly analyse the obligations of developed to less developed countries in terms of rights. James Sterba argues that "distant peoples" (e.g. persons in Third World countries) enjoy welfare rights that members of the developed countries are obliged to respect.[8] Welfare rights are defined as rights to whatever is necessary to satisfy "basic needs", and "basic needs", in turn, as needs "which must be satisfied in order not to seriously endanger a person's health and sanity".[9] It follows that multinationals are obliged to avoid workplace hazards that seriously endanger workers' health.

A similar notion is advanced by Henry Shue in his book, *Basic Rights*. The substance of a basic right for Shue is "something the deprivation of which is one standard threat to rights generally".[10] He considers it a "minimal demand" that "no individuals or institutions, including corporations, may ignore the universal duty to avoid depriving persons of their basic rights".[11] Since one's physical security, including safety from exposure to harmful chemicals or pollution, is a condition for one's enjoyment of rights generally, it follows that the right to physical security is a basic right that imposes specific obligations on corporations.

Equally important for our purposes is Shue's application elsewhere of the 'no harm' principle to the actions of US multinationals abroad.[12] Associated with Mill and traditional liberalism, the 'no harm' principle reflects a rights-based approach emphasising the individual's right to liberty, allowing maximal liberty to each so long as each inflicts no avoidable harm on others. Shue criticises as a violation of the 'no harm' principle a plan by a Colorado-based company to export millions of tons of hazardous chemical waste from the US for processing and disposal in the West African nation of Sierra Leone.[13] Using the same principle, he is able to criticise any US asbestos manufacturing corporation which, in order to escape expensive regulations at home, moves its plant to a foreign country with lower standards.[14]

Thus the Shue–Sterba rights-based approach recommends itself as a candidate for evaluating multinational conduct. It is irrelevant whether the standards of B comply or fail to comply with home country standards; what is relevant is whether they meet a universal, objective minimum. In the present context, the principal advantage of a rights-based approach is to establish a firm limit to appeals made in the name of host country laws and morals – at least when the issue is a clear threat to workers' safety. Clear threats such as in-plant asbestos pollution exceeding levels recommended by independent scientific bodies are incompatible with employees' rights, especially their right not to be harmed. It is no excuse to cite lenient host country regulations or ill-informed host country public opinion.

But even as a rights-oriented approach clarifies a moral bottom line for extreme threats to workers' safety, it leaves obscure not only the issue of less extreme threats, but of harms other than physical injury. The language of rights and harm is sufficiently vague so as to leave shrouded in uncertainty a formidable list of issues crucial to multinationals.

When refined by the traditions of a national legal system, the language of rights achieves great precision. But left to wander among the concepts of general moral theory, the language proves less exact. Granted, the celebrated dangers of asbestos call for recognising the right to workers' safety no matter how broadly the language of rights is framed. But what are we to say of a less toxic pollutant? Is the level of sulphur-dioxide air pollution we should demand in a struggling nation, say one with only a few fertiliser plants working overtime to help feed its malnourished population, the same we should demand in Portland, Oregon? Or, taking a more obvious case, should the maximal level of thermal pollution generated by a poor nation's electric power plants be the same as West Germany? Since thermal pollution raises the temperature of a given body of water, it lowers the capacity of the water to hold oxygen and in turn the number of 'higher' fish species, e.g. salmon and trout. But whereas the trade-off between more trout and higher output is rationally made by the West German in favour of the trout, the situation is reversed for the citizen of Chad, Africa. This should not surprise us. It has long been recognised that many rights, e.g. the right to medical care, are dependent for their specification on the level of economic development of the country in question.[15]

Nor is it clear how a general appeal to rights will resolve issues that turn on the interpretation of broad social practices. For example, in the Italian tax case mentioned earlier, the propriety of submitting an 'Italian' vs. 'American- style' tax return hinges more on the appraisal of the value of honesty in a complex economic and social system, than on an appeal to inalienable rights.

IV. AN ETHICAL ALGORITHM

What is needed, then, is a test for evaluating P more comprehensive than a simple appeal to rights. In the end nothing short of a general moral theory working in tandem with an analysis of the foundations of corporate existence is needed. That is, ultimately, there is no escape for the multinational executive from merging the ordinary canons of economic decision-making, of profit maximisation and market share, with the principles of basic moral theory.[16] But this formidable task, essential as it is, does not preclude the possibility of discovering lower-order moral concepts to clarify the moral intuitions already in use by multinational decision-makers. Apart from the need for general theories of multinational conduct there is need for pragmatic aids to multinational decision-making that bring into relief the ethical implications of views already held. This suggests, then, the possibility of generating an interpretive mechanism, or algorithm, that managers of multinationals could use in determining the implications of their own moral views about cases of the form, 'Is P permissible for C when P is acceptable in B but not in A?'.

The first step in generating such an ethical algorithm is to isolate distinct senses in which the norms of A and B conflict. Now, if P is morally and/or legally permitted in B, but not in A then either:

1. The moral reasons underlying B's view that P is permissible refer to B's relative level of economic development; or
2. The moral reasons underlying B's view that P is permissible are independent of B's relative level of economic development.

Let us call the conflict of norms described in (1) a 'type 1' conflict. In such a conflict, an African country that permits slightly higher levels of thermal pollution from electric power generating plants, or a lower minimum wage, than those prescribed in European countries might do so not because higher standards would be undesirable *per se*, but because its level of economic development requires an ordering of priorities. In the future, when it succeeds in matching European economic achievements, it may well implement the higher standards.

Let us call the conflict of norms described in (2) a 'type 2' conflict. In such cases levels of economic development play no role. For example, low-level institutional nepotism, common in many underdeveloped countries, is justified not on economic grounds, but on the basis of clan and family loyalty. Presumably the same loyalties will be operative even after the country has risen to economic success – as the nepotism prevalent in Saudi Arabia would indicate. The Italian tax case also reflects an Italian cultural style with a penchant for personal negotiation and an unwillingness to formalise transactions, more than a strategy based on level of economic development.

When the conflict of norms occurs for reasons other than relative economic development (type 2), then the possibility is increased that there exists what Richard Brandt has called an "ultimate ethical disagreement".[17] An ultimate disagreement occurs when two cultures are able to consider the same set of facts surrounding a moral issue while disagreeing on the moral issue itself. An ultimate disagreement is less likely in a type 1 case since after suitable reflection about priorities imposed by differing economic circumstances, the members of A may come to agree that *given* the facts of B's level of economic development, P is permissible. On the other hand, a type 2 dispute about what Westerners call 'nepotism' will continue even after economic variables are discounted.

The status of the conflict of norms between A and B, i.e. whether it is of type 1 or 2, does not fix the truth value of B's claim that P is permissible. P may or may not be permissible whether the conflict is of type

1 or 2. This, however, is not to say that the truth value of B's claim is independent of the conflict's type status, for a different test will be required to determine whether P is permissible when the conflict is of type 1 rather than type 2. In a type 1 dispute, the following formula is appropriate:

> P is permissible if and only if the members of A would, under conditions of economic development relevantly similar to those of B, regard P as permissible.

Under this test, excessive levels of asbestos pollution would almost certainly not be tolerated by the members of A under relevantly similar economic conditions, whereas higher levels of thermal pollution would be. The test, happily, explains and confirms our initial moral intuitions.

Yet, when, as in type 2 conflicts, the dispute between A and B depends upon a fundamental difference of perspective, the step to equalise hypothetically the levels of economic development is useless. A different test is needed. In type 2 conflicts the opposing evils of ethnocentrism and ethical relativism must be avoided. A multinational must forgo the temptation to remake all societies in the image of its home society, while at the same time rejecting a relativism that conveniently forgets ethics when the payoff is sufficient. Thus, the task is to tolerate cultural diversity while drawing the line at moral recklessness.

Since in type 2 cases P is in conflict with an embedded norm of A, one should first ask whether P is necessary to do business in B, for if not, the solution clearly is to adopt some other practice that is permissible from the standpoint of A. If petty bribery of public officials is unnecessary for the business of the Cummins Engine Company in India, then the company is obliged to abandon such bribery. If, on the other hand, P proves necessary for business, one must next ask whether P constitutes a direct violation of a basic human right. Here the notion of a right, specifying a minimum below which corporate conduct should not fall, has special application. If Polaroid, an American company, confronts South African laws that mandate systematic discrimination against non-whites, then Polaroid must refuse to comply with the laws. Thus, in type 2 cases, P would be permissible if and only if the answer to both the following questions is 'no'.

> (a) Is it possible to conduct business successfully in B without undertaking P?
> (b) Is P a clear violation of a basic human right?

What sorts of practice might satisfy both conditions (a) and (b)? Consider the practice of low-level bribery of public officials in some under-developed nations. In some South American countries, for example, it is impossible for any company, foreign or national, to move goods through customs without paying low-level officials a few dollars. Indeed, the salaries of such officials are sufficiently low that one suspects they are set with the prevalence of the practice in mind. The payments are relatively small, uniformly assessed, and accepted as standard practice by the surrounding culture. Here, the practice of petty bribery would pass the type 2 test and, barring other moral factors, would be permissible.

A further condition, however, should be placed on multinationals undertaking P in type 2 contexts. The companies should be willing to speak out against, and be willing to work for a change of P. Even if petty bribery or low-level nepotism passes the preceding tests, it may conflict with an embedded norm of country A, and as a representative of A's culture, the company is obliged to take a stand. This would be true even for issues related exclusively to financial practice, such as the Italian tax case. If the practice of underestimating taxes due is (1) accepted in B, (2) necessary for successful business, and (3) does not violate any basic human rights, then it satisfies the necessary conditions of permissibility. Yet in so far as it violates a norm accepted by A, C should make its disapproval of the practice known.

To sum up, then, two complementary tests have been proposed for determining the ultimate permissibility of P. If P occurs in a type 1 context, then P is not permissible if:

> *The members of A would not, under conditions of economic development relevantly similar to those of B, regard P as permissible.*

If P occurs in a type 2 context, then P is not permissible if either:

1. *It is possible to conduct business successfully in B without undertaking P, or*
2. *P is a direct violation of a basic human right.*

Notice that the type 1 test is not reducible to the type 2 test. In order for the two tests to have equivalent outcomes, four propositions would need to be true: (i) If P passes (1) it passes (2); (ii) if P fails (1), it fails (2); (iii) if P passes (2), it passes (1); and (iv) if P fails (2), it fails (1). But none of these propositions is true. The possibility matrix below lists in rows A and B the only combinations of outcomes that are possible on the assumption that the two tests are equivalent. But they are not equivalent because the combinations of outcomes in C and D are also possible.

	Criterion 1	Criterion 2
A	Fail	Fail
		equivalent outcomes
B	Pass	Pass
C	Fail	Pass
		non-equivalent outcomes
D	Pass	Fail

To illustrate, P may pass (2) and fail (1); for example, the practice of petty bribery may be necessary for business, may not violate basic human rights, but may nonetheless be unacceptable in A under hypothetically lowered levels of economic development; similarly, the practice of allowing a significant amount of sulphur-dioxide pollution (sufficient, say, to erode historic artefacts) may be necessary for business, may not violate basic rights, yet may be hypothetically unacceptable in A. Or, P may fail (2) and pass (1); for example, the practice of serving alcohol at executive dinners in a strongly Muslim country may not be necessary for business in B and thus impermissible by criterion 2 while being thoroughly acceptable to the members of A under hypothetically lowered economic conditions.

It follows, then, that the two tests are not mutually reducible. This underscores the importance of the preliminary step of classifying a given case under either type 1 or type 2. The prior act of classification explains, moreover, why not all cases in row C or in row D will have the same moral outcome. Consider, for example, the two Fail–Pass cases from row C mentioned above, i.e. the cases of artefact-damaging, sulphur-dioxide pollution and petty bribery. The former might be classified properly (depending upon circumstances) as a type 1 practice, and hence would be permissible, while the latter might be classified as a type 2 practice, and would be impermissible.

V. SOME PRACTICAL CONSIDERATIONS AND OBJECTIONS

The algorithm does not obviate the need for multinational managers to appeal to moral concepts both more general and specific than the algorithm itself. It is not intended as a substitute for a general theory of morality or even an interpretation of the basic responsibilities of multinationals. Its power lies in its ability to tease out implications of the moral presuppositions of a manager's acceptance of 'home' morality and in this sense to serve as a clarificatory device for multinational decision-making. But in so far as the context of a given conflict of norms categorises it as a type 1 rather than type 2 conflict, the algorithm makes no appeal to a universal concept of morality (as the appeal to basic human rights does in type 2 cases) save for the purported universality of the ethics endorsed by culture A. This means that the force of the algorithm is relativised slightly in the direction of a single society. When A's morality is wrong or confused, the algorithm can reflect this ethnocentricity, leading either to a mild paternalism or to the imposition of parochial standards. For example, A's oversensitivity to aesthetic features of the environment may lead it to reject a given level of thermal pollution even under hypothetically lowered economic circumstances, thus yielding a paternalistic refusal to allow such levels in B, despite B's acceptance of the higher levels and B's belief that tolerating such levels is necessary for stimulating economic development. Or, A's mistaken belief that the practice of hiring twelve-year-olds for full-time, permanent work, although happily unnecessary at its relatively high level of economic development, would be acceptable and economically necessary at a level of economic development relevantly similar to B's, might lead it both to tolerate and undertake the practice in B. It would be a mistake, however, to exaggerate this weakness of the algorithm; coming up with cases in which the force of the algorithm would be relativised is extremely difficult. Indeed, I have been unable to discover a single, non-hypothetical set of facts fitting this description.

The algorithm is not intended as a substitute for more specific guides to conduct such as the numerous codes of ethics now appearing on the international scene. A need exists for topic-specific and industry-specific codes that embody detailed safeguards against self-serving interpretations. Consider the Sullivan Standards, designed by the black American minister, Leon Sullivan, drafted for the purpose of ensuring non-racist practices by US multinationals operating in South Africa. As a result of a lengthy lobbying campaign by US activists, the Sullivan principles are now endorsed and followed by over half of all American multinationals with South African subsidiaries. Among other things, companies complying with the Sullivan principles must:

> *Remove all race designation signs.*
> *Support the elimination of discrimination against the rights of*
> *   Blacks to form or belong to government-registered unions.*
> *Determine whether upgrading of personnel and/or jobs in the lower*
> *   echelons is needed (and take appropriate steps).*[18]

A variety of similar codes are either operative or in the process of development, e.g. the European Economic Community's Vredeling proposal on labour-management consultations; the United Nation's Code of Conduct for Transnational Corporations and its International Standards of Accounting and Reporting; the World Health Organisation's Code on Pharmaceuticals and Tobacco; the World Intellectual Property Organisation's Revision of the Paris Convention for the Protection of Industrial Patents and Trademarks; the International Chamber of Commerce's Rules of Conduct to Combat Extortion and Bribery; and the World Health Organisation's Infant Formula code against advertising of breast-milk substitutes.[19]

Despite these limitations, the algorithm has important application in countering the well documented tendency of multinationals to mask immoral practices in the rhetoric of 'tolerance' and 'cultural relativity'. Utilising it, no multinational manager can naïvely suggest that asbestos standards in Chile are permissible because they are accepted there. Nor can he infer that the standards are acceptable on the grounds that the Chilean economy is, relative to his home country, underdeveloped. A surprising amount of moral blindness occurs not because people's fundamental moral views are confused, but because their cognitive application of those views to novel situations is misguided.

What guarantees that either multinationals or prospective whistleblowers possess the knowledge or objectivity to apply the algorithm fairly? As Richard Barnet quips, "on the 56th floor of a Manhattan skyscraper, the level of self-protective ignorance about what the company may be doing in Colombia or Mexico is high."[20] Can Exxon or Johns Manville be trusted to have a sufficiently sophisticated sense of 'human rights', or to weigh dispassionately the hypothetical attitudes of their fellow countrymen under conditions of 'relevantly similar economic development'? My answer to this is 'probably not', at least given the present character of the decision-making procedures in most global corporations. I would add, however, that this problem is a contingent and practical one. It is no more a theoretical flaw of the proposed algorithm that it may be conveniently misunderstood by a given multinational, than it is of Rawl's theory that it may be conveniently misunderstood by a trickle-down capitalist.

What would need to change in order for multinationals to make use of the algorithm? At a minimum they would need to enhance the sophistication of their decision-making mechanisms. They would need to alter established patterns of information flow and collection in order to accommodate moral information. The already complex parameters of corporate decision-making would become more so. They would need to introduce alongside analyses of the bottom line, analyses of historical tendencies, nutrition, rights, and demography. And they would need to introduce a new class of employee to provide expertise in these areas. However unlikely such changes are, I believe they are within the realm of possibility. Multinationals, the organisations capable of colonising our international future, are also capable of looking beyond their national borders and applying – at a minimum – the same moral principles they accept at home.

NOTES

1 An example of disparity in wages between Mexican and US workers is documented in the case study by John H. Haddox, 'Twin-plants and corporate responsibilities', in Patricia Werhane and Kendall D'Andrade (eds.), *Profits and Responsibility,* New York, 1985.

2 Richard D. Robinson, *International Business Management: A Guide to Decision Making,* second edition, Hinsdale, Ill., 1978, p. 241.

3 Robinson, *International Business Management,* p. 241.

4 Charles Peters and Taylor Branch, *Blowing the Whistle: Dissent in the Public Interest,* New York, 1972, pp. 182–5.

5 Arthur Kelly, 'Italian bank mores', in T. Donaldson (ed.), *Case-Studies in Business Ethics,* Englewood Cliffs, N.J., 1984.

6 Arnold Berleant, 'Multinationals and the problem of ethical consistency', *Journal of Business Ethics,* III, 1982, pp. 185–95.

7 One can construct an argument attempting to show that insulating the economies of the less developed countries from the highly developed countries would be advantageous to the less developed countries in the long run. But whether correct or not, such an argument is independent of the present issue, for it is independent of the claim that if P violates the norms of A, then P is permissible.

8 James Sterba, 'The welfare rights of distant peoples and future generations: moral side constraints on social policy', *Social Theory and Practice,* VII, 1981, p. 110.

9 Sterba, 'Welfare Rights', p. 111.

10 Henry Shue, *Basic Rights: Subsistence, Affluence, and US Foreign Policy,* Englewood Cliffs, N.J., 1980, p. 34.

11 Shue, *Basic Rights,* p. 170.

12 Henry Shue, 'Exporting hazards', *Ethics,* XCI, 1981, pp. 579–606.

13 Shue, 'Hazards', pp. 579–80.

14 Considering a possible escape from the principle, Shue considers whether inflicting harm is acceptable in the event overall benefits outweigh the costs. Hence, increased safety risks under reduced asbestos standards might be acceptable insofar as the economic benefits to the country outweighed the costs. The problem, as Shue correctly notes, is that this approach fails to distinguish between the 'no-harm' principle and a naïve greatest happiness principle. Even classical defenders of the 'no harm' principle were unwilling to accept a simple-minded utilitarianism that sacrificed individual justice on the altar of maximal happiness. Even classical utilitarians

did not construe their greatest happiness principle to be a "hunting licence" (Shue, 'Hazards', pp. 592–3).

Still another escape might be by way of appealing to the rigours of international economic competition. That is, is it not unreasonable to expect firms to place themselves at a competitive disadvantage by installing expensive safety equipment in a market where other firms are brutally cost-conscious? Such policies, argue critics, could trigger economic suicide. The obligation not to harm, in turn, properly belongs to the government of the host country. Here, too, Shue's rejoinder is on-target. He notes first that the existence of an obligation by one party does not cancel its burden on another party; hence, even if the host country's government does have an obligation to protect their citizens from dangerous workplace conditions, its duty does not cancel that of the corporation (Shue, 'Hazards', p. 600). Second, governments of poor countries are themselves forced to compete for scarce foreign capital by weakening their laws and regulations, with the result that any 'competitive disadvantage' excuse offered on behalf of the corporation would also apply to the government (Shue, 'Hazards', p. 601).

15 Sterba himself reflects this consensus when he remarks that for rights ". . . an acceptable minimum should vary over time and between societies at least to some degree" (Sterba, 'Distant Peoples', p. 112).

16 For the purpose of analysing the moral foundations of corporate behaviour, I prefer a social contract theory, one that interprets a hypothetical contract between society and productive organisations, and which I have argued for in my book, *Corporations and Morality,* Englewood Cliffs, N.J., 1982, see especially ch.3. There I argue that corporations are artefacts; that they are in part the products of our moral and legal imagination. As such, they are to be moulded in the image of our collective rights and societal ambitions. Corporations, as all productive organisations, require from society both recognition as single agents, and the authority to own or use land and natural resources, and to hire employees. In return for this, society may expect that productive organisations will, all other things being equal, enhance the general interests of consumers and employees. Society may reasonably expect that in doing so corporations honour existing rights and limit their activities to accord with the bounds of justice. This is as true for multinationals as it is for national corporations.

17 Richard Brandt, 'Cultural relativism', in T. Donaldson and P. Werhane (eds.), *Ethical Issues in Business,* second edition, Englewood Cliffs, N.J., 1983.

18 See 'Dresser industries and South Africa', by Patricia Mintz and Kirk O. Hanson, in Thomas Donaldson (ed.), *Case Studies in Business Ethics,* Englewood Cliffs, N.J., 1984.

19 For a concise and comprehensive account of the various codes of conduct for international business now under consideration, see 'Codes of conduct: worry over new restraints on multinationals', *Chemical Week,* July 15, 1981, pp. 48–52.

20 Richard J. Barnet and Ronald Muller, *Global Reach: The Power of Multinational Corporations,* New York, 1974, p. 185.

Is enduring good order between 'states' really possible?

PETER INGRAM

Queen's University of Belfast

I

States relate to each other in complex ways and in many different areas bearing on people's social lives. These relationships include some that could be politically insignificant or neutral, like sport (though now this seldom is) or communication and travel (which seem neutral in themselves, though instrumentally important). Some cultural areas have a varying ideological relevance, while the numerous departments of science and technology, together with the social sciences and economics, have far-reaching effects on the material conditions of life: all may present serious political implications. Other areas of activity, such as access to resources, interstate diplomacy, and the disposition of power itself, have indisputably direct consequences for the life of the state. Although political activities like diplomacy must always have significance for the state, the categorisation of different areas as politically significant is not at issue in this paper; what matters is that almost no aspect of human behaviour can be sure of not acquiring at some time international political significance through its importance for the state. This point is essential to a full understanding of the way in which the state and the states-system are conceptualised at present, and particularly of the impasse that has been created for the betterment of international (but, more correctly, interstate) relations.

Despite the diversity of international relations there is at their core a special area of importance – international law – which attempts to systematise and order relations between states in a consistent and enduring way. If it were as sucessful as it has been claimed to be it would provide a secure and comprehensive underpinning of international existence generally. For the most part, public international law has as its subjects states.[1] It takes two main forms: rules which are (or are held to be) binding on all states; and treaties and other agreements arrived at by consent between two or more states, which are not binding on states not parties to the agreement (although it may have serious results for them).[2] The traditional two chief weaknesses of international law are readily apparent in any jurisprudential approach: the lack of centrally organised sanctions to give reality to the claim that international law has the authority to bind its subjects; and the pervading voluntaristic character of the international system, which extends not just to interstate agreements but throughout.

It is this second weakness on which I shall concentrate. If there are exceptions to the voluntaristic character of international law – as with the claims of customary international law – these exist more in theory than in practice, although it is doubtful how far even theory can be taken: states, for example, frequently reserve the right of holding to their own interpretation of the rules.[3] Where (from a realist's point of view) states really are compelled to act as the rules require – as individuals may be compelled by law to act against their own self-interest – the compulsion arises all too frequently from the realities of power and not from a duty conditional on the authoritative character of the rules themselves. It is important to stress too that the voluntaristic character of the system is evidenced not just in the necessity for consent and agreement to be given and upheld in practice, but also in the many possibilities the rules themselves provide for reservation, derogation and repudiation, either directly or by default. The latter concepts give principled support for arrangements that not even the most ardent contract theorists would wish to admit in a general way into a municipal system. Otherwise, the practice of relations between states seems in some of its main features to follow in reality certain lines of the traditional social contract theory devised to explain and justify the formal obligations found in domestic political relationships between individuals.

Even if they are present for the contractarians in domestic society, voluntaristic features are of course circumscribed, if not abolished, by the existence of sanctions[4] – not the pragmatic sanctions issuing from power, but effective sanctions grounded in authority, which, if they are to maintain a properly legal character, must be provided for according to general rules. These rules, though they may not directly emanate from or be executed by a central body, must nevertheless find their validity in, and be ultimately controlled by an organised central administration. Such a central body has to act as a guarantor of their effectiveness, that is to say, that rules will be upheld and infractions punished. As already stated, the first weakness of international law is its lack of dependable, centrally organised sanctions, and so there can be no delimitation of its voluntaristic character by means of the standard method for municipal law. While there have been attempts at centrally organised sanctions (mostly of an economic kind),[5] they have suffered from an ineffectiveness created not by the object-state's self-sufficiency but rather by their reliance on individual voluntary enforcement by each sovereign state either directly or through international organisations. And voluntarism degenerates into the worst kind of self-help when resort is had to the so-called sanction of war.[6]

The two weaknesses of international law are not separate but linked. The lack of centrally organised sanctions renders unavoidable a practical dependence on voluntary agreement between states and voluntary adherence to rules. But there is an independent need to maintain a voluntaristic character for the international system which precludes the imposition of centrally organised sanctions. Voluntarism has come to be associated with the indispensability of sovereignty for the full-fledged state. So, centrally organised sanctions are difficult to organise in practice because of the existence of over 150 sovereign states and the consequent impossibility of getting the voluntary agreement and active cooperation of all these states in order that sanctions should be effective. But in addition, they are precluded in principle, since an imposed demand that sanctions be enforced by some state would derogate from its authority as a sovereign state. To organise sanctions centrally and effectively would itself be an implicit statement that the autonomy of states could be circumscribed. Therefore the international system fails as a legal system delivering order and security, not for a lack of rules about behaviour – these it does possess – but for the lack of effective rules about compulsion, sanctions against defaulters, and contingency arrangements for others in the case of default.

The need to maintain an essential voluntary aspect to international agreements is an inevitable outcome of the commitment to the concept of sovereignty. Anything less than a voluntary agreement (although admittedly it may be less voluntary in practice than in theory) is a derogation from the ideal of total autonomy which is not just associated with sovereignty but – much more – is its very embodiment.

The concept of sovereignty cannot be examined in detail here. But it is necessary to say a few words to deal with possible arguments that sovereignty can be reconciled with centrally organised – and imposed – sanctions, or that non-voluntary agreements do exist (as with customary international law). There are two approaches to be considered. One accepts the claim that sovereignty would in no wise be diminished by the existence of some central – and real – authority, like a United Nations with substantial power of its own origination. The other (perhaps more plausibly) agrees that a central authority must diminish each state's sovereignty in an absolute sense; but since each state would, or should, be affected equally, it would remain the equal of others in the matter of relative sovereignty. All states would (in theory) be equals in their relationships with each other, and sovereign in their relations among themselves as individual states.

Can sovereignty survive undiminished the existence of an effective central authority? As with unanimous direct democracy, individual autonomy is not diminished so long as each and every member voluntarily accedes to each and every arrangement in the society to which he belongs. He may accede directly because he is committed to the content of the rule or course of action decided on, or he may accede because he accepts the principle that he should be guided by the majority view.[7] But with this argument the commitment to majoritarianism belongs to the individual's autonomous system of beliefs: and so it is not a principle to which the majority can appeal in order to justify imposition of their decision on a recalcitrant minority. If they attempt to do this, they thereby seek to diminish individual autonomy; and if this is the case, we may say that any imposition – however justified – diminishes actual autonomy.

However, even if everybody seems to be agreeing all the time, adherence to unanimous direct democracy cannot provide the certainty that is necessary for a developed system to have full practical value for those who belong to it. If we leave acceptance of decisions up to each individual on every occasion, the system will develop massive indeterminacy, and its members a feeling of chronic insecurity. For a system to be useful, its members have to have some sort of sureness about the arrangements it purports to provide. It is good to know that a particular person has always kept his word in the past, and one may sincerely believe that he will keep his word in the future; but if the worst came to the worst, one would like to be sure of being able to depend on his being made to keep his word. Additionally, it is a reasonable requirement that there should be effective contingency arrangements in the event that he actually succeeds in defaulting. Such arrangements are needed by even the most harmonious and cooperative society, since just the possibility of collapse diminishes the feeling of security which itself is a necessary part of real security. An ordered society needs arrangements which say that if a person chooses to behave differently from what is required of him (however unlikely that may be) he will be made to do what he does not wish to do, or at least, others will not suffer innocently by his default. So the exercise of autonomy is conditional, and not absolute, by virtue of the existence of such arrangements. The threat alone of imposition destroys complete autonomy; and effective authority cannot avoid providing such arrangements, and by doing so it must curtail real autonomy, and at the international level this would mean a sovereignty that was conditional or circumscribed.

So it is impossible from a theoretical point of view to reconcile effective central authority with an undiminished state sovereignty, if sovereignty is coterminous with autonomy. And this is still to neglect the transfer of material power which must take place for any central body to possess truly effective authority – a point which remains to be considered.

II

Sovereignty requires to be effective. In this, sovereignty is more than authority. To talk of 'a moral authority' that lacks, or is unassociated with, coercive power is not, as it may seem to the cynical, to make use of an empty phrase. Still, states hardly want to have the status of a moral authority only. The whole point of laws and legal systems, nationally and internationally, would be lost if beneath the apparatus of administration, government, and social regulations there lay nothing more than moral authority. For states it is vital that their authority should be real and effective: what the state lays down for rules must have the force of law. Their authority must be recognised internally by their citizens and externally by other states as their equals in the world. Voluntarism, therefore, cannot be prized by states just for its own sake, as it is in the context of some individual moralities, because it enshrines a feature of human life (like autonomy) of deep moral value; it is prized as much (or more) because it declares where in principle actual power (as well as authority) should lie – that is, firstly and finally with the state. To make their authority effective, to give their autonomy substance, states must have power. If their sovereignty is to be found in all-encompassing authority, it is necessary that the power accomanying sovereignty should in principle be absolute too. The power should always be there to be called on, even if it is not always used. (In any case, it is quite often called on, as in times of war.)

Stated like this, the possession of power seems to be a practical necessity – and an overwhelming one, perhaps – but still not a necessity dictated by conceptual logic. I wish to argue, however, that this all-important possession of power is the latter kind of necessity, given the concept of the state as we understand it. (There may be other conceptualisations of 'state' in both historical and contemporary thought, but they are not conceptualisations which the international system works with, or which could prove hermeneutically useful in describing international affairs at the present time.)

The effective possession of power as the criterion (and the aspiration too) of statehood is grasped by Kelsen (among others) when he suggests that efficacy within a specific geographical territory is in fact the norm of recognition for national states in the international legal order.[8] But in the context of relations between states this is to be seen not as an artifically devised rule but as a norm constituted by international practice – the practice, of course, of power-holding states. In other words, the conceptual logic of 'state' could be different, but – as a matter of fact – the logic of the word is at present understood to demand the possession of effective power.[9]

Can effective power actually be a variety of limited power? From the point of view of abstract theory 'effective power' might be understood as signifying only that power which was sufficient for the conduct of political affairs and the preservation of social order. But can political power be partitioned off into a separate department of public life quite independent of other public, social and even private affairs? Is the realm of practical politics easily bounded? On the contrary, the relationship between sovereignty and power is such that a relative or limited sovereignty is an unacceptable idea, not because an international system based on relations between equals with limited power would not be viable, but because internal necessities for the state require sovereignty and its accompanying claim to power to be residually absolute and unlimited.[10] Why is this?

Modern life has become increasingly complex. A technologically developed society, with its individual members possessing specialised functions, needs scope for effective public intervention, if only for administrative and coordinative purposes. The activities of social life are interlocked in such a way that many of them have, or could have, political significance for the state. (Indeed, it can be said that they do have significance just because they could have.) Since political life may be affected by what goes on in numerous areas of social behaviour, few areas remain safe from politics. The result of modern social developments is that the state is impelled to claim an omnicompetence in all matters; and it has come therefore not only to extend its truly political power but also to acquire, necessarily, a power that pervades, through the legal system, every aspect of social life. The reality of state power is such that it should be there to meet all contingencies, and the complexity of modern life is such that potential shortcomings in power, once they are recognised, render the state actually vulnerable. Although it may not use it, the state must have access to all the power that may be available to it.

Furthermore, the state's identification with a nation (though often a constructed nation, especially in the developing world) means that its support of national sentiment can be, if not essential, a very practical contribution to its own identity. The general development of a national identification with the state is too useful a source of strength to be ignored, for the state as well as the nation. The idea of the state has moved from embracing constrained internal political and external diplomatic functions, embodying a concern to protect strictly political interests, to the position where every activity that has a 'national' character and a general social relevance can have both domestic and international significance for the state. Clearly, areas like economics and technology would already be of vital interest to the state because of their practical effects. But the identification of state and nation has also created a concern on the state's part with activities relating more to the nation, most obviously those with a cultural or ideological content. This has led to claims by states to authority not only in matters like the structure and content of education, linguistic policy, or the writing of history,[11] but also over politically 'innocent' activities carrying, so to speak, a national tag, like sport.[12]

However inappropriate the categorising of this or that activity may seem to be, the actuality is that no aspect of social life can be sure of not acquiring political significance at some time or other.[13] Which areas of behaviour are of significance as a matter of fact will in part have a culturally relative, in part a genuinely pragmatic cause, but above all – in the end – this will be determined by the present-day concept of the state itself, and the ways in which particular states choose to actualise it. What needs emphasising is that the state's claims about the activities over which it may exercise legitimate authority, and over which it accordingly needs appropriate power, have become very extensive indeed.

The realities of power refer not only to the current amount of power the state deems properly its own, but also to the extent of activities in which it seems proper for that power to be exercised. No more than internal requirements might demand that the state possess an all-encompassing power in its own interests. But of course it is nothing too profound to mention that if the state cannot risk possible constraints on its power arising internally, it can hardly be prepared to tolerate constraints arising from some external source either – that is to say, constraints that are not self-imposed but really imposed by others. Internal requirements have external consequences precluding the realisation of a diminished but equal sovereignty between states. The external alienation of power for the purposes of international relations would mean a loss for the state of the proper power it needs to be assured of, if it is to have ultimate control over its internal affairs. External sovereignty – the autonomy and self-determination of states – is not simply an expression of a moral statement about authority but also a normative statement about where power must be located for a state to be properly a state. Sovereignty cannot allow an irrevocable alienation of power from the state internally or externally.

The relationship between states at present is based not so much on unconstrained power – for the reality is that it is constrained, even for the superpowers – as on an aspiration by states to unconstrained power in regard to their own interests. An idealisation of power is therefore built normatively into the system. The possession of an unfettered power to act on their own behalf is a desire of all states, a desire which they seek to achieve, and one endorsed by the present conceptualisation of the international system. This is not to deny that states wish very largely to behave in the international arena in a constructive way; but still, obligations incurred internationally are to be (in principle) self-imposed and freely chosen obligations. The harmony of an ideal international system is to be based on cooperation not subjection.

In the practical way of things, constraints on power have sometimes to be accepted as unavoidable, but they are not willingly accepted if they frustrate a state's pursuit of its own ends. Of course, they are accepted if they instrumentally promote the self-interest of the state concerned (though all too often according to seemingly short-term considerations). The wish to possess unconstrained power, to surrender power only partially and recoverably, is easily explained by the state's desire not to render itself vulnerable to oppression of any indirect kind or, worse, to direct attack by another state. But this fear does not explain the unwillingness to adopt systems which could offer a reasonably good guarantee of protection but at the cost of a loss of sovereignty. As with the individual in the supposed state of nature there is a desire to preserve the widest possible freedom to act in one's own interest – in the case of the state, to protect and further most efficiently the state's own interests (and for some states at least, the interests of its citizens too) at home and abroad.

III

Against the theoretical weaknesses of international law on paper, supporters of the international system ask us to set its successes in practice.

Frankly, many of these successes ought to be achievable by rational parties acting in their own self-interest; the system only acts to smooth the process. Many of the regulatory features of the international system likewise represent measures which promote cooperation or secure co-ordination rather than recognise at least a residual need for compulsion. The system's rules are for the most part undemanding. They often do not threaten real loss to any of the states concerned, and they usually advance the self-interest of most of the parties. Impressive though some achievements of international law have been, the test of a legal system is its ability to control self-interested behaviour, to maintain – consistently – order against the odds, and in the last resort to succeed in requiring its subjects to act against their own narrow self-interest. The international system does not look so effective in this respect. That we have been kept from a world war for nearly forty years is one boast, but this is no very long period; and moreover, it has been a period when there have been perhaps some two hundred serious armed conflicts around the world, at the same time as there have been continual deep tensions even for peaceful nations. The adherence to a belief in legitimate, just war does not save the system morally or conceptually: developed municipal systems have long since abandoned a general principle of legitimate self-help in domestic affairs (though there are exceptions) even when narrowly justified.

The embedding of power in the concept of the state (as that is presently understood) means that the transfer of power and authority away from the state, as something that might be deliberately undertaken, is not simply very difficult in a practical way but is (one should say) conceptually obstructed. The ideas that seem worth applying as a possible basis for a revised world order reflect what has been said elsewhere about possibilities for revising the internal order of the state itself. "The state is not something which can be destroyed by a revolution, but is a condition, a certain relationship between human beings, a mode of human behaviour; we destroy it by contracting other relationships, by behaving differently."[4]

In international affairs the activities of states consist too often in no more than self-interested actions. A sound international system requires ethical behaviour, just as any comprehensive social system does; and ethical behaviour requires us to act for social purposes sometimes against our own genuine interests. This paper has deliberately resorted to an exaggerated picture of the international system in terms of power and self-interest, but not a false one. It is not to be denied that for the most part the system works smoothly overall from one week to the next, from one year to the next, by cooperation and agreement. But what must be faced is the problem of what is to happen when cooperation fails and breakdown threatens. Legal systems are intended both to keep things running smoothly in an atmosphere of obedience to rules and to deal with impending or actual failures in such overall obedience. It is in regard to the latter function that the international system is seriously deficient; and no states-system can provide us with a good guarantee that normality will be maintained or restored in an orderly fashion when breakdown occurs. Because of their commitment to power and the promotion of their own interests we cannot in the end depend on states alone always to act properly in the context of the system as a whole, or voluntarily to act to save the system at serious cost to themselves. Nor can the international system in an orderly, straightforward and dependable fashion ensure that states do act against their own particular interests where appropriate, because the very idea of state sovereignty militates against this.

Change is required, but it cannot be effected by a direct assault on the power of the state, or by direct attempts to transfer its power and authority to other organisations. There is greater opportunity to bring about change by ensuring that where power remains apart from the state, it continues to do so, and by constructing and developing networks of power relationships that do not involve states as parties. The international system is only contingently a business of arranging relations between states: in the end it exists to further relationships between people, to optimise the conditions of life for human beings. So reform must be engaged in not just at the institutional level, but at the level of individual relationships too. In the end it is up to people to create and foster new relationships between themselves at all levels, as well as to support appropriate non-state institutions.

So long as virtually every activity of life is actually or potentially subordinate to control by the state through the legal system, the disadvantages of an international system constructed on – and dependent on – a network of interstate relationships seem inescapable. States "are means of organising people for participation in the international system".[15] They are conceptually integrated in a necessary way into the system, through the identification of the state as either the source or at least the embodiment of authority. Alternatives to the present international system are most often propounded in terms merely of other kinds of states-systems. Theorists attempt to get away from the apparent excesses of the large state by suggesting that large units could be broken up into smaller federated or altogether independent units, or that existing large states could be counterbalanced by the formation of stronger regional group-ings by the smaller states. The idea of a single world authority is a radical solution to the states problem, but one that is unrealisable as a direct move from present conditions. Other possibilities do not provide for major changes but present only rearrangements of states.

However, whether we wish to move towards one single large author-ity, a collection of many small authorities, or any one from a number of complex federal systems, such suggestions, though adroitly moving 'authority' around, tend not to take full account of the realities of power. These present a formidable practical obstacle; but worse, the concepts of authority and power are meshed together for laws and legal systems both nationally and internationally. While the two concepts are certainly distinct, their connection is so strong (as I have argued in emphasising the importance of effective authority) that to try and shift authority around while paying no attention to power is not simply to attempt some-thing that is very difficult but something that is conceptually contra-dictory. While sovereignty must remain intact, that power which creates and supports state autonomy whether in reality or in recognised principle must remain intact too. There can be no change in the structure of authority without a change, not to the realities of power, but to the manner in which power is idealised for the state; and there can be no change here without a change in the idea of sovereignty, or a total aban-donment of the concept of it as it is currently understood.

Sovereignty is immune to direct assault. Its abandonment could only be accomplished through the surrender of their own sovereignty by all states together. Such a supreme sacrifice can be imagined, but not con-vincingly. With even a mere handful of states in the world it would seem an unlikely achievement. With the number of sovereign states seemingly approaching two hundred a coordinated surrender of sovereignty seems as impossible a happening in reality as the move from Hobbes's state of nature to political society. A more plausible way of shifting the interna-tional system into a new mode would be to concentrate on the realities of power rather than the abstract disposition of authority, forbearing from a straight demand on states to surrender their power. The aim must be to change the actualities of power as it exists in the world, and thereby to confront states with a real and permanent, *de facto* loss of power which must be recognised in the way international institutions and relationships are constructed.

There are power sources and power relationships of a material as well as a non-material kind which are to some degree independent of control by the state. In the past as well as today the state has sought to increase its control of power in all its manifestations. I would wish to argue that whatever the intrinsic merits or demerits of sources of power distinct from the state, there is a prima-facie case for valuing them positively, protecting them from further encroachments by the state, and even augmenting them at least as a necessary counterbalance to the state's power. The last is already enough to act as an effective counterweight to the over-aggrandisement of other power sources, although it is perhaps not always sufficient to be able actively to control them. Where direct control is necessary, it should be possible to explore dealings with transnational organisations and relationships in ways that do not directly involve states as the agents of control.

A multiplex balancing of power with power may seem like nothing more than the present system made worse, with greater potential for unruliness and the eventual anarchy of war. On the contrary, it is intended as presenting two advantages. A greater compexity of power relationships could plausibly lead to greater stability – or at least less instability – than the present system, because a diversification of power must promote the dissociation of interest from the state. The pattern of developments could progress to a state where individuals, institutions and corporations large and small would have created patterns of relationships in which much diminished states were only one kind of party among others. Such a system would also enhance the roles and powers of parties for whom resort to military force was not a historically conditioned response to some situations. Real power takes other forms than brute physical coercion and military force. There are, among others, economic forms of power, power in education, the morally coercive power of small communities, the power of religion, all of which can be stronger than the power of the state in appropriate circumstances.

In addition, a more complex system of power would serve as a staging-post on the road to developing the source of a single world authority, by initiating structural developments that would not be merely changes rung on the present states-system. The creation of new forms of authority cannot be successfully carried out against established patterns of power. And the redistribution of power should be seen as a preparation for new forms of authority and not as an end in itself. Indeed, in itself – in its reliance on the physical force of power rather than the moral force of authority – it is to be seen as, if anything, intrinsically worse than the present system, which at least expresses a commitment to morality in the claims it makes about authority and legitimacy. Yet it still presents a possible opening for a diversion past obstruction to progress in the present system. Future developments must be towards the eventual establishment of a world authority: the stress is rightly on 'authority' and not 'power', but authority cannot be effective without power, or exist for long against power. A supposed authority cannot control unitary sources of excessive power; but a supreme authority mught be better placed to control complex and numerous power relations with great diversity of origins, and to uphold in a dependable way some universal value for the world. Keeping power divided into small elements could mean easier control by a world authority with sufficient power to act effectively; and keeping it diversified would help to ensure too that a world authority could never gather enough power to itself to be able to abuse it.

It hardly needs mentioning that such developments are conjectural, and hazily so, at this point. To leave the development of ideas at a stage where stress is laid on the allocation of power, the uses of power, the advantages of power, may seem nakedly amoralistic, especially as it goes against a received belief in the legitimacy of the state in principle. Yet the realities of the world are as they are; and any theory of international reform has to put itself forward as a workable one. To concoct an ideal world order in theory is not at first sight too difficult a task. Many writers have painted pictures of the form which international developments ought to take and the way in which international law might work. They have been able to depict a sometimes splendid world structure, about which, unfortunately, one can only say that if one wanted to get there, one would not start from here. We, however, have no choice but to start from here. If permanent good order is not possible between states as they are currently conceptualised, and if it is believed that good order is desirable in itself and in the way in which it facilitates many worthwhile human endeavours, then one must be prepared to work out ideas for change which, through their presentation of a principled but feasible scheme, offer to realise promises in practice. Though a situation of power against power seems, on its face, to incline us towards greater disorder, it seems paradoxically that this is the only way in which we can have the possibility of an enduring orderly world. This point was grasped by the old idea of a 'balance of power'. But to leave almost all significant power with states alone has had, and is liable to have again, unhappy consequences.

NOTES

1   This statement requires some important qualifications, but it does not misrepresent the international attitude, whereby international organisations and other agencies occupy a very secondary position in international law. Cf. Ian Brownlie, *Principles*

of Public International Law, second edition, Oxford, 1973, pp. 60–72.

2 Other sources of international law, or more strictly evidence of the state of the law, include judicial decisions and the writings of jurists. See Brownlie, *Principles,* pp. 1–32.

3 Even enthusiasts for international law have to concede the "voluntary basis" of international jurisdiction, which "arises from a persistent reluctance to accept the consequences and risks of impartial judgment" (C. Wilfred Jenks, *A New World of Law?,* London, 1969, p. 157).

4 One assumes, *pace* Hobbes, and some modern writers who advocate moral heroism, that duress and true consent cannot co-exist.

5 The Katanga affair and the peace-keeping operations in the Congo in 1960–61 provided a notable exception, in so far as they involved a centrally organised and more or less generally supported use of coercive power by the United Nations in an effective way. Even so, there was considerable disagreement about the financing of the operations.

6 Attempts to conceptualise war as a sanction seemingly fail to appreciate the positive function of organised sanctions in expressing the collective will of society. The punishment of a criminal is a reaffirmation of the domestic system of rules to emphasise the authority and integrity of society. War constitutes a breakdown (if only a temporary one) of international order and the rules which support it. It is the very abnegation of a system of rules.

7 This allows a little more leeway for associating individual autonomy with actual government than does, for example, R. P. Wolff, *In Defence of Anarchism,* New York, 1976, pp. 18–19.

8 Hans Kelsen, *General Theory of Law and State,* New York, 1961, p. 121.

9 The most notable case of Rhodesia, with its failure to obtain international recognition, remains an exception and does not seem to represent a change in the rule. The converse recognition of governments that have ceased to possess effective power within their territory, though not infrequently practised by states because of their ideological commitments, continues to seem anomalous.

10 By 'residually' I mean that in the last resort a state will claim that it is right for it to reject the demands of international law, and call back any delegated power, in order to protect its own vital interests.

11 A lack of interest in a given area seems often simply to imply that the state does not consider it worth taking seriously. The seeming persecution of Aristotelian philosophy in Czechoslovakia, in one paradoxical way, does the state credit.

12 It should nevertheless be conceded that sport can be seen as of some practical importance for the state, in promoting the health and collective spirit of its citizens.

13 Even religion can lose its political significance for the state, as is increasingly the case in most Western countries, though the situation is quite the opposite in Islamic states.

14 Gustav Landauer, quoted by David Miller, *Anarchism,* London, 1984, p. 151.

15 F. S. Northedge, *The International Political System,* London, 1976, p. 141.

Equal pay for equal work in the Third World[*]

HUGH LEHMAN

University of Guelph, Ontario

I

Transnational corporations have found it profitable to establish manufacturing operations in Third World nations in part because labour costs are considerably reduced. The practice of paying workers in a Third World nation at a lower rate apparently conflicts with a principle which has gained widespread support in other contexts, the principle of equal pay for work of equal value. For example, it has been claimed that certain jobs traditionally performed by women are of equal value to employers as other jobs traditionally performed by men but that since the women are paid at a lower rate they are being unjustly treated. The argument is that since the jobs are of equal value and since jobs of equal value should be remunerated at the same rate, the salaries for the traditional women's jobs should be equal to the salaries for the comparable men's jobs.

If the principle of equal pay for work of equal value is valid as a principle of justice, then it appears that the practice of paying workers in Third World countries at a lower rate than workers doing the same jobs in industrialised nations is unjust. Recently, however, Henry Shue has argued that the principle of equal pay for equal work is unacceptable because it has unacceptable implications.[1] His argument is open to several criticisms. In order to express these criticisms I shall first state his argument as I understand it. After criticising his argument I shall suggest alternative criticisms of the equal pay for work of equal value principle. I shall argue that Shue is correct in thinking that this principle is valid only with a restriction in scope. Outside such restrictions, violations of the equal pay for equal work principle may be in accord with more basic moral principles such as either the difference principle or utilitarian principles concerning the satisfaction of interests.

[*] This paper has previously been published in the *Journal of Business Ethics,* 1985 (Copyright ©1985 by D. Reidel Publishing Company, Dordrecht, Holland).

II

Shue suggests three possible interpretations of the equal pay for equal work principle. The alternative interpretations arise in light of different ways of construing 'equal pay'. The claim that workers should receive equal pay could mean either that they should receive the same number of dollars per hour (or per week or per item, etc.); or it could mean that workers in Third World nations should be paid enough so that their standard of living in the Third World country was the same as that of workers at comparable jobs in industrialised nations; or it could mean that workers in Third World nations should be paid enough so that their standard of living relative to other people in the same country was the same as the standard of living of the workers in the industrialised nation relative to other people in the industrialised nation.

Shue argues that on any of the three interpretations the equal pay for equal work principle is unacceptable. Given the third interpretation of the principle, the salary paid to workers in Third World nations might be so low that it would not provide for the physical needs of the workers or other people dependent upon them. I have no criticism to make of Shue's objection to the principle interpreted in this third way. According to Shue, if the principle is interpreted in either the first or the second way, then the pay that a corporation is required to pay to workers in Third World nations is too high. Applying the equal pay for equal work principle under either of the first two interpretations, according to Shue, is unrealistic. Further, he maintained, paying workers in Third World nations at such a high rate would give them salaries sufficient to give them a standard of living equivalent to the *élite* of those nations. To pay workers in Third World countries at such a high rate would mean that such workers would earn more in a week than most workers in such countries earn in a year. Shue objects that, intuitively, such salaries are too high. He concludes that the equal pay for equal work principle ought not to be understood as applying regardless of social context.

While I have a certain amount of sympathy with Shue's remarks, these objections to the equal pay for equal work principle are poorly formulated. The claim that applying some moral principles yields 'unrealistic' consequences is not, so far as I can see, a sound objection to the principles. On many occasions people opposed to the implications of a moral principle have claimed that the principle is unrealistic. I suspect that all that they mean is that people will not voluntarily conform to the principle. However, to say that people or corporations will not voluntarily conform to the principle of equal pay for equal work is not necessarily a good reason for saying that the principle is mistaken or that it ought not to be applied.

Shue's other objection, namely that to pay the workers in Third World countries at a rate which would give them a standard of living equivalent to the *élite* of those countries, is poorly formulated also. Surely, we ought to ask, why would it be wrong for these people to be paid at such a relatively high rate? To suggest, as Shue does, that such a high rate of pay is counter-intuitive does not explain why it would be wrong to require that workers in such countries be paid at such a high rate.

III

Is there a serious objection then to the principle of equal pay for work of equal value, if that principle is interpreted in either of the first two ways that Shue suggests? I am inclined to agree with Shue that the principle, interpreted in either of these ways, is open to serious criticism. In arguing against the principles, I shall on the one hand appeal to utilitarian considerations and on the other hand argue that justice does not require that workers in Third World nations be paid such high salaries. Henceforth when I refer to the principle, I shall understand it as interpreted in either the first or the second way.

I shall assume that, under proper restrictions, if a transnational corporation moves a manufacturing, mining or agricultural operation to a Third World nation, that can lead to increases in the quality of life of a significant number of the poor people of that nation. Such increases in the quality of life will be reflected in an increase in total utility. Improving the quality of life of the poorest people in such a manner need not reduce the quality of life of the wealthy people of the nation. Thus, the increase in the quality of life of these poor people will increase utility overall, at least within the Third World nation. However, in some cases, if a corporation opens a commercial operation in a Third World nation, there will be some loss of employment by workers in the First World nation. Thus, it is possible that the increase in total utility within the Third World nation would be negatively balanced by a loss of utility elsewhere. Indeed, not only is this possible, it has, of course, occurred repeatedly. However, in many cases there is good reason for believing that the increase in utility which may occur in the Third World nation is not counterbalanced by the increased unemployment and consequent loss of utility in the First World nation. The workers in the First World nation, even while unemployed, do not suffer a decrement in their utility equal to the increment in the utility of the Third World workers who would be employed in their place.

Of course, if a corporation begins a business operation in the Third World, it does not automatically lead to significant increases in the quality of life of poor people there. The poor people may remain essentially as poor as they were, while any benefits that accrue in that world accrue to the wealthiest people. Of course, such a result is not inevitable. In light of this, what can be argued is that if there are restrictions on the operation of a corporation so that if it were to set up operations in a Third World nation it would lead to significant improvements in the quality of life of the people in the Third World, then it is morally right or desirable that corporations set up such operations in the Third World. Now, we may ask, should the corporations who are considering setting up such operations be required to pay workers in the Third World at a rate equal to that which they pay comparable workers in the industrialised parts of the world? The answer, I believe, is probably negative. The requirement that workers in Third World nations be paid at such a high rate would, in many cases, have the consequence that there would be no economic incentive for the corporation to transfer operations to the Third World. The decision not to make such a transfer would produce less overall utility than would be produced by making a transfer and paying workers at the lower rate. Thus, on utilitarian grounds, we can argue that subject to the conditions indicated, the adoption of the equal pay for equal work rule would be morally wrong. Indeed, it appears that on utilitarian grounds, corporations should be encouraged to transfer operations to Third World nations subject to the condition indicated, namely, that there be significant improvements to the quality of life of the poorest people of those nations.

If we think about the conditions in some Third World nations that make life miserable there we find that major contributing factors to the poor quality of life are such things as the level of health care, the level of nutrition, the level of education, and the like. If one were a benevolent dictator in such a country, one would presumably maximise utility in that country by bringing about significant improvements in some of these areas. Thus, rather than requiring corporations to provide equal pay for equal work, one would choose to require corporations to make signifant improvements to the native water supply, sewerage, hospitals, etc. Such improvements would improve the quality of life far more than the greater salaries required by the equal pay for equal work principle since, even with those greater salaries, a worker in a Third World nation could not buy decent hospitals, sewage treatment, water, etc. Thus,

again, we see that the principle of equal pay for equal work is unacceptable on utilitarian grounds. Total utility would be maximised by paying
lower salaries.

Now, it may be objected that, while it is true that acting in accord
with the principles of equal pay for equal work would not maximise utility, that is irrelevant. Those who appeal to the principle in arguments
concerning women's rights apparently believe that accepting the principle would improve the quality of life of women relative to that of men.
They appear to argue, for the most part, that the basic reason for adopting the equal pay for equal work principle is that the lower quality of life
of women as compared to men's is unjust. Such injustice, they may
argue, should be eradicated regardless of whether this leads to an
increase in total utility. We may wonder then whether the utilitarian
arguments offered above for rejecting the principle of equal pay for equal
work would be undercut by similar appeals to justice in this case. In my
view, such is not the case. Arguments in favour of Shue's intuitions may
be grounded on several distinct fundamental moral principles.

Shue suggests that the principle of equal pay for equal work may be
valid only within social contexts within which the difference between the
highest and lowest standards of living is restricted within certain limits.
Where one is comparing conditions within a modern welfare state with
those in a Central American country in which, among other things,
people drink untreated water which they and their animals use for
bathing and other purposes, the principle does not apply. We suggest
that the reason why the principle does not apply is that it is indeed a
derivative moral principle which is limited in scope. The precise character of the limitations of the principle is a controversial matter. How one
formulates such limitations depends on his more basic moral principles.
I shall argue however that on the basis of either of two moral principles
one can provide explanations which tend to justify Shue's intuitions.

One may argue, in accord with John Rawls's difference principle,
along the following lines: unequal treatment is justified, according to the
difference principle, providing that the inequality benefits the poorest
people in the community and providing there is equality of opportunity.
In countries with a large middle class, as in the industrialised democracies, unequal pay for equal work does not benefit the poorest workers.
Unequal pay for equal work may benefit, for example, male workers
who receive higher pay than women doing comparable jobs, or it may
benefit white workers who receive higher pay than black workers who do
comparable jobs. It would be arguable that it benefited the poorest workers only if the alternative for them was a significantly lower living stan-

dard. In industrialised democracies this is not normally the case. If people are unemployed, their essential needs are satisfied through various forms of social welfare. This is true, for the most part, even in the United States and Canada, although some people do slip through the social welfare net.

When we consider the question at issue concerning the salary for workers in Third World countries, the case is clearly not the same. Living conditions for many people in many such countries are deplorable. Industrialisation can provide a significant alternative. The inequality in pay for workers in these countries as compared to workers in Europe or North America is justifiable, in accord with the difference principle, on the grounds that it yields a significant benefit for the workers in the Third World countries.

We can argue for a similar conclusion in a second way – in accord with utilitarian principles concerning the satisfaction of interests to which many philosophers subscribe. It is assumed that people's interests differ in weight. One's interest in sufficient nourishing food has greater weight than one's interest in casual entertainment. Given a choice, one ought to try to satisfy weightier interests prior to attending to less weighty interests. If we assume that in general people's interest in their own survival and in the survival of their close relatives is weightier than their interest in equal treatment, we can argue that we ought to accept wage scales in the Third World countries which are lower than those in industrialised countries. The argument, of course, depends on the assumption that the alternative to working and being paid at the lower rate for the worker in the Third World country is that the corporation won't set up operations in that country and that, in consequence, it is far more likely that his life or the lives of his family and friends will be nasty, brutish and short.

We should consider two objections to the above argument. We have been considering the issue of whether salary scales for workers in Third World countries which are lower than for workers at comparable jobs in the industrialised countries are unjust to the workers in the Third World countries. We have argued that it is not unjust to those workers. However, it may be objected that by allowing corporations to pay workers in Third World countries at a lower rate we are permitting an injustice to workers in the industrialised democracies who, in consequence of corporations moving to Third World nations, become unemployed and suffer in significant ways as a result of that.

In replying to this objection, I would argue along the following lines: the policy of permitting lower wage scales for workers in Bangladesh and comparable places need not be unjust. We have argued that it is in accord with the difference principle. It is also in accord with the principle of equal consideration of interests. Since the interests of workers in Third World countries in survival are weightier than the interests of workers in First World countries in having a job, we ought to take steps to satisfy the interests in survival where this can be done prior to satisfying interests in employment. However, we have not yet considered the possibility that workers have a right to their job. A worker may claim that he has a right to his job and thus that when this job has been taken from him and given to someone else, he is being treated unjustly. This objection raises many issues and is too complex to fully answer here. However, if the objection is valid, it means at most that an employer ought not to shut down a manufacturing operation which is profitable and re-open in another location and hire new workers at lower salaries. In other words, it may be that a worker who has had a job has a right to that job. He ought not to be replaced by another worker if he is doing the job well. However, for new jobs, it is not at all clear that workers in one country have a right to those jobs – unless of course the new jobs were created with the benefit of tax or other incentives on the part of the government of that country.

Our reply to this objection does not, of course, imply that the interests of workers in First World countries in having jobs are not weighty. They are indeed weighty. They ought to be satisfied prior to other less weighty interests. This may require that within First World countries social policies be adopted which contribute to elimination of unemployment. The unemployment of workers in First World countries cannot be traced to one cause only. While we have spoken above in ways that suggest that the unequal wage scales are the cause of unemployment of workers in First World countries, this is an over-simplification. The unequal wage scales are not a sufficient condition for people in First World countries being unemployed. At most, the unequal wage scales are a part of a set of conditions which is sufficient for that effect. Other factors are also part of the same set of conditions. Modification of these other factors would reduce or eliminate any unemployment which is associated with corporations transferring operations to Third World countries.

Another objection to the position we have supported is that the considerations we have cited as allowing corporations to pay Third World workers less for work of equal value appear also to permit exploitation of people who are extremely poor. Thus, it might be argued that reasoning such as I have defended would provide a justification for a corporation doing business in South Africa to pay black or coloured workers at a lower rate than white workers in that country. It might be argued that the coloured or black workers will be significantly better off if they are employed regardless of the fact that their salary is less than that of white workers doing the same or closely similar work.

In reply I would say that the question of investment in South Africa is a complex issue and the principle of equal pay for equal work is a middle-level moral principle. Presumably other moral principles would have a bearing on the question of investment in South Africa. The South African political system is fundamentally unjust. I would argue that corporations ought not to set up shop at all in South Africa unless their doing so contributes in a significant way towards eliminating the injustices practised in that country. It is not at all clear that a multinational corporation that set up shop in South Africa but paid black or coloured workers at the low salaries paid such workers by South African business would make any contribution towards eliminating that unjust system. However, were it reasonable to believe that a foreign corporation could contribute towards the reduction or elimination of injustice in South Africa while paying black or coloured workers in that country less than workers in industrialised countries are paid for doing the same job then I believe such investment should be encouraged.

Similarly, I would argue that failing to satisfy the equal pay for equal work principle is not the same as exploiting people who are extremely poor. The term 'exploitation' is an emotive term. This is not the place to engage in a full analysis of this term. However, we might note that failing to pay workers in Third World countries at the same rate as workers in countries in the industrialised world is not necessarily equivalent to treating such workers *merely* as means to our ends. Thus, this second objection is not really an objection to the thesis that I have defended.

NOTES

1 Henry Shue, 'Transnational transgressions', in Tom Regan (ed.), *New Introductory Essays in Business Ethics,* New York, 1984, pp. 274 ff.

Institutional rights and international duties: some reflections on Henry Shue's argument

DAVID S. SCARROW
Kalamazoo College, Michigan

In his *Basic Rights*[1] Henry Shue aims to establish (1) that subsistence rights are as 'basic' as the right to physical security, (2) that therefore enjoyment of physical security and subsistence are inseparable, and (3) that the duties to provide and protect subsistence around the world are inseparable from the duties to promote and protect the right of physical security. This third point suggests the main policy objectives of Shue's book: to conclude that the United States should be as concerned to promote and protect the subsistence rights of people around the world as it professes to be concerned about protecting the civil rights of those people. My aim in this paper is not to challenge Shue's policy recommendations; but I do intend to examine and question the premises which Shue uses to justify them.

I

Shue opens his book with a sketch of his conception of a "moral right":

> A moral right provides (1) the rational basis for a justified demand (2) that the actual enjoyment of a substance be (3) socially guaranteed against standard threats. [p. 13]

And rights are basic

> ... only if enjoyment of them is essential to the enjoyment of other rights... When a right is basic, any attempt to enjoy any other right by sacrificing the basic right would be quite literally self-defeating, cutting the ground from beneath itself. [p. 19]

That is, no right can be enjoyed unless all basic rights are enjoyed. Hence, no basic right can be enjoyed without the enjoyment of all other basic rights. On Shue's view, both the right to physical security and the right to subsistence are basic rights. Persons cannot enjoy either right without enjoying the other.

Shue moves from this conclusion to a claim about duties. His primary

concern is to argue that the duty to secure subsistence rights is as important as the duty to secure the right to physical security. He argues that if
it is impossible to secure one right without securing the other, then it is
impossible to have the duty to secure one right without having the duty
to secure the other. But both the premise of this argument and its conclusion are false.

II

Shue's claim that physical security and subsistence are basic rights has a
certain plausibility. At least it is plausible that other rights can hardly be
enjoyed if these rights are not protected. Shue sometimes uses the non-
basic right to assemble as an example of a right which would be virtually
meaningless if assembling aroused the threat of physical violence either
on the part of the civil authorities or others. Likewise, the right to assemble would be seriously curtailed if assembling aroused serious threats to
one's capacity to obtain subsistence for oneself and one's family – such as
the threat of losing the only available job in a society where public
assistance is not provided.

But Shue's thesis becomes less plausible when it maintains the
inseparability of those rights which he has identified as basic. For if, as
Shue claims, one can enjoy a right only if that right is institutionally
protected from standard threats, then it looks as if it is entirely possible
to enjoy one basic right without enjoying another. For example, in
pioneer days there often was no problem in obtaining sufficient food and
water, but there was considerable threat to physical security. Thus the
right to subsistence was realised, since there were few standard threats
to subsistence; but the right to physical security was not realised, since
there were as yet no effective political institutions to guard against the
standard threats of violent attack. Again, there are other situations where
the right to physical security is realised while the right to subsistence is
not. Some would maintain that this in fact describes the present social
reality in the United States.

These objections are similar to one raised by Marc Wicclair and discussed by Shue in a long footnote (note 13, pp. 178–81). Against Shue,
Wicclair argued that it was possible for a people to enjoy the right not to
be tortured while not enjoying any subsistence rights. Hence, Wicclair
concluded, it would be possible for a people to 'enjoy' the right not to be
tortured even though they were severely deprived of the necessities of
subsistence.

In response to this objection Shue argued that a person who was starving might agree to submit to torture in return for securing food, and that in this case the person's right to be protected from torture would not be protected after all. And Shue anticipated the reply that doing this would be a case of renouncing a right rather than a case of not enjoying a right by saying that the objection is "fairly obviously mistaken" (p. 180). But here it is Shue's reply which seems mistaken. Although he correctly says that the starving man was coerced into renouncing his right not to be tortured, he is wrong in concluding that the man was not enjoying the right. Indeed, the very fact that he could trade his right in order to obtain food shows that he was enjoying the right. The fact that we can be faced with the choice of our money or our life (to use Shue's example) does not mean that our money is counterfeit.

The same point can be made by a more realistic example. Instead of thinking of the right not to be tortured, consider the right of not submitting to medical experimentation or the right not to donate a bodily organ or the right not to give one's own blood. Yet even as one enjoys these rights, one also has the right to submit oneself to experimentation or to donate an organ or to give blood. And one has the right to do these things for money. If one needs money for subsistence one has the right to get money by donating an organ or by giving blood. Yet a society's failure to realise the right of subsistence does not *eo ipso* mean that it has failed to protect people's rights to maintain the integrity of their own body.

Perhaps Shue would reply that a right is never adequately secured – protected against standard threats – if it is possible for people to be coerced into renouncing the substance of the right. Thus he might argue that the right not to submit to medical experimentation or to donate a bodily organ is not adequately protected as long as the right to subsistence is not adequately protected. For the point of there being rights is to protect people not simply from deprivations caused by other people but also to protect them from situations where they will be faced with the choice of giving up something which is vital to them as persons. So in order to protect any vital interest every vital interest must be protected. As Shue says:

> But one of the chief purposes of morality in general, and certainly of conceptions of rights, and of basic rights above all, is indeed to provide some minimal protection against utter helplessness to those too weak to protect themselves. [p. 18]

However, this defence raises a problem which Shue wanted to avoid. For this defence specified basic rights in terms of vital interests: those human interests which need to be fulfilled and protected for the flourishing of any sort of decent life. For it would be most implausible for Shue to go so far as to say that people should never be forced to make choices among any of their interests – that they should be protected from all coercive situations. Rather, his demand for protection is plausible only in so far as it is a demand for protection of vital interests. And then he might argue that in order to protect any vital interest every vital interest must be protected. In order to protect one's interest in not being tortured one's interest in having the wherewithal of subsistence must be protected.

But although there is considerable plausibility in the claim that both the enjoyment of physical security and the enjoyment of subsistence are fundamental for a minimally satisfactory life, this claim does not give Shue what he wants and what he needs to establish his claim that people have basic rights to these things. In the first place, it does not give him the basis he needs for arguing for the correlative duties. To have a right, Shue tells us, is to be able to make a justifiable demand that the substance of the right be secured. But to have a vital need does not give a basis for such a demand. The fact that I have a vital need for something does not justify me in demanding of you that you provide it. And if I respond to someone's vital need, I do so out of considerations of humanity rather than to satisfy a claim against me. My act is one of beneficence, not an act of duty.

Nor, secondly, does appeal to vital needs accomplish what Shue wanted to accomplish. By speaking of basic rights rather than of vital interests Shue wanted to avoid the issue of defending a universal and thus culturally independent specification of what are the truly vital interests. For example, he wanted to avoid defending the claim that enjoyment of subsistence is more vital than the satisfaction of an ideological interest – e.g. the interest in being part of a fundamentalist Islamic state. He wanted to avoid this difficult task of specifying universal primary goods by directing his argument at anyone who admits that there are some rights which all people have. He appeals to them with the principle: If people have any rights, then people have basic rights. Then, by arguing that the right to subsistence is inseparable from the right to physical security – that the latter right cannot be enjoyed without enjoying the former – he aims to persuade his reader that the right to subsistence is as universal as the right to physical security. I have challenged this strategy by taking Shue's conception of a moral right seriously and arguing that the rights to physical security and the rights to subsistence are separable. In doing this I have implicitly argued that in Shue's sense of 'basic right' no rights are basic.

III

Shue intends his thesis about the inseparability of basic rights to provide a ground for establishing the equal urgency of the duties which are correlative to those rights. When that thesis about rights is put aside, the claim about duties loses much of its *a priori* plausibility.

Shue distinguishes those duties which are correlative with rights into three kinds: (1) the duty not to deprive people of the enjoyment of the substance of a right; (2) the duty to protect people from those who would deprive them of that substance; and (3) the duty to aid those who are deprived. Against such advocates of human rights as Cyrus Vance and Hugo Bedau, Shue wants to argue that we have as much duty to promote the enjoyment of subsistence rights as we have to protect and promote the enjoyments of physical security – duties which we would carry out by putting pressure on foreign governments to desist from wanton killing within their own populations and to abstain from the torture, imprisonment, and murder of dissidents. Shue wants to argue that we have as much duty to work toward securing the enjoyment of subsistence as we have to work toward the securing of these rights to physical security.

But that conclusion simply does not follow from whatever may plausibly be claimed about the inseparability of the enjoyment of these rights. For it may be that we – i.e. the people of the Western democracies – can have some effect in modifying the repressive and murderous policies of a regime and yet have virtually no power with regard to the subsistence of the people in that nation. It *may* be! Of course, whether or not this is so depends upon the details of the situation. But that is just the point. No quick argument based upon the inseparability of the enjoyment of the substance of rights can lead to a conclusion about the inseparability of duties with respect to those rights.

Indeed, the fact is that even the duties corresponding to a single right can be separated. For example, a wealthy nation and other corporate entities may have the duty to aid foreign peasants who have been deprived of subsistence; but it is wildly implausible to say that a nation or a corporation has the duty to protect foreign peasants from such deprivation – for they do not have the power or even the right to provide such protection. Only the foreign government itself can do that. Moreover, a failure of that government to provide such protection may even undermine the *prima-facie* duty not to adopt policies which will deprive the foreign peasant of subsistence. For if a nation's restraint upon itself and its corporations only helps other nations to enrich themselves by investment policies similar to the exploitative ones it eschewed, then the nation will have acted foolishly. As Shue himself remarks:

> Organizations and individuals who will voluntarily avoid deprivation that would otherwise be advantageous to them because they know that their potential victims are protected, cannot be expected to behave the same way when they know that their potential victims are without protection. [p. 61]

Such "individual [or national] restraint would be too much to ask" (p. 59).

This suggests that, although a nation does not have the duty to protect the subsistence of the citizens of other countries, it may have a duty both to put pressure upon foreign governments to do a better job in providing such protection and to refrain from practices which tempt those governments to weaken whatever protection they do give. And analogous considerations apply in the realm of physical security. It would be absurd to say that one nation has a duty to protect the physical security of citizens of other nations: that duty belongs to the government of that other nation. But it is not absurd to say that a nation has a duty not to assist foreign governments in their murderous and repressive practices and a duty to put pressure on foreign governments to reform. But even here we cannot give *a priori* answers, uninformed by the facts of a particular case. Before we decide to pressure a foreign government into stopping its repressive practices we must decide that such relaxation will not lead to a revolutionary regime which is even more murderous and repressive. At least we must make this determination if we would justify our pressuring in terms of increasing the enjoyment of physical security among the inhabitants of another country. As we know, it requires considerable experience and wisdom to even begin to make such a determination.

With respect to duties, then, there are two general points to be made. First, the international duties of individuals, of nations, and of other corporations with respect to promoting the values associated with human rights are for the most part the duties of influencing foreign governments to give increasing protection for those rights. Second, an individual, a nation, or a corporation may have more power to bring effective pressure for enhancing the protection of some of these values than it has for promoting the protection of others. Thus it may have more power to persuade a government to reform its practices with respect to civil rights than it has to reform its practices with respect to subsistence rights. And if this were the case, then the individual or nation or corporation would be justified in concentrating its efforts on the former rather than in wasting its energies on the latter. In this sense, at least, the duties are separable.

IV

Shue's argumentative strategy is to begin with the claim that a person's right to physical security and a person's right to subsistence are equally 'basic' and to conclude that our duty to secure subsistence for people around the world is as urgent as our duty to secure their physical security. Having questioned the truth of both premises and conclusion, I now want to question Shue's way of grounding his claims about our international duties in his claims about rights.

According to Shue, a moral right "provides a rational basis for a justified demand that the actual enjoyment of a substance be socially guaranteed against standard threats" (p. 13). But this definition blurs an important distinction, namely, the distinction between the justification of an institution and justification within an institution. That people have the right to physical security justifies the creation and maintenance of institutions which will protect physical security against standard threats. And once such institutions are in place a member of that institution has a rational basis for "demanding" that his or her physical security be protected against a particular threat. But it makes no sense to speak of someone as *demanding* the creation of an institution which will provide such protection. Within an institution there are identifiable persons or offices who are responsible for protection. But in a state of nature there is no one who has the responsibility for creating institutions. In such a state there will be pleas for aid and there will be proposals for cooperation. And perhaps institutions will emerge if acceptance of such proposals for cooperation become habitual. But no one outside that situation could provide those institutions for those persons. No one could be the object of a demand to do so.

This confusion – this failure to distinguish explicitly between the demands one can justifiably make within an institution and the justification of the institution – plays an important part in Shue's argumentation. For he argues as if the duties connected with rights were all intra-institutional duties, as if our duty to assist the inhabitants of other nations to enjoy their basic rights were the corollary of their rationally justifiable demand upon us. Thus in speaking of the duty to protect he says:

> The duty to protect is, then, a secondary duty of enforcing the primary duty of avoiding the destruction of a people's means of subsistence. In this respect it is analogous to, for example, the duty of police to enforce the duty of parents not to starve their children. [p. 55]

But a bit later he says that the duty to protect includes the duty to design "laws and institutions that avoid reliance upon unreasonable levels of self-control" (p. 59). And here the analogy with the duties of the police is entirely inappropriate. Even if I have some sort of duty to help design (and establish) institutions which will protect – or will better protect – the rights of others, this duty is not in response to a 'demand' which those others impose upon me. They have no more licence to demand that I do my duty than anyone else has.

But Shue's confusion does more than flaw his argument. For by obscuring the vast difference between institutional duties and extra-institutional duties he obscures the leap from the fact that governments have the duty to protect the security and subsistence of their own citizens to the cosmopolitan claim that they have duties to secure these values for everyone, those outside their own nation as well as those within it. But this leap is made implausible by Shue's own insistence that these values can only be secured by established institutions powerful enough to ward off "standard threats". For what can an outsider do to design or establish an institution for a foreign community? Because the possibilities are so limited, the duties seem minimal.

Thus, as Shue's own recognition of the moral importance of political institutions suggests, justifying duties by reference to rights is plausible only for intra-institutional duties. Whatever inter-institutional – international – duties there are are more plausibly justified by reference to reciprocity or equity or humanity. It is out of humanity that we have reason to influence foreign governments to improve their performance in protecting the subsistence and physical security of their citizens. And considerations of equity may ground the duties of the affluent nations towards the poorer ones. Yet even considerations of equity recognise that the complex interdependence of a nation's economic and social practices with its economic status precludes simple judgements about what is owed to a poorer country or what can be done to improve its status. The institutional context necessary for the enjoyment of any rights and any human values – a context which Shue emphasises – can often be just the fact that minimises the duties of those outside an institution to promote those values for the people within it. There simply may be very little that an outsider can do.

NOTES

1   Henry Shue, *Basic Rights: Subsistence, Affluence and U.S. Foreign Policy*, Princeton, N.J, 1980.

Conflicting conceptions
of deterrence*

HENRY SHUE
University of Maryland

I. THE BAPTISM OF THE BOMB

Here is a two-step plan to rescue nuclear war from immorality. First, the United States should build the most moral offensive nuclear weapons that money can buy and bring nuclear warfare into compliance with the principle of non-combatant immunity. Then it should build a defensive 'shield' that will make offensive nuclear weapons 'obsolete' and take the world 'beyond deterrence'. In this second stage, called the 'Strategic Defence Initiative' by believers and 'Star Wars' by doubters, anti-missile technology will confront missile technology like Hegelian antithesis confronting its thesis, and we will all be lifted up out of the age of nuclear war into a realm made safe for conventional war.[1] Even according to believers in the SDI, however, intermediate deployment, not to mention full deployment, of a strategic defence is some time away, pending breakthroughs on technological problems at which public money is now being thrown. Meanwhile, during the intervening decades we must look to the morality of our offensive missiles, and on the offensive front too there is good news: nuclear weapons are becoming more discriminate. The bomb has been born again. Now it is more just, and it need not indiscriminately slaughter the innocent. Thus spake, for example, Wohlstetter.

Writing a wide-ranging article in *Commentary*, eminent theorist of deterrence Albert Wohlstetter decries how some "moralists" have blithely embraced the threat of the nuclear incineration of women and children in the adversary society on the mistaken assumption that the most – perhaps, the only – credible form of deterrence was mutual assured

* Early ancestors of this paper were read at Davidson College, at a Third Thursday Briefing and a Workshop for Teachers conducted by the Center for Philosophy and Public Policy at the University of Maryland, and at the Second Fulbright Anglo-American Colloquium on Ethics and International Affairs of the Centre for Philosophy and Public Affairs at St. Andrews University. I benefited so much from the discussions at these occasions that I doubt whether those present will recognise the paper now, least of all its conclusion. For the financial support of this work I am grateful to the Ford Foundation, which bears no responsibility for my views.

destruction: destruction, not of enemy forces, but of enemy families.[2] "Not even Genghis Khan," Wohlstetter notes, "avoided combatants in order to focus solely on destroying noncombatants."[3] Seriously intended assured destruction is neither moral nor credible. Further, Wohlstetter's critique of mutual assured destruction as "self-confessed suicidal bluff" and of "the insanity of deception labelling itself deception", strengthens his essay as a powerful and worthy successor to Fred Iklé's classic critique of mutual assured destruction.[4]

Moralists who have opposed assured destruction have, according to Wohlstetter, been part of the problem in a different way. (Few, if any, 'moralists' seem to have been part of the solution.)

> Moralists who have chosen to emphasise the shallow paradoxes associated with deterrence by immoral threats against population have been at their worst when they have opposed any attempts to improve the capability to attack targets precisely and discriminately. . . They have often stopped research and engineering on ways to destroy military targets without mass destruction; and they have done collateral damage to the development of precise, long-range conventional weapons. . . . They have tried to stop, and have slowed, the development of technologies which can free us from the loose and wishful paradoxes involved in efforts to save the peace with unstable threats to terrorize our own as well as adversary civilians.[5]

While I certainly do not think that all the paradoxes of deterrence are shallow, loose, and wishful,[6] I shall have nothing to say in response to Wohlstetter's internal criticisms of mutual assured destruction. I want to concentrate instead on Wohlstetter's positive thesis, his good news about "the revolution in precision" on the part of offensive nuclear missiles. This good news is that we now have a morally superior alternative to mutually assured destruction as either murderous intent or suicidal bluff. The new generation of precision guided munitions (nuclear and non-nuclear) restores a morally significant choice "between killing innocent bystanders with nuclear weapons or attacking means of aggression and domination" – "a choice between destroying military targets and destroying innocents".[7]

I am not persuaded that we have any such choice between a form of nuclear war that could more or less satisfy the just-war requirement of avoiding harm to the innocent and another form of nuclear war that alone involves mass slaughter. Worse, I fear that in pursuit of a way to fight a nuclear war with clean hands we may undermine what little hope we still have of avoiding nuclear war. In order to see the depths of the difficulties we first need to take a few steps back.

II. FOUR POLAR POSTURES

Whenever people discuss the reason for possessing nuclear weapons, they say 'deterrence', but increasingly they do not mean deterrence, or at the very least, they do not mean deterrence in its classic, i.e. early post-World War II sense. Your reasons for wanting to possess nuclear weapons depend upon how you would use them, if you chose to use them. Almost everyone, although not quite literally everyone, says that he or she would never wish actually to use nuclear weapons. But possession is pointless unless some use is not only conceivable but, in some sense, feasible. I do not mean that the possession of nuclear weapons is pointless unless you will, or even would, use them. I mean it is pointless unless you might use them – unless there are circumstances in which you could use them and might do it, whether or not you actually would. If there are no circumstances in which you might use nuclear weapons, then you cannot even effectively bluff that you would use them – you can, as Wohlstetter emphasises, only bluff suicidally. So, any given rationale for the possession of nuclear weapons turns upon their conceivable use.

Use has at least two essential components: what and when. What are the targets and when might they be attacked? I shall call these two elements of any planned use of nuclear weapons 'target' and 'time'. Oversimplifying considerably, we can divide conceptions of deterrence into four types with reference to choice of target and choice of time (Figure 1). The targets of a nuclear attack can be either predominantly 'countervalue' (cities and other civilian areas) or 'counterforce' (weapons, troops and command centres). The launching of the attack can be either earlier (before the other side has launched nuclear weapons) or later (after the other side has launched nuclear weapons).[8]

Any plan to attack civilian targets, but only in retaliation, I call retaliatory deterrence. Any plan to attack military targets in an initial use of nuclear weapons I call initiatory deterrence. I am introducing these new labels, which I shall explain more fully in due course, as part of an effort to take a fresh look at some issues. Nevertheless, reciprocal policies of retaliatory deterrence would obviously constitute what is ordinarily called mutual assured destruction, and NATO's declared policy of first use of nuclear weapons in response to a successful conventional attack in Europe is one form (among several possible forms) of initiatory deterrence.[9] I want, however, to stick to the fundamentals here rather than to enter the thickets of actual policies just yet. Next, we must see why we seem to be driven into choosing between retaliatory deterrence and initiatory deterrence. Then, we can concentrate upon that disagreeable dilemma and, in the end, try to escape it.

Nuclear deterrence is one method for stopping an adversary nation from doing things you do not want it to do without, if the deterrence succeeds, actually having to go to war. Nuclear deterrence is a form of international coercion for nation-states that are politically sovereign but understand, to some extent, nuclear vulnerability. Deterrence succeeds if it stops your adversary from doing what you did not want done without getting you into a war. In its specific form, between the Soviet Union and the United States, its goal is containment without conflict. Each superpower is attempting to protect its own sphere of influence without being forced to fight World War III in order to do so. If avoiding war were the policy's only purpose, deterrence would not be such a delicate balancing act: the trick is avoiding war *and* getting what you most want (what the speeches call 'vital interests'). One may well decide, in the closing words of the film *War Games*, that "the only winning move is not to play the game". If one chooses to play, however, it is essential to see that the game is ineradicably in part military. Doctrines of deterrence are politico-military: (1) here is how we will stop them without a war and (2) here is how we will fight the war if (1) does not work. Accounts of deterrence that ignore the question 'and what if deterrence fails?' are deceptions, self-deceptions, or both – and 'it had better not fail' is not an answer to the question.

The military and the moral debates are alike in being fundamentally about what would have to be done if deterrence fails. The military question is: if your adversary can in fact be coerced only by means of a successful war effort, in how good a position are you left by the deterrence policy you pursue to conduct a successful effort after the policy has failed? The military assessments obviously admit of degrees, but for our purposes very rough and obvious standards will serve. Moral criteria apply to both the threat, and the military implementation if the threat should fail to deter, but judgements about the threat are in some (difficult to specify) fashion dependent upon judgements about what will happen if the threat fails. And it would seem prudent to give a lot of attention to the case of failure.[10]

FIGURE I

Polar offences

		TIME	
		Earlier	Later
	Civilian	(Terroristic)	RETALIATORY
TARGETS			
	Military/command	INITIATORY	(Damage-limiting)

Looking at Figure 1 with military and moral considerations in mind, then, we can fairly quickly see why terroristic deterrence is the most objectionable militarily and morally. We can next turn to its diametrical opposite, damage-limiting retaliation, which is more appealing militarily in that it plans for attacks upon the opposing forces rather than upon civilians, and more appealing morally in that it respects the nuclear taboo by using nuclear weapons only in retaliation. This appealing combination will turn out, however, to suffer centrifugal tendencies. The combination of counterforce targeting and second-strike timing seems driven apart: if we demand counterforce targeting, we are pushed toward first-strike timing, that is, initiatory deterrence; if we demand second-strike timing, we are pushed toward civilian targets, that is retaliatory deterrence. And we seem to be left with these two unappealing choices. First, then, we acknowledge terroristic deterrence; next we struggle with damage-limiting retaliation; and then comes our confrontation with the only two choices that seem to be left.

III. MILITARY PRESSURES FOR EARLY LAUNCH

TERRORISTIC DETERRENCE. What is militarily sensible can be of human interest only if it is morally sensible as well. Nevertheless, be it ever so moral, a position about nuclear deterrence is unacceptable unless it makes military sense. Satisfaction of both military criteria and moral criteria is necessary for an acceptable policy. To attack first and to attack the civilians on the other side (upper left box of Figure 1) is militarily nonsensical – more precisely, instrumentally irrational – not to mention morally abominable. Terroristic deterrence is a disastrous failure by both military and moral criteria. From a military point of view, one does not start a war by consuming substantial numbers of one's most sophisticated and powerful weapons in a manner certain to enrage and embitter the political and military leader of one's adversary while leaving the adversary's best weapons and leadership untouched – this would be true military madness. From any recognisable moral point of view, this would be true terrorism as well. What terrorists – as well as most torturers, which is why most torture is a species of terrorism[11] – do is assault defenceless civilians who are not in control of what the terrorists oppose.

Terroristic deterrence will, I hope, strike ordinary readers as bizarre. Nevertheless, it is well to remember that the only two actual military uses of nuclear weapons so far, the American attacks upon Hiroshima and Nagasaki, were and were intended to be terroristic, war crimes unpunished because committed by the victors but unsurpassed in calculated cruelty by the most dastardly war crimes of the Japanese. The purpose of the nuclear strikes on Hiroshima and Nagasaki was "to induce a sense of hopelessness in a people, still resisting despite immense suffering, by impressing upon them their vulnerability to an unprecedented form of horror".[12] As George Marshall maintained before the attacks on the two cities: "It's no good warning them . If you warn them there's no surprise. And the only way to produce shock is surprise."[13] We consciously implemented a policy of terrorising civilians. In one sense it 'worked', but presumably only because the adversary could not defend itself in kind.

DAMAGE-LIMITING RETALIATION. A retaliatory strike against military targets (lower right box of Figure 1) is a deterrent threat that would be welcomed, or at least tolerated, by some moralists, namely those whose overriding criterion is the principle of non-combatant immunity interpreted to mean not targeting civilians. Indeed, from this point of view one might judge that the only form of retaliation the implementation of which could possibly be morally justified (after deterrence had already failed) would be an attack upon the military forces, not the civilians of the other society. I readily acknowledge that damage-limiting retaliation is in an entirely different moral realm from terroristic deterrence and that the appropriate moral assessment of it is not obviously negative. Let us say for now that we will not exclude it on moral grounds.

How to assess damage-limiting retaliation by military criteria is a difficult question. In destroying any remaining forces on the other side, especially any nuclear forces that had been held in reserve out of the initial attack, one would be limiting the future damage that one could suffer (in a subsequent round). Thus, a military rationale might well generally support the choice of military targets for any strike, retaliatory or not. Professional military leaders tend greatly to prefer to fight the opposing military forces rather than to attack unarmed civilians. Since it is the other side's military forces, not its non-combatants, who can destroy your own forces, it is eminently sensible to prefer to deal with the opposing military first. It is the threat to you – and to the civilians you are defending.

The trouble is, first, that the feasibility of counterforce retaliation lies largely in the hands of the adversary, who can eliminate many potential nuclear targets and many other non-nuclear military targets from your retaliatory attack by the simple expedient of using them in its own initial attack.[14] An adversary who has decided to launch a nuclear attack is unlikely to be very cooperative about saving you targets. Second, if one were seen by the adversary to be building the capability for damage-limiting retaliation, it would have an added incentive to make any first-strike a massive one. Both these difficulties result from the fact that military targets tend to be movable targets. The first aspect of movability is that you can do less damage to the enemy in your second-strike – and the enemy decides how much less and which – while the second is that the enemy has an added reason to do more damage to you in its first-strike in order to put its capabilities to good use instead of merely letting you destroy them where they sit. Worst of all, whatever you were actually planning, an objective capability to conduct any very significant damage-limiting retaliation might appear to even an only moderately suspicious adversary as evidence of plans for a disarming first-strike, since any counterforce capability that could be used second could also be used first. It will always be difficult to convince an adversary that any major counterforce capability is only for retaliating, not for disarming.[15]

It turns out, then, that any plan for damage-limiting retaliation suffers at least three significant military defects:

1. *Enemy-selected targets.* Your adversary decides what you can attack (quantity and quality) in your second-strike in deciding what to use in its first-strike.
2. *Magnitude incentive.* An adversary who observes that you have counterforce capabilities has a strong reason to make any first-strike it would otherwise have made more massive than it would otherwise have been in order not to 'waste' its weapons by leaving them for you to destroy with your second-strike.
3. *Pre-emption incentive.* An adversary who observes that you have counterforce capabilities has a reason to make a first-strike it would not otherwise have made in order not to be vulnerable to a disarming first-

strike, even though you may not currently plan a first-strike.

The second and third defects mean that any significant capability for damage-limiting retaliation provides an adversary with some reason (of indeterminate strength – and indeterminate net strength, when contrary incentives are balanced in) to launch a massive, pre-emptive counter-force strike. These are two respects in which damage-limiting retaliation *cannot be* militarily *superior* to initiatory deterrence – the third point, indeed, consists of damage-limiting retaliation's being treated by a cautious adversary as if it were initiatory deterrence, as a result of the inexorable (and understandable) tendency to engage in worst-case planning when faced with a capability for pre-emptive disarming. The militarily rational response to the capability for pre-emptive disarming can be, other things equal, pre-emptive disarming of that very capability – more about this vicious circle later.

The first defect, enemy control of the quantity and quality of targets available for a second-strike, is a respect in which damage-limiting retaliation is irretrievably inferior to initiatory deterrence, in military terms, because at best it can destroy only 'left-over' targets – *how* inferior depends of course on how massive the initial attack was. Against an adversary who actually has the plans that NATO claims to have – beginning nuclear war with a limited first use – it might be, in military terms, quite a good plan, only marginally inferior to initiatory deterrence; against an adversary whose first-strike would in any case be massive, which is the announced Soviet policy, damage-limiting retaliation would be radically inferior. The essence of the first point, however, is just that how inferior the implementation of damage-limiting retaliation would be to the implementation of initiatory deterrence is under the control of your enemy, who gets the first 'move'.

Therefore, while I would not claim that the military assessment is conclusive, the case in the abstract for considering damage-limiting retaliation unacceptable by military criteria is very strong: on points (2) and (3) it cannot be superior to initiatory deterrence, and on the first point it must be *inferior to a degree to be determined by an attacking adversary*. Damage-limiting retaliation is *ineradicably* inferior (to an indeterminate degree) in permitting the adversary to control targets because, after all, it is a second-strike, which brings us back to the two underlying features of time and target.

Of the three military defects of damage-limiting retaliation we have considered, only the first is determined by time; the second and third are determined by target. *Any* plan for a retaliatory strike allows the adversary to move what is movable, if it chooses. *Any* plan for a very large counterforce strike provides the adversary with some reason to strike first and with considerable reason to do so massively, if at all. It should now be abundantly clear why the only serious options appear to be initiatory deterrence and retaliatory deterrence, if you do not simply assume that deterrence will be effective indefinitely and ignore the consequences of its failure.

Looking at Figure 1, we can say that if you are going to be in the bottom row, you should be in the left column. That is, if your targets are to be military, you should plan to strike first – this is the only way to prevent the adversary from placing a very low ceiling on the effectiveness of your attack. This is clear from our discussion of damage-limiting retaliation, compared to initiatory deterrence. It is especially clear for the concrete case in which your adversary's first-strike will, either because of your counterforce targeting or for other reasons of its own, not be limited.

From our earlier discussion of terroristic deterrence, on the other hand, military and moral reasons combine into a conclusive case for saying that the upper left box is absolutely to be avoided, although the moral reasons are for choosing the right column and the military reasons are for choosing the bottom row. That is, from a moral point of view, if you are ever going to slaughter civilians, you should surely do it only in retaliation; and from a military point of view, if you are ever going to slaughter civilians, you should surely eliminate the forces defending them (and capable of attacking you) first. Putting the military point less perversely, we can say simply that military considerations argue for attacking the opposing military forces, whenever it is that you attack. There are no sound military reasons for attacking non-combatants.[16]

Faced, then, with an apparent residual dilemma between initiatory deterrence and retaliatory deterrence, I shall try in the remainder of this essay to move through the following four steps: a brief indication of the sharp difference in doctrine (whatever the historical continuity in military policy) represented by the doctrine of initiatory deterrence; a catalogue of four implausible premises on which the thesis of the moral superiority of initiatory deterrence (over retaliatory deterrence) rests; some speculative arguments for the thesis that initiatory deterrence is morally inferior; and the introduction of "finite deterrence" as possibly the least evil form of nuclear deterrence.

IV. THE DOCTRINE OF INITIATORY DETERRENCE

Retaliatory deterrence is a doctrine that threatens only retaliation. Retaliatory deterrence never requires your side to be the first to go nuclear.[17] Initiatory deterrence is a doctrine that threatens to initiate nuclear war. The implementation of initiatory deterrence depends upon your side's using your nuclear forces first, before your adversary has used its nuclear forces – indeed, against its nuclear forces (among other military targets).

'Deterrence' was once sharply defined as what I am calling 'retaliatory deterrence', for example, in 1959 by one Albert Wohlstetter: "To deter an attack means being able to strike back in spite of it. It means, in other words, a capability to strike second."[18] As a point about Wohlstetter's views, my thesis is that his 1983 position about *targets* is incompatible with his 1959 position about *time* and is forcing him away from the doctrine of retaliatory deterrence toward the doctrine of initiatory deterrence. This may be a shift that he himself would not welcome.

I am giving the benefit of the doubt to Wohlstetter specifically and to advocates of counterforce targeting generally by treating their doctrine as a form of deterrence, and I have manufactured the clumsy name 'initiatory deterrence' in order to do so. Many critics of counterforce targeting would simply say that all the associated doctrines are doctrines of war-fighting, not deterrence doctrines at all. These are doctrines of war-fighting, it is said, because they are doctrines about how actually to employ nuclear weapons in a militarily fruitful way by engaging the military forces on the other side.

Now, the critics are quite right to notice a radical doctrinal difference between the retaliatory deterrence of Wohlstetter's 1959 position and the intiatory deterrence that is, or is implied by, his 1983 position. It is this difference that my labels are intended to mark. It is inaccurate, however, simply to label all doctrines of counterforce targeting, or even all doctrines of first-strike counterforce targeting – that is, of initiatory deterrence – as 'nuclear war-fighting', if the implication is that the advocates of these doctrines are all planning for the fighting of a nuclear war so that as soon as they are ready, they can go ahead and get one started.

A doctrine of initiatory deterrence is a doctrine about the circumstances in which nuclear weapons would be used, and a full-blown account of initiatory deterrence, which Wohlstetter does not pretend to offer, would specify how the nuclear weapons would be used – against which targets, etc. In this sense, namely that it discusses when and how to use nuclear weapons, initiatory deterrence is a doctrine about war-fighting. Doctrines of retaliatory deterrence, however, also specify when and how nuclear weapons would be used. The time is: only as a second-strike. The targets are: civilians.

What is different about initiatory deterrence, then, is not that it specifies when and how to use nuclear weapons, but the specific answers it gives: early and against military forces, including nuclear forces. These answers do not keep initiatory deterrence from being a doctrine of deterrence – they simply make it, as I shall soon try to show, a misguided form. It is perfectly possible for people, perhaps including Wohlstetter, to believe that the best way to preserve peace is to be prepared for war – thereby *deterring* aggression! This 'lesson of Munich' too, I believe, is misguided as a universal rule, but it is a perfectly coherent and widely held belief – it is, for example, the basic justification given to Americans and Russians alike every year for gargantuan military budgets.

Initiatory deterrence is the nuclear species of the generic belief that the best way to prevent wars is to be prepared to fight them:

> The best way to prevent a nuclear war is to be prepared to fight one. The doctrine of retaliatory deterrence is not a plan for fighting a war – it is a plan for murdering the civilians on the other side after the enemy forces have already defeated you: why should the enemy leaders believe that after your threat to slaughter their civilians has failed to achieve its purpose (of deterring their forces) you will execute the threat anyway? Why would you? Indeed, morally, how could you?

This is a very fundamental challenge to the received wisdom, for it is, at bottom, the thesis that threats to retaliate will not actually deter: you do not deter the first move by threatening to make the (by that time point-less) second move. You deter the other side from making the first move by being ready to make the first move yourself and by being ready to make it in a militarily rational way.

Now, the preceding paragraph is all just rhetoric – it is all conclusions without any supporting data, political, historical, psychological, or of any other kind. This is a first, very important point to be made against initiatory deterrence: like all doctrines of deterrence, it is ninety-nine per cent speculation. What the preceding paragraph claims is that initi-atory deterrence will more effectively deter. Such speculative assertions are difficult to assess, but there is no particular reason to believe them. It adds nothing, however, to label initiatory deterrence 'war-fighting', merely because it answers the questions of time and target. What we must do is to examine critically the specific answers given by this form of deterrence policy, and the rationale for choosing just these answers.

V. IS COUNTERFORCE TARGETING LESS MURDEROUS?

Albert Wohlstetter says that we should choose counterforce targeting because it is, among other things, morally superior to the targeting of civilians. I have already explained why I think targeting military forces leads to planning to go nuclear first, that is, leads to the choice of initiatory deterrence rather than damage-limiting retaliation. However, the criticisms of the claim of moral superiority in this section of the essay apply to much counterforce targeting; they would also apply to damage-limiting retaliation if it could be sustained against my earlier criticisms.

Anthony Kenny has lucidly summed up the objections to all doctrines of deterrence by saying that deterrence is "murderous, dangerous, and wasteful": murderous, because we risk killing innocent people; dangerous because we run a high risk of getting ourselves killed; and wasteful, because in the process we are misguidedly spending billions."[19] Wohlstetter assures us that counterforce targeting is less murderous than countervalue targeting. (He clearly also believes that it is less dangerous, because more credible, and that the research and development on precision-guided munitions are an excellent investment.) Why is that?

At first, the moral superiority of counterforce targeting seems too obvious to deserve discussion. Superficially it may appear to be perfectly apparent that the best way to prevent a certain category of people from being killed is to prevent anyone's aiming nuclear weapons at them. Not only is this not obviously true, however, but whether it is true at all is one of the central issues about the effectiveness of deterrence. What the correct relation is between targeting certain people and killing those same people is at the heart of the arguments about whether, and how, deterrence actually works.

The central thesis in the doctrine of retaliatory deterrence is that, given that both sides do now possess nuclear weapons, the civilians on both sides are safer if they are the targets of the weapons, because – roughly – no leader in his right mind wants to get the civilians on both sides killed and so the situation is stable in the sense that neither side has any persuasive reason to use its weapons. I am far from trying to defend retaliatory deterrence with reference to effectiveness. All that I claim is that retaliatory deterrence is not obviously mistaken and that, therefore, to ignore the distinction between who is targeted and who, if anyone, is actually killed is question-begging.

I maintain, then, only that *if* the doctrine of retaliatory deterrence should somehow turn out to be meaningful and correct, it would emerge that those who were targeted were not killed and were not killed because they were targeted – this is one of the many 'paradoxical' aspects of retaliatory deterrence. This is also a *very* big 'if'. The doctrine of retaliatory deterrence bears a remarkable structural similarity to the air-force fantasy. The original fantasy concerns conventional city-bombing and says: the way to break the morale of the enemy forces is to threaten to bomb their families. The original fantasy turned out in World War II and Vietnam to be false, but retaliatory deterrence could be different, since it depends upon a threat, not upon punishment already inflicted. Perhaps, as Bernard Brodie reasoned, there is "more strategic leverage to be gained in holding cities hostages than in making corpses".[20] My only point now is: who knows?

And that is to say: I am unwilling at this point either to try to defeat Wohlstetter's thesis of the moral superiority of counterforce targeting by invoking the alleged greater effectiveness of countervalue targeting or to accept Wohlstetter's thesis because he invokes the alleged greater effectiveness (credibility, etc.) of counterforce targeting. Either way the moral issue would be settled by appeal to supposed knowledge about what will work – actually deter the specific decision-makers on the other side. If anyone had such concrete knowledge, that would be fine. Given the difficulties that the CIA has in making accurate predictions about simple questions like who will be the next Soviet Defence Minister, however, any pretensions to knowing even which Soviet leaders have which degree of influence on which issues, much less how each thinks and what the dynamics of the interactions of the various leaders are, would be a joke. So, we must turn elsewhere.

Before we do, however, we can formulate the first premise needed to support the thesis of the moral superiority of counterforce targeting, a premise which, I submit, is in the foreseeable future unverifiable and unfalsifiable:

> *First premise for moral superiority: greater effectiveness.* Counterforce targeting by the United States, which it has the capability and will to execute, will deter present and future leaders of the Soviet Union from aggressive actions outside the sphere of influence already conceded to the USSR by the US in the absence of aggressive actions by the United States outside the sphere of influence already conceded to the US by the USSR, and countervalue targeting would not have deterred them.

Obviously the details of this formulation could be debated endlessly, but in our current state of knowledge about the specific workings, if any, of nuclear deterrence, it does not seem worth the trouble.

The second premise needed concerns a considerably better-defined issue, although its formulation too is subject to debate:

> *Second premise for moral superiority: separable targets.* Collocation of counterforce and countervalue targets in the Soviet Union is morally negligible, that is, the number of Soviet non-combatants who would be killed in the smallest counterforce strike that it would be militarily rational for the United States to make is significantly smaller than the number who would be killed in the smallest countervalue strike required by retaliatory deterrence.

My understanding is that this second premise is as completely and straightforwardly false as any statement about nuclear matters can be. Many of the most essential Soviet military targets are located in or near major concentrations of population.

> Assuming the urban population was ninety per cent sheltered. . . estimated Soviet fatalities from a US counter-ICBM attack would range from 3.7 million to 13.5 million, depending on the attack parameters; if the urban population were only ten per cent sheltered, fatality estimates for the same set of attacks ranged from 6.0 million to 27.1 million.
>
> A comprehensive US counterforce attack would kill many more people than this. Two of the three Soviet FBM submarine bases are located within urban areas (Severomorsk near Murmansk, and Vladivostok). More than seventy per cent of the Soviet air bases are in the western USSR south of Leningrad. And about 500 IRBMs and MRBMs are deployed west of the Urals. . . Attacks on these could well double the fatality estimates cited in the previous paragraph ... In the case of a US counterforce attack against the Soviet Union, the fatalities could well approximate those of the Second World War, when the Soviet Union suffered about 20 million fatalities (some 10 million of them were civilians), but they were lost over a period of four years – rather than a few hours, days or perhaps weeks – and they were considered as being nothing less than a holocaust.[21]

Countervalue destruction is guaranteed. The only question is whether to *add counterforce* targets as well.

Further, on many versions of counterforce targeting, including Wohlstetter's, the targeting would in addition be counter-command, that is, the political and military leadership who could order a retaliatory strike against the United States and Western Europe would be included as prime targets. Given the poor quality of intelligence about such crucial details as the physical movements of specific Soviet leaders, those choosing the targets would presumably have to include secondary and tertiary targeting options if there was to be any serious hope of preventing retaliation by killing everyone who could order it.

In addition, Wohlstetter relies on the theoretical possibility that the yield of warheads could be reduced because the precision of missile guidance is so much improved. If you can deliver a warhead right on top of its target, you need less explosive force to destroy the target than if you can only come close. The question remains: will yields actually be reduced to such a degree that 'collocated', that is, nearby, non-combatants will not be killed? Presumably yields will not be reduced below a force that will reliably destroy command bunkers and missile silos that have been 'super-hardened' to the maximum extent feasible. Moreover, even an extremely low-yield warhead which strays over a 'soft', that is, civilian, target will wreak awful destruction. Whatever the *average* degree of precision, no one can be expected to believe that there will be no stray missiles – it is well to remember that the old Army acronym SNAFU stands for Situation *Normal*. . . (. . . All Fouled Up)! The moral superiority claimed must turn out to be a feature of the actual attack, not of an ideal attack on paper.

In sum, the question is not: how precisely guided are individual missiles? The questions are: how much destruction altogether would you need to try to inflict in order for an attack not to be suicidal (by inviting and leaving possible a retaliatory attack); and how much destruction would you probably actually cause? There may be precise individual missiles – there are no militarily rational precise missile attacks. Actual United States battle plans (for example, the Single Integrated Operational Plan) have in fact included a thorough mixture of kinds of targets.[22]

Speaking of suicide, we come to the third premise, which is considerably more important than the second was:

> *Third premise for moral superiority: no escalation.* The initial counterforce strike would be militarily decisive (while remaining small enough to satisfy the second premise of *separable targets*), that is, neither the massive response promised by official Soviet policy statements nor further rounds of escalation by the United States would occur – at best, the entire nuclear war would consist of a single attack by the United States, which the Soviet Union would then lack either the capability or the will to answer; and, at worst, the United States would endure any Soviet military responses without resorting to retaliation against Soviet civilians.

If the second premise (separable targets) is as clearly and totally false as

I believe it is, the third premise does not even make sense: it is impossible to avoid 'escalating' to civilian targets if civilian targets will already
be destroyed by missiles nominally aimed at military (and command)
targets. Let us, nevertheless, assume that an initial nuclear attack large
enough to make sense militarily could also somehow be 'clean' enough to
satisfy the second premise – perhaps targets would be restricted to troop
concentrations on the great plains between Moscow and Warsaw. (If it
included missile silos around Moscow, it would be indistinguishable
from a countervalue attack on Moscow.) So, an initial counterforce strike
by the United States has been sufficiently restrained to be clearly distinguishable from a countervalue strike (as required by the second
premise), with the result that missiles near cities have been voluntarily
spared (not to mention submarine-launched missiles involuntarily
spared).

Now what? Are we really supposed to believe that the surviving Soviet
leaders would calmly say 'OK. . . you win'? They might. On the dis-
play-of-determination hypothesis so dear to NATO they would. Much of
the world would be praying that they would. They would be assured a
place of special honour in human history – for having kept human history
in business – if they did. But, would they really leave all those expensive
gleaming missiles sheathed in their silos? The unlocatable submarines
harmlessly submerged? I am not claiming to know – this is yet another
example of the pointless tennis-without-a-net that masquerades as
deterrence 'theory'. My only point here too is my previous one: who
knows? It is for those who are so confident about counterforce targeting
to shore up their premises.

It should simply be added explicitly that the civilians at risk from
escalation include the civilians in the society whose government breaks
the nuclear taboo. The Soviet Union has *never*, to my knowledge,
claimed that it knows how to conduct a nuclear strike that will not
slaughter civilians – it only claims that it will not use nuclear weapons
first.

> *Fourth premise for moral superiority: no nuclear winter.* The initial
> counterforce strike, plus any Soviet retaliation and any further
> exchanges between the two sides, will remain below the (currently
> unknown and probably unpredictable) threshold for nuclear
> winter.

Although I think that the findings about nuclear winter are important,
primarily because they demonstrate the significance of factors that were
previously totally ignored in government studies on the effects of nuclear

war, I shall only mention them, for two reasons. First, clear, non-technical accounts of their significance are readily available.[23] Second, although I am treating nuclear winter as the subject of a fourth premise in order to acknowledge its importance, the satisfaction of the fourth premise is directly dependent upon the satisfaction of the second and third premises. As the reports of the findings about nuclear winter have stressed, the suspended soot in the smoke from burning cities is much more critical to the blockage of sunlight than is the suspended dust from blasted military targets. If a militarily meaningful counterforce strike cannot avoid causing conflagrations in metropolitan centres (i.e. satisfy the second premise), the jig is up for everyone in the Northern Hemisphere after the first-strike. This would be the so-called 'self-retaliation' – the soot clouds could be at least as thick over the attacker as over the attacked in a few days. The judgement of Carl Sagan is: "A major strike would be clearly in the vicinity of, and perhaps well over, the climatic threshold."[24]

If we nevertheless assume the absence of 'self-retaliation', we then face, in effect, questions about the satisfaction of the third premise: if you add the smoke from the burning of United States cities set afire (even if not nominally targeted) by a retaliatory strike, how great and how persistent would the temperature drop from blocked sunlight be? Would the Soviet leaders just decide that if the initial American attack on them had so far left the hemisphere below the threshold of climatic catastrophe, they should refrain from retaliating and keep us all below the threshold, leaving themselves defeated and the United States not only victorious but unscathed? Perhaps. Or perhaps they would choose what is called victory-denial. In any case: the questions about the fourth premise are simply a re-run of the questions about the second and third premises.

It may be objected that the findings about the phenomena of nuclear winter are too speculative and based on too many debatable assumptions to be relied upon. Indeed, the nuclear winter findings are certainly hypothetical, but they are not one whit more speculative than what passes for 'deterrence theory', which is part elegant game theory and part inelegant conjecture about actual Soviet political interests: the Rational Russian meets the Real Russian. Actual discussions of deterrence tend to be like a caviar and peanut-butter sandwich: the elegant bits of game theory sink into the mire of conjecture about Soviet decision-making.[25] We have no reason to believe that the mathematical models of particle suspension and reflectivity used by the scientists working on nuclear winter are any farther from the actual phenomena than the rational agents in war games are from Soviet Air Force generals. Cautious agnosticism seems to me to be the order of the day all round.

VI. IS INITIATORY DETERRENCE LESS DANGEROUS?

In the preceding section I have not actually kept separate what Kenny calls "murderous" and "dangerous". I have emphasised, as Wohlstetter did, the murderous, that is, the killing of civilians on the side attacked, but especially when we considered retaliation in the discussion of premises three (*no escalation*) and four (*no nuclear winter*), we were discussing the dangerous, that is, the killing of civilians on the attacking side. For the most part, I think a civilian is a civilian, and it is immaterial whether he is a powerless member of the aggressive state or a powerless member of the state aggressed upon – after all, one of the main purposes of the laws of war has always been to prevent slaughters of non-combatants committed in the name of punishing the guilty.[26] To the extent that all non-combatants are to be treated the same, the distinction between murderous and dangerous does not cut much ice. It would certainly not recommend a United States policy that its ultimate effect was not to kill a lot of civilians on the other side but to get a lot of American civilians killed.

In the preceding section the main doubts I raised focused generally on counterforce targeting. In this section I concentrate specifically upon the early-use version of counterforce targeting, which is initiatory deterrence. I want, in other words, to focus upon the choice about timing that makes the most military sense out of counterforce targeting. I shall lay out what might be called the objective incentive structure of initiatory deterrence. So far I have concentrated upon the military and moral considerations which apply when deterrence fails. Now we must consider the much more obscure issue of whether deterrence will in fact fail, and more specifically whether either initiatory or retaliatory deterrence is in any way clearly more likely to be effective than the other is. At the beginning of the preceding section we simply noted that the first premise for the moral superiority of initiatory deterrence is indeed greater effectiveness. I confessed there that the similarity between retaliatory deterrence and the air-force fantasy gives me great doubt about whether retaliatory deterrence 'works'.

Now I want to lay out the strongest reason I know for believing that initiatory deterrence may not only not 'work' but may be strongly counter-productive, that is, may produce nuclear war. Since all arguments about the effectiveness of international nuclear deterrence directed by two superpowers at each other are highly speculative, I have no great faith in arguments about effectiveness in either direction – hence, my earlier emphasis on the moral and military results of deter rence failure. The following abstract argument is recounted here with two particular limitations. First, I claim only to be describing the objec- tive incentives created by initiatory deterrence. What will happen subjec- tively – or, if you like, whether Soviet and American actors will decide rationally – I do not claim to predict. I maintain only that initiatory deterrence unnecessarily creates a situation in which a response that *would* be rational for the other side is very bad for the side with this policy. Second, I once again do not so much attempt to establish any- thing positive as to urge deep hesitations about the accelerating Ameri- can and Russian plunges into initiatory deterrence by showing that one can tell just as good a story on the contrary side of the argument about effectiveness.

Whatever else can be said about retaliatory deterrence, that policy gives the other side no additional reason to attack. Retaliatory deterrence may or may not 'work' – that is, deter attack – and it obviously creates possibilities for accidental nuclear war and provides each side with a capacity for enormous harm to the other. Thus, it gives the other side much serious cause to *worry*. But it gives them no cause to *attack*, if they believe that our strategy is genuinely retaliatory. They could be assured that our strategy is strictly retaliatory if we built no weapons with counterforce capability. If our force is survivable, an attack by them is even more pointless. Hence, it might be immaterial with a policy of retaliatory deterrence whether our force had any positive deterrent effect, as long as it did not have the negative effect of being provocative.

And what have the Americans been building lately? Counterforce weapons of the kind needed for a first-strike. And what have the Soviets been building lately? Counterforce weapons of the kind needed for a first-strike.

Now, it is essential to see that the issue is not whether leaders on either side are gratuitously scheming to launch a first-strike out of a clear blue sky. The issue is the incentive structure that is being created in the form of objective military capabilities. The problem is what the insiders call 'crisis stability'. I do not think that the United States now intends a first-strike against the Soviet Union, nor that the Soviets intend one against it, etc. Yet the fact remains that Americans are building weapons that are objectively capable of destroying Soviet weapons before they are fired, and Soviets are building weapons that are objectively capable of destroying American weapons before they are fired. Objective capabilities can remain, while intentions change. Intentions are most likely to change when people have powerful incentives to change them. Let us look at the incentives the Soviets and the Americans are creating by building these weapons with counterforce capability. This will show why enhancing a counterforce capability in the direction of a first-strike capability, and the strategy of initiatory deterrence that can rationalise it, could add greatly to whatever the probability of nuclear war would be if both sides had only the capability for retaliatory deterrence.

Our counterforce weapons threaten their strategic nuclear weapons, which are the only nuclear weapons that protect them from our nuclear weapons. They would not want to lose their weapons. Unfortunately, there is an obvious way not to lose weapons that is not a way not to lose cities. Use them. Soviet development of an effective capability to destroy American weapons in the ground is an incentive for their use and vice versa.

I am not suggesting for a minute that either leadership is crazy enough simply to go ahead one day and calmly use its missiles on the other side for no other reason than that they *might* otherwise lose their own missiles. The great danger is that in a period of heightening tension between the US and the USSR we might reach a point at which war seemed inevitable – or at least, very likely – and the leadership on one side or the other decided that it should act before it was too late. A number of scholars have argued, very roughly, that World War I began because of mutual belief in its inevitability (and brevity) and mutual desire to get a jump on the other side militarily once attempts at prevention seemed quixotic.[27]

I do not know, or claim to know, *how* likely this phenomenon of use-them-before-you-lose-them is. The point is simply that development of an objective capacity to destroy a major portion of the other side's forces is in itself an incentive for use – it is a stimulant and a provocation. A capacity to destroy virtually all the other side's forces – that is, a capacity to disarm – would be a severe provocation, and it is important also to notice that the incentive pulls on both sides and that it creates a vicious circle. It is not merely that the Soviets who shot down KAL 007 might, if you will pardon the expression, jump the gun. The Americans too might jump the gun: who would want to go down in history as the American president who 'let the Communists repeat Pearl Harbour on his watch'? And it is not just that one or the other might jump the gun, it is also that each side must worry that the other side will. One of the most terrible features of counterforce warfare is, as we saw earlier, that there can be enormous advantages for the side that is ruthless enough to strike early – if going late means going with only what is left after you have suffered a counterforce strike. You cannot fire off your *cities* and thereby avoid losing them. The essential point was recognised as early as November 1945 by Jacob Viner, who asked: "What difference will it then make whether it was country A which had its cities destroyed at 9 a.m. and country B which had its cities destroyed at 12 a.m., or the other way around?"[28] This creates a radical difference in incentive structure between countervalue targeting and counterforce targeting (with large numbers of warheads).

Thus, developing a counterforce capability appears actively to undermine any actual deterrence there might be. The unrestrained development of a counterforce capability inherently tends toward the attainment of superiority, because it moves in the direction of a capacity to attack your adversary in such a way that it will be made unable to attack you back. A fully successful counterforce attack would deprive the other side of even the capacity to retaliate. In so far as the stability of deterrence depends upon its mutuality – that is, depends upon each side's being able to retaliate after having absorbed a first-strike (an axiom of deterrence theory) – a full counterforce capability is the capacity to deprive the other side of the ability to retaliate. The other side is rendered unable to strike second. They could not rely on the strategy of retaliatory deterrence even if they wanted to.

Once again, this does not mean that they will just gratuitously go ahead and strike first. One intermediate possibility is to adopt the policy of launch-on-warning, or launch-under-attack. Launch-on-warning is not a first-strike policy. Missiles are not launched until there is an indication that the other side has already attacked, but they are launched very promptly. Adopting launch-on-warning amounts to putting nuclear forces on a hair-trigger. There is not a lot of time for checking around to confirm whether the signals indicating incoming missiles are false, if the missiles have military targets including your own retaliatory force. If they have civilian targets or your retaliatory force will survive for some other reason, such as hardening, you have all the time in the world.

This is an additional specific manner by which development of counter-force capability might increase the probability of nuclear attack. It provides a strong incentive for the adoption of a policy of launch-on-warning, and the policy of launch-on-warning might enormously raise the probability of accidental nuclear war. Only panic, not malevolence, is required. Here too the incentive pulls on both sides and creates a vicious circle. If both sides were on hair-trigger settings, we might never know who made the mistake and fired first, thinking they were firing second. But, then, we would not need to know.

Now, since I can see no reason why concrete policies for the real world should be based on disembodied scenarios like those in the preceding few paragraphs, I cannot honestly recommend taking this abstract argument about crisis instability as definitive. Many firm advocates of retaliatory deterrence seem to find it a devastating demonstration that initiatory deterrence is more dangerous. In the abstract one can equally well speculate, however, that the complete attainment of a counterforce capacity great enough for a non-suicidal first strike would immobilise the other side with fear.

Who knows? – I primarily want to emphasise the methodological point that the arguments about effectiveness are awash in ignorance and uncertainty. The most magisterial treatment of attempts to construct a coherent theory of deterrence ends with foreboding:

> This legion of uncertainties ought to have created a common humility – to be so much in the dark with so much at stake. Unfortunately the frustration with this predicament led many strategists to show astonishing confidence in their own nostrums, combined with vindictiveness against those who differed. The question of what happens if deterrence fails is vital for the intellectual cohesion and credibility of nuclear strategy. A proper answer requires more than the design of means to wage nuclear war in a wide variety of ways, but something sufficiently plausible to appear as a tolerably rational course of action which has a realistic chance of leading to a satisfactory outcome. It now seems unlikely that such an answer can be found. No operational nuclear strategy has yet to be devised that does not carry an enormous risk of degenerating into a bloody contest of resolve or a furious exchange of devastating and crippling blows against the political and economic centres of the industrialised world. . . Those who have responsibility for unleashing nuclear arsenals live by the motto that if they ever had to do so they would have failed. Remarkably, up to now they have succeeded. C'est magnifique, mais ce n'est pas la stratégie.[29]

Nevertheless bearing in mind that we are in great danger of drifting away from solid ground, we can pursue the debate about crisis instability a few steps farther. One rejoinder to the above thesis that initiatory deterrence is crisis-unstable is as follows. What is being criticised is counterforce targeting, but what is being shown to be unstable is a situation containing a first-strike capacity on at least one side. Having even a large number of counterforce weapons may, however, be far from having a first-strike capability. One has a genuine first-strike capability only when one has so many counterforce weapons of such high reliability that one can launch a first-strike that is non-suicidal, that is, will not simply invite and allow a devastating retaliation. One must be capable of a virtually *disarming* first-strike, or it would be suicidal to launch one. There is no 'window of vulnerability' – neither the Americans nor the Soviets are anywhere near the capability to disarm the other. So what is the harm in building more counterforce weapons as long as neither side has a true first-strike capability?

A competition in building counterforce weapons has two possible outcomes. Either one side will 'get ahead' and attain the capacity for a non-suicidal first-strike or the competition will continue indefinitely without either side's attaining enough superiority to embolden it to launch. If it is more likely that one side or the other will actually attain the capability of destroying enough weapons on the other side to make any retaliation then still possible 'acceptable', then the objection about crisis instability will at that time apply. And prevention is surely better than a cure attempted within the unstable situation. The argument against the current counterforce competition is then simply that it will probably lead to an unstable situation that is easier to head off than to repair later.

If, on the other hand, it is more likely that the competition in counterforce weapons will continue indefinitely, the policy of initiatory deterrence is the formula for an endless arms race. The situation may never become a great deal more unstable than it is now, if neither side achieves a 'break-out'. The new counterforce weapons on one side simply become new targets for the other side, which then needs more warheads, which then become new targets for the first side, etc. This obviously is another vicious circle.

This, I believe, reveals the fundamental problem concerning the effectiveness of initiatory deterrence: pursuit of it leads to one or the other of two vicious circles.[30] If one side or the other can attain a genuine first-strike capacity, the result is the vicious circle of crisis instability, created by the military incentive for attacking first. (The incentive applies as well to the weaker side, which lacks first-strike capacity, because it will be weaker still if it lets the superior side go first – indeed, partially disarming the adversary before being more or less totally disarmed may seem the only hope.) How strong this incentive will be, relative to other considerations, I do not, as I have emphasised, claim to know. If neither side can attain a genuine first-strike capability, on the other hand, the result is the vicious circle of an unending, highly competitive arms race. How strong the incentive to keep trying to attain a first-strike capability will be, I once again do not claim to know. How effective is a policy that leads only to vicious circles?

VII. FINITE DETERRENCE: ESCAPE FROM THE DILEMMA?

Maybe there is something a little more positive here. The answer to the question, 'what is an acceptable conception of deterrence?' must surely be: 'none of the above'. Retaliatory deterrence is supremely murderous. Initiatory deterrence is supremely dangerous and supremely wasteful – and, unless escalation could be controlled, equally murderous in the end as well. We committed in Hiroshima and Nagasaki the kind of civilian slaughters that terroristic deterrence would threaten to commit, and have been haunted by our massive unpunished war crimes ever since. Damage-limiting deterrence involves severe military compromises. Decency and honour would suggest, however, that rather than make moral compromises of the magnitude we have canvassed, we should consider military compromises.

The worst feature of damage-limiting deterrence is that it may be perceived as, or by worst-case reasoning treated as, initiatory deterrence, which in turn feeds crisis instability. Yet, of the four polar tendencies among conceptions of deterrence, late use against military targets – second-strike counterforce – seems morally least awful. Is there a form of later military use that could be threatened without being mistaken for initiatory deterrence, as damage-limiting deterrence is liable to be?

Once again, I do not really know. If there can be an acceptable form of nuclear deterrence – it is nowhere written that there necessarily can be – it would seem likely to lie farther than damage-limiting deterrence in the direction of second-strike counterforce. We would have to go, so to speak, out through the lower right-hand corner of Figure 1. Is there in reality such a position?

We saw at the end of the last section that there is a critical distinction between counterforce capability and first-strike capability. A first-strike capability is a counterforce capability so extensive that it would disarm the adversary, leaving it with no nuclear forces with which to retaliate. The trouble is that counterforce tends to move in the direction of first-strike, as more and more counterforce is built. The distinction tends to be eroded. All ordinary counterforce tends to be destabilising because it tends to grow toward first-strike capability, which would be very destabilising indeed.

No form of counterforce capability can be acceptable unless it is clearly distinguishable from initiatory deterrence, especially by a suspicious adversary. Perhaps, however, maintaining this distinction may be easier than one might have feared. What is needed is counterforce with a low ceiling on quantity. Both initiatory deterrence and damage-limiting deterrence involve relentless competition in arms building, because each of the weapons on the other side becomes a target for the weapons on this side. As the other side builds new weapons/targets, this side needs new weapons. But these weapons are, for the other side, also targets, and against these new weapons/targets the other side needs new weapons/targets against which this side needs new weapons/targets, *ad infinitum*. This is what I mean in saying that a counterforce competition is *relentless*. It becomes impossible even to explain what adequacy could mean – enough is never enough, except temporarily until the other side responds, or seems to respond. In an all-out competition in acquiring capacity for counterforce it becomes literally impossible even to specify an end, much less to reach it (except by seizing any temporary opportunity to conduct a disarming strike).

President Eisenhower, however, is often quoted as having said, "We need only what *we* need." The wisdom of this comment is the insight that adequacy for deterrence can be specified in a manner that does not twist adequacy into the endless pursuit of superiority. Relentlessly competitive counterforce, in which every new weapon for side B becomes a new target for side A, begins by assuming: side A can deter side B only if A's forces could defeat B's forces. This means, however, that side A could have an *adequate* force only if it had a *superior* force. Presumably, however, any such 'laws of deterrence' are symmetrical, and side B could have an adequate force to deter side A only if it too had a superior force. Therefore, mutual deterrence would depend upon *each* side's being superior to the other side, which is simply nonsense. Relentless counterforce competition is not merely empirically unstable. Worse, it makes *mutual* deterrence logically incoherent. It can in fact only be the pursuit of superiority by both sides.

The goal of counterforce would not have to be incoherent, however, if adequacy were given a sensible interpretation that sharply distinguished the pursuit of genuine adequacy from the pursuit of superiority. If 'enough' is not defined in practice as 'more than the other side has', it can be possible to have enough (and more than enough). It can be possible to impose a ceiling. Any arms competition will always remain competitive – as Lenin might have said (but did not): 'An arms race is not a dinner party'. The competition need not, however, be relentless in the sense of each side's endlessly pursuing superiority over the other side.

How much is enough? What would an adequate counterforce capacity look like? This is not the place, and I am not the person, to launch that discussion. Here, I want only to provide an example of how it can begin

– and is beginning. In the Fortieth Anniversary issue of the *Bulletin of the Atomic Scientists* Harold A. Feiveson, Richard H. Ullman, and Frank von Hippel are proposing ninety per cent reductions in the current US nuclear forces, which would still leave the US with an awesome arsenal of two thousand warheads in a triad consisting of five hundred single-warhead intercontinental ballistic missiles, five hundred single-warhead submarine-launched ballistic missiles, and one thousand air-launched cruise missiles, which they call an illustrative finite deterrence force.[31] Naturally the details of what Feiveson, Ullman, and von Hippel themselves consider only an illustrative proposal need further debate, and I no more than they intend to endorse precisely this proposal. My only point now is that this suggestion from the Princeton Project on Finite Deterrence, as it is called, is one plausible way of saying: 'This is adequate – stop here'.

The members of the Princeton Project do not explicitly discuss the question of first-use, although they do propose the elimination of all 'tactical' nuclear weapons from Europe. Nor do they claim that the forces they suggest could only be used purely for counterforce attacks – on the contrary, they explicitly concede that their "finite deterrence" is still a "balance of terror". This concession, however, puts them light years ahead of Wohlstetter's illusions about fine-tuning and the "revolution in precision".

As I noted above in criticising the incredible second premise of Wohlstetter's argument for the moral superiority of his kind of counterforce – the premise of separable targets – countervalue destruction is always guaranteed. The kinds of surgical nuclear strikes that Wohlstetter must assume are utterly imaginary. It is that kind of groundless enthusiasm about precision that can allow one to embrace the deep tendencies in counterforce toward the pursuit of superiority – superiority which can pay off in conflict only if used early while still retained. Incautious optimism about an illusory kind of counterforce without tears can lead one to give in to the pressures toward superiority and early use.

If it is foolish to pursue counterforce with a human face, but is wrong, as Wohlstetter insists, simply to embrace the slaughter of civilians, is there any form of nuclear deterrence that is left?

The only hope for a tolerable conception of deterrence that I can see is in the direction of a kind of counterforce without illusions, specifically without the twin – and mutually supportive – illusions that morality is thereby attainable and superiority is therefore desirable. When one sees that the premise is false, one can resist the mischievous inference, which is: if you can fight a nuclear war in a morally discriminating manner, you might as well prepare to win it. If instead the best that can be said for counterforce morally is that the slaughter of civilians would be a little less than if you made a special point of slaughtering civilians – that is, adopted retaliatory deterrence – then you would retain even a relatively small counterforce capacity with the utmost reluctance and in the clear-eyed realisation that ever to use it might unleash a holocaust. In addition, you would retain only the smallest force compatible with nuclear stability. We might call this 'finite counterforce', but such a name would encourage the self-deception that civilians could be spared. The targeting ought in fact to be as purely counterforce as possible, I would agree with Wohlstetter, but better to stick with 'finite deterrence', especially since the limitation on numbers of warheads would probably do more to spare civilians than any efforts at discrimination in targeting possibly could. Indeed, I think we have seen that in the end choice of targets, which was a fundamental dimension in Figure 1, is far less significant than choice of numbers. If real attacks cannot be discriminate, what you attack is less important than how much you attack with.

Militarily this is almost as unsatisfactory as it is morally. Of the three military defects of damage-limiting retaliation – enemy-selected targets, magnitude incentives, and pre-emption incentives – finite deterrence would largely eliminate the last two by demonstrating through its acceptance of minimally adequate numbers of warheads that it was genuinely not aiming at the capability for a disarming first-strike. These are extremely important gains for stability in crises. Enemy-selection of targets, on the other hand, is the military price one pays for not being the one who begins a nuclear war. If the illusion of becoming able to launch a disarming first-strike has been abandoned, however, the real price for not going first is less than it seems. Against a nation whose first nuclear attack was massive, it would nevertheless be high.

Indeed, many will argue that a force of around two thousand warheads is not enough militarily. Others will argue that it is too much morally. It could be the worst of both worlds: not enough militarily (so that nuclear war will come) and too much morally (so that the war will be unprecedentedly murderous). On the other hand, to leave the purists on both sides unhappy may not be a bad rule-of-thumb.

NOTES

1   For some of the doubts, see Sidney D. Drell, Philip J. Farley, and David Holloway, 'Preserving the ABM Treaty: a critique of the Reagan strategic defence initiative', *International Security*, IX, 1984, pp. 51–91; John Tirman (ed.), *The Fallacy of*

Star Wars, New York, 1984, especially the chapters by Hans Bethe and Richard Garwin; and Ashton B. Carter, *Directed Energy Missile Defence in Space*, Washington, 1984. For advocacy of SDI, see Zbigniew Brzezinski, Robert Jastrow, and Max M. Kampelman, 'Defence in space is not "Star Wars"', *New York Times Magazine*, January 27, 1985, pp. 28–9, 46, 48, and 51.

2 Albert Wohlstetter, 'Bishops, statesmen, and other strategists on the bombing of innocents', *Commentary*, June 1983, pp. 15–35.

3 Wohlstetter, 'Bishops', p. 16.

4 Wohlstetter, 'Bishops', p. 31. See Fred Iklé, 'Can nuclear deterrence last out the century?', *Foreign Affairs*, LI, 1973, pp. 267–85. A reply to Iklé then was: Wolfgang Panofsky, 'The mutual hostage relationship between America and Russia', *Foreign Affairs*, LII, pp. 109–18. A reply to (Iklé and) Wohlstetter recently is: McGeorge Bundy, 'Existential deterrence and its consequences', in Douglas MacLean (ed.), *The Security Gamble*, Maryland Studies in Public Philosophy, Totowa, N.J., 1984, pp. 3–13.

5 Wohlstetter, 'Bishops', p. 29.

6 The most sophisticated discussions of the paradoxes I know are: David Gauthier, 'Deterrence, maximisation and rationality'; Gregory S. Kavka, 'Nuclear deterrence: some moral perplexities'; David Lewis, 'Devil's bargains and the real world'; and Gregory S. Kavka and David Gauthier, 'Responses to the paradox of deterrence'; all in Douglas MacLean (ed.), *The Security Gamble*, Maryland Studies in Public Philosophy, Totowa, N.J., 1984, pp. 100–61.

7 Wohlstetter, 'Bishops', p. 19 and p. 31.

8 Sometimes it is difficult to decide when one is clarifying by sticking to the fundamentals and when distorting by over-simplifying. Obviously far more than four basic options can be, and repeatedly have been, worked out. Counterforce targets, for example, could be divided into nuclear and non-nuclear, e.g. troop concentrations; or they could be divided into military strictly speaking (which could be subdivided into nuclear and non-nuclear) and politico-military, including the whole Soviet and American chain of command right up to the top. Initial uses could be sub-divided into limited and massive, etc. Besides targets and timing, one could also consider a third dimension: type of weapons used, nuclear or non-nuclear. Soviet nuclear missiles could, perhaps, someday be struck with American precision-guided conventional weapons, thereby observing the taboo on nuclear *use*.

I do not mean to deny that at least some of these other distinctions are important or even to deny that something is lost when they are left aside. I maintain only that I am focusing on *some* of the fundamental issues, and I am trying to discuss them in an uncluttered way. Much else could usefully also be said, but I do not think it would require essential changes in what is said. In the final section of the paper I introduce one simple additional factor that I take to be crucial.

9 For a clear account of the major differences between first-use and first-strike, and an explanation of why the current combination of first-strike on one side and first-use on the other is one of the worst possible combinations, see Freeman Dyson, *Weapons and Hope*, New York, 1984, pp. 250–3.

10 For a comprehensive examination of the varieties of deterrence theories, and their intellectual failure to face the question of what happens if deterrence fails, see Lawrence Freedman, *The Evolution of Nuclear Strategy*, London, 1981.

11 See Manuel Velasquez and Cynthia Rostankowski (eds.), *Ethics: Theory and Practice*, Englewood Cliffs, N.J., pp. 150–68.

12 Freedman, *Evolution*, pp. 18–9.

13 Freedman, *Evolution*, p. 19.

14 See Desmond Ball, *Can Nuclear War be Controlled?*, Adelphi Paper No. 169, London, 1981, section V, 'Soviet strategic doctrine: implications for the control of nuclear war', pp. 30–35. "The doctrine that, once the nuclear threshold is passed, it is the task of the nuclear forces to terminate the war by achieving military victory through massive, crippling strikes is deeply rooted in Soviet strategic culture, and the preferences and habits of the military bureaucracy would tend to rule out any possibility of improvisation in favour of 'American-formulated rules of intra-war restraint'" (34–5). Also see note 9 above, on the difference between NATO first-use and USSR first-strike – and the tragedy of their being combined.

15 It will be impossible to convince anyone when the counterforce capability is itself vulnerable to an initial counterforce strike, as will be the MX when based in Minuteman silos.

16 It may be worth mentioning what I would call the 'air-force fantasy', which contradicts this Clausewitzian point. Fans of air-force city bombing often advance the false hypothesis that if the civilians are subject to terror-bombing the morale on the other side will be broken. After the megatonnage dropped from the skies, there never yet has been a clear positive example. The disconfirming cases include: German bombing of the British during World War II, British bombing of the Germans during World War II, American bombing of Japan during World War II, and American bombing of Vietnam. The unfalsifiable counter-argument always is: it wasn't terrible enough – next time, unleash us (e.g. Vietnam). On Vietnam, see John Mueller, 'The search for the single "breaking point" in Vietnam: the statistics of a deadly quarrel', *International Studies Quarterly*, XXIV, 1980, pp. 497–519.

   And don't Hiroshima and Nagasaki show that if it is *nuclear* terror, morale will break? What if they show, instead, that morale will break if nuclear attacks are made on a *non*-nuclear power, which cannot retaliate in kind?

17 You might fire back before you are hit, if you have a policy of launch-under-attack, but not before you are fired upon with nuclear weapons. And if your own force is survivable – that is , will remain available for use even after you have been attacked – as it ought to if your strategy actually is retaliatory deterrence, you will have no need for the dangerous hair-trigger policy of launch-under-attack, or launch-on-warning. You can wait to assess what actually resulted from the attack before you make the decision to retaliate.

18 Albert Wohlstetter, 'The delicate balance of terror', *Foreign Affairs*, XXXVII, 1959, p. 215. I am not implying a criticism of inconsistency – everyone is allowed to change his mind once every quarter-century – I simply want to emphasise the magnitude of the change between the 1959 article and the 1983 article.

19 Anthony Kenny, 'The logic and ethics of nuclear deterrence' in this volume.

20 Bernard Brodie, 'Schlesinger's old-new ideas', unpublished paper, *Bernard Brodie Papers*, Box 33, folder 8, quoted in Fred Kaplan, *The Wizards of Armageddon*, New York, 1983, p. 47.

21 Desmond Ball, *Can Nuclear War be Controlled?*, Adelphi Paper No. 169, London, 1981, p. 28 – in this extremely careful analysis, see generally section IV, 'The control of damage in nuclear war', pp. 26–30. For the effects of a Soviet counter-ICBM attack on the US, see Sidney D. Drell and Frank von Hippel, 'Limited nuclear war', *Scientific American*, CCXXXV, no. 5, November 1976, p. 27; more generally, see Frank von Hippel, 'The effects of nuclear war', in David W. Hafemeister and Diet-

rich Shroeer (eds). *Physics, Technology and the Nuclear Arms Race*, New York, 1983, pp 1–46.

22 See David Alan Rosenberg, 'The origins of overkill: nuclear weapons and American strategy, 1945–1960', *International Security*, VII, 1983, pp. 3–71; reprinted in a highly useful collection, *Strategy and Nuclear Deterrence,* an *International Security* Reader, ed. Steven E. Miller, Princeton, N.J., 1984, pp. 113–81. Also in the Miller anthology, see Desmond Ball, 'US strategic forces: how would they be used?' pp. 215–44; and see Desmond Ball, *Targeting for Strategic Deterrence*, Adelphi Paper No. 185, London, 1983.

23 The most accessible account of the findings about nuclear winter and their implications for policy is Carl Sagan, 'Nuclear war and climatic catastrophe: some policy implications', *Foreign Affairs* LXII, 1983–84, pp. 257–92. The most recent account, which uses three-dimensional models of the atmosphere, is S. L. Thompson, V. V. Aleksandrov, G. L. Stenchikov, S. H. Schneider, C. Covey, and R. M. Chervin, 'Global climatic consequences of nuclear war: simulations with three dimensional models', *Ambio*, XIII, pp. 236–43. Pioneering articles appeared in a special double issue, 'Nuclear war: the aftermath', *Ambio*, XI, nos. 2 and 3, 1982. The one-dimensional study that first attracted widespread public attention was reported in R. P. Turco, O. B. Toon, T. P. Ackerman, J. B. Pollack, and Carl Sagan, 'Nuclear winter: global consequences of multiple nuclear explosions' *Science*, CCXXII, 1983, pp. 1283–92. A more readable account appeared as Richard P. Turco, Owen B. Toon, Thomas P. Ackerman, James B. Pollack and Carl Sagan, 'The climatic effects of nuclear war', *Scientific American*, CCLI, no. 2, August 1984, pp. 33–43. The original report from *Science* and a collection of other relevant articles is available as Paul R. Ehrlich, Carl Sagan, Donald Kennedy and Walter Orr Roberts, *The Cold and the Dark: The World after Nuclear War*, New York, 1984. A study requested by the Department of Defense was unable to fault the basic methodology of the original studies – see National Research Council, National Academy of Sciences, *The Effects on the Atmosphere of a Major Nuclear Exchange*, Washington, 1985.

24 Carl Sagan, 'Nuclear war and climatic catastrophe', p. 276. Then there would be the climatic effects of the retaliatory strike.

25 Perhaps I ought to provide an example. Here is an almost randomly selected one, in no way worse than average but interesting in that the 'argument' is said in an accompanying footnote to go back to 1967, thus demonstrating how groundless speculations become orthodox dogmas of deterrence: "Presumably people believe the Soviet Union is interested in annihilating the United States because this would make it the dominant world power. The analogy, if us defences had eliminated the Soviet ability to annihilate the United States, would be a countervalue attack designed to weaken the United States. To deter this type of attack the United States would need a retaliatory capability that could weaken the Soviet Union as much as the Soviet countervalue attack could weaken the United States. A countervalue capability roughly equivalent to the Soviet countervalue capability should be sufficiently large to satisfy this requirement." – Charles L. Glaser, 'Why even good defences may be bad', *International Security*, IX, 1984, pp. 103–4. This deterrence requirement of 'equal countervalue capability' is, thus, derived from the assumptions that the Soviet Union is simultaneously (1) devoted to dominating the world by doing as much damage to the United States as the us lets it and (2) devoted to making military decisions using benefit–cost analysis and the principle of maximising expected util-

ity. That a demonically power-mad regime would use BCA to set its strategy is logically possible, but what reasons do we have to believe it is true? How do we know that an equal amount of damage "should be sufficiently large"? If they are such wild annihilators, perhaps the US would need to be capable of doing them twice as much damage in order to deter them. If they are such careful reasoners, perhaps they would not risk half as much damage in an uncertain adventure. Why exactly equal amounts? Are they just like us? If so, why are we contemplating destroying each other?

26   Thus, although I generally admire the pioneering philosophical work on deterrence by Gregory Kavka, I utterly reject his thesis that Soviet civilians "are partially responsible and hence partly liable" (to threatened attack) – see Gregory S. Kavka, 'Nuclear deterrence: some moral perplexities', in Douglas MacLean (ed.), *The Security Gamble: Deterrence Dilemmas in the Nuclear Age*, Maryland Studies in Public Philosophy, Totowa, N.J., 1984, p. 132. It is the rare Soviet civilian, I would suggest, who has even the slightest responsibility for any of the policies of the dictatorial state to which she is subjected, and few indeed who have enough responsibility to be placed justly at risk of death. The vast majority of the civilians in the Soviet Union (as in many nations) are women and children with no power and no voice at all.

27   "Russia, Germany and France each misjudged the extent of the other's military preparations and mobilised, fearful that failure to do so would enable their opponents to gain a decisive military advantage" – Richard Ned Lebow, 'Practical ways to avoid superpower crises', *Bulletin of the Atomic Scientists*, XLI, 1985, p. 25. For a full study of how crises issue in wars, see Richard Ned Lebow, *Between Peace and War: The Nature of International Crisis*, Baltimore, 1981. On World War I, see especially 'The July crisis: a case study', pp. 119–47. However, also see Richard Ned Lebow, 'Windows of opportunity: do states jump through them?', *International Security*, IX, 1984, pp. 147–86, as well as other articles in the same number of *International Security* on 'The great war and the nuclear age'.

28   Jacob Viner, 'The implications of the atomic bomb for international relations', *Proceedings of the American Philosophical Society*, January 29, 1946, p. 54, quoted in Fred Kaplan, *The Wizards of Armageddon*, New York, 1983, p. 27.

29   Freedman, *Evolution*, pp. 395 and 400.

30   This point has become clear to me from repeated – not to say endless – conversations with my colleague Robert K. Fullinwider.

31   Harold A. Feiveson, Richard H. Ullman, and Frank von Hippel, 'Reducing U.S. and Soviet nuclear arsenals', *Bulletin of the Atomic Scientists* XLI, 1985, pp. 144–50.

The poor against the rich: the case for action welfare rights

JAMES P. STERBA

University of Notre Dame, Indiana

I

Libertarians today are strongly united in opposition to welfare rights. According to Robert Nozick, "the state may not use its coercive apparatus for the purpose of getting some citizens to aid others".[1] For Murray Rothbard, "the libertarian position calls for the complete abolition of governmental welfare and reliance on private charitable aid".[2] In this paper I argue that this libertarian opposition to welfare rights is ill-founded. Welfare rights, I argue, can be given a libertarian justification, and once this is recognised, opposition to welfare rights can be seen as inconsistent with a moral point of view.

Now libertarians have defended their view in basically two different ways. Some libertarians, following Herbert Spencer, have (1) defined liberty as the absence of constraints, (2) taken a right to liberty to be the ultimate political ideal, and (3) derived all other rights from this right to liberty. Other libertarians, following John Locke, have (1) taken a set of rights, including, typically, a right to life or self-ownership and a right to property, to be the ultimate political ideal, (2) defined liberty as the absence of constraints in the exercise of these fundamental rights, and (3) derived all other rights, including a right to liberty, from these fundamental rights.

Each of these approaches has its difficulties. The principal difficulty with the first approach is that unless one arbitrarily restricts what is to count as an interference, conflicting liberties will abound, particularly in all areas of social life.[3] The principal difficulty with the second approach is that as long as a person's rights have not been violated, her liberty would not have been restricted either, even if she were kept in prison for the rest of her days.[4] Now I don't propose to try to decide between these two approaches. What I do want to show, however, is that on either approach welfare rights are morally required.

II. SPENCERIAN LIBERTARIANISM

Thus suppose we were to adopt the view of those libertarians who take a right to liberty to be the ultimate political ideal. According to this view, liberty is usually defined as follows:

The want conception of liberty: Liberty is being unconstrained by other persons from doing what one wants.

Now this conception limits the scope of liberty in two ways. First, not all constraints whatever their source count as a restriction of liberty: the constraints must come from other persons. For example, people who are constrained by natural forces from getting to the top of Mount Everest do not lack liberty in this regard. Second, constraints that have their source in other persons, but that do not run counter to an individual's wants, constrain without restricting that individual's liberty. Thus, for people who do not want to hear Beethoven's Fifth Symphony, the fact that others have effectively proscribed its performance does not restrict their liberty, even though it does constrain what they are able to do.

Of course, libertarians may wish to argue that even such constraints can be seen to restrict a person's liberty once we take into account the fact that people normally want, or have a general desire, to be unconstrained by others. But other philosophers have thought that the possibility of such constraints points to a serious defect in this conception of liberty,[5] which can only be remedied by adopting the following broader conception of liberty:

The ability conception of liberty: liberty is being unconstrained by other persons from doing what one is able to do.

Applying this conception to the above example, we find that people's liberty to hear Beethoven's Fifth Symphony would be restricted even if they did not want to hear it (and even if, perchance, they did not want to be unconstrained by others) since other people would still be constraining them from doing what they are able to do.

Yet even if we accept all the liberties specified by the Ability Conception, problems of interpretation still remain. The major problem in this regard concerns what is to count as a constraint. On the one hand, libertarians would like to limit constraints to positive acts (i.e., acts of commission) that prevent people from doing what they are otherwise able to do. On the other hand, welfare liberals and socialists interpret constraints to include, in addition, negative acts (i.e., acts of omission) that prevent people from doing what they are otherwise able to do. In fact, this is one way to understand the debate between defenders of 'negative liberty' and defenders of 'positive liberty'. For defenders of negative liberty would seem to interpret constraints to include only positive acts of others that prevent people from doing what they otherwise are able to do, while defenders of positive liberty would seem to interpret constraints to include both positive and negative acts of others that prevent people from doing what they are otherwise able to do.[6]

Now suppose we interpret constraints in the manner favoured by libertarians to include only positive acts by others that prevent people from doing what they are otherwise able to do, and let us consider a typical conflict situation between the rich and the poor.

In this conflict situation, the rich, of course, have more than enough resources to satisfy their basic needs. By contrast, the poor lack the resources to meet their most basic nutritional needs even though they have tried all the means available to them that libertarians regard as legitimate to obtain such resources. Under circumstances like these, libertarians usually maintain that the rich should have the liberty to use their resources to satisfy their luxury needs if they so wish. Libertarians recognise that this liberty might well be enjoyed at the expense of the satisfaction of the most basic nutritional needs of the poor. Libertarians just think that a right to liberty always has priority over other political ideals, and since they assume that the liberty of the poor is not at stake in such conflict situations, it is easy for them to conclude that the rich should not be required to sacrifice their liberty so that the basic nutritional needs of the poor may be met.

From a consideration of the liberties involved, libertarians claim to derive a number of more specific requirements, in particular, a right to life and a right to property.

Here it is important to observe that the libertarian's right to life is not a right to receive from others the goods and resources necessary for preserving one's life; it is simply a right not to be killed unjustly. Correspondingly, the libertarian's right to property is not a right to receive from others the goods and resources necessary for one's welfare, but rather a right to acquire goods and resources either by initial acquisition or by voluntary agreement.

Of course, libertarians would allow that it would be nice of the rich to share their surplus resources with the poor. Nevertheless, according to libertarians, such acts of charity should not be coercively required, because the liberty of the poor is not thought to be at stake in such conflict situations.

In fact, however, the liberty of the poor is at stake in such conflict situations. What is at stake is the liberty of the poor to take from the surplus possessions of the rich what is necessary to satisfy their basic nutritional needs. When libertarians are brought to see that this is the case, they are genuinely surprised, for they had not previously seen the conflict between the rich and the poor as a conflict of liberties.[7]

Now when the conflict between the rich and the poor is viewed as a conflict of liberties, we can either say that the rich should have the liberty to use their surplus resources for luxury purposes, or we can say that the poor should have the liberty to take from the rich what they require to meet their basic nutritional needs. If we choose one liberty we must reject the other. What needs to be determined, therefore, is which liberty is morally preferable: the liberty of the rich or the liberty of the poor.

I submit that the liberty of the poor, which is the liberty to take from the surplus resources of others what is required to meet one's basic nutritional needs, is morally preferable to the liberty of the rich, which is the liberty to use one's surplus resources for luxury purposes. To see that this is the case we need only appeal to one of the most fundamental principles of morality, one that is common to all political perspectives, namely, the *'ought' implies 'can'* principle. According this principle, people are not morally required to do what they lack the power to do or what would involve so great a sacrifice that it would be unreasonable to ask them to perform such an action.[8] Now it seems clear that the poor have it within their power to willingly relinquish such an important liberty as the liberty to take from the rich what they require to meet their basic nutritional needs. Yet it would be unreasonable to ask them to make so great a sacrifice. In the extreme case, it would involve asking the poor to sit back and starve to death. Of course, the poor may have no real alternative to relinquishing this liberty. To do anything else may involve worse consequences for themselves and their loved ones and may invite a painful death. Accordingly, we may expect that the poor would acquiesce, albeit unwillingly, in a national or international political system that denied them the welfare rights supported by such a liberty, at the same time that we recognise that such a system imposed an unreasonable sacrifice on the poor – a sacrifice that we could not morally blame the poor for trying to evade.[9] Analogously, we might expect that a woman whose life was threatened would submit to a rapist's demands, at the same time that we recognise the utter unreasonableness of those demands.

By contrast, it would not be unreasonable to ask the rich to sacrifice the liberty to meet some of their luxury needs so that the poor can have the liberty to meet their basic nutritional needs. Of course, we might expect that the rich for reasons of self-interest might be disinclined to make such a sacrifice. Yet, unlike the poor, the rich could not claim that relinquishing such a liberty involved so great a sacrifice that it would be unreasonable to ask them to make it; unlike the poor, the rich could be morally blameworthy for failing to make such a sacrifice.

Consequently, if we assume that however else we specify the requirements of morality, they cannot violate the 'ought' implies 'can' principle, it follows that, despite what libertarians claim, the right to liberty endorsed by libertarians actually favours the liberty of the poor over the liberty of the rich.

Yet couldn't libertarians object to this conclusion, claiming that it would be unreasonable to ask the rich to sacrifice the liberty to meet some of their luxury needs so that the poor could have the liberty to meet their basic nutritional needs? As I have pointed out, libertarians don't usually see the situation as a conflict of liberties; but suppose they did. How plausible would such an objection be? Not very plausible at all, I think.

For consider: what are libertarians going to say about the poor? Isn't it clearly unreasonable to ask the poor to sacrifice the liberty to meet their basic nutritional needs so that the rich can have the liberty to meet their luxury needs? Isn't it clearly unreasonable to ask the poor to sit back and starve to death? If it is, then there is no resolution of this conflict that would be reasonable to ask both the rich and the poor to accept. But that would mean that the libertarian ideal of liberty cannot be a moral ideal; for a moral ideal resolves conflicts of interest in ways that it would be reasonable to ask everyone affected to accept. Therefore, as long as libertarians think of themselves as putting forth a moral ideal, they cannot allow that it would be unreasonable *both* to ask the rich to sacrifice the liberty to meet some of their luxury needs in order to benefit the poor *and* to ask the poor to sacrifice the liberty to meet their basic nutritional needs in order to benefit the rich. But I submit that if one of these requests is to be judged reasonable, then, by any neutral assessment, it must be the request that the rich sacrifice the liberty to meet some of their luxury needs so that the poor can have the liberty to meet their basic nutritional needs; there is no other plausible resolution, if libertarians intend to be putting forth a moral ideal.

It should also be noted that this case for restricting the liberty of the rich depends upon the willingness of the poor to take advantage of whatever opportunities are available to them for satisfying their basic needs by engaging in mutually beneficial work, so that failure of the poor to take advantage of such opportunities would normally either cancel or at least significantly reduce the obligation of the rich to restrict their own liberty for the benefit of the poor.[10] In addition, the poor would be required to return the equivalent of any surplus possessions they have taken from the rich once they are able to do so and still satisfy their basic needs. Nor would the poor be required to keep the liberty to which they are entitled. They could give up part of it, or all of it, or risk losing it on the chance of gaining a greater share of liberties or other social goods.[11] Consequently, the case for restricting the liberty of the rich for the benefit of the poor is neither unconditional nor inalienable.

Even so, libertarians would have to be disconcerted about what turns out to be the practical upshot of taking a right to liberty to be the ultimate political ideal. For libertarians contend that their political ideal would support welfare rights only when constraints are 'illegitimately' interpreted to include both positive and negative acts by others that prevent people from doing what they are otherwise able to do. By contrast, when constraints are interpreted to include only positive acts, libertarians contend, no such welfare rights can be justified.

Nevertheless, what the foregoing argument demonstrates is that this view is mistaken. For even when the interpretation of constraints favoured by libertarians is employed, a moral assessment of the competing liberties still requires an allocation of liberties to the poor that will be generally sufficient to provide them with the goods and resources necessary for satisfying their basic nutritional needs.

Of course, libertarians might respond that even supposing welfare rights could be morally justified on the basis of the liberty of the poor to take from the rich in order to meet their basic nutritional needs and the liberty of third parties to take from the rich in order to provide for the basic nutritional needs of the poor, the poor still would be better off without the enforcement of such rights.[12] For example, it might be argued that when people are not forced through taxation to support a system of welfare rights, they are both more productive, since they are able to keep more of what they produce, and more charitable, since they tend to give more freely to those in need when they are not forced to do so. As a result, so the argument goes, the poor would benefit more from relying on charity alone.

Yet, surely it is difficult to comprehend how the poor could be better off without a guaranteed minimum, assuming, as seems likely, that they would experience a considerable loss of self-respect once they had ultimately to depend upon charity rather than a guaranteed minimum for the satisfaction of their basic needs. It is also difficult to comprehend how people who are so opposed to a guaranteed minimum would turn out to be so charitable to the poor when there is no guaranteed minimum.

Nevertheless, it might still be argued that where there is no guaranteed minimum the greater productivity of the more talented people would provide increased employment opportunities that would benefit the poor more than would a guaranteed minimum. But this simply could not occur. For if the more talented members provided sufficient employment opportunities to enable the poor to meet their basic needs then the conditions for invoking a right to a guaranteed minimum would not arise, at least for those capable of working, since the poor are first required to take advantage of whatever employment opportunities are available to them before they can legitimately invoke such a right. Consequently, given the conditional nature of the right to a guaranteed minimum, and the practical possibility and in most cases the actuality of insufficient employment opportunities obtaining, there is no reason to think that the poor would be better off without the enforcement of welfare rights.

In brief, what this shows is that if a right to liberty is taken to be the ultimate political ideal, then, contrary to what libertarians claim, not only would a system of welfare rights be morally required, but also such a system would benefit the poor more than would reliance on charity alone.

III. LOCKEAN LIBERTARIANISM

Yet suppose we were to adopt the view of those libertarians who do not take a right to liberty to be the ultimate political ideal. According to this view, liberty is defined as follows:

> *The rights conception of liberty:* liberty is being unconstrained by other persons from doing what one has a right to do.

And the most important ultimate rights in terms of which liberty is specified are, according to this view, a right to life understood as a right not to be killed unjustly and a right to property understood as a right to acquire goods and resources either by initial or voluntary agreement. Now in order to evaluate this view, we must determine what are the practical implications of these rights.

Presumably, a right to life understood as a right not to be killed unjustly would not be violated by defensive measures designed to protect one's person from life-threatening attacks. Yet would this right be violated when the rich prevent the poor from taking what they require to satisfy their basic nutritional needs? Obviously, as a consequence of such preventive actions poor people sometimes do starve to death. Have the rich, then, in contributing to this result, killed the poor, or simply let them die; and, if they have killed the poor, have they done so unjustly?

Now sometimes the rich in preventing the poor from taking what they require to meet their basic nutritional needs would not in fact be killing the poor, but only causing them to be physically or mentally debilitated. Yet since such preventive acts involve resisting the life-preserving activities of the poor, when the poor do die as a consequence of such acts it seems clear that the rich would be killing the poor, whether intentionally or unintentionally.

Of course, libertarians would want to argue that such killing is simply a consequence of the legitimate exercise of property rights, and hence, not unjust. But to understand why libertarians are mistaken in this regard, let us appeal again to that fundamental principle of morality, the *'ought' implies 'can'* principle. In this context, the principle can be used to assess two opposing accounts of property rights. According to the first account, a right to property is not conditional upon whether other persons have sufficient opportunities to satisfy their basic needs. This view holds that the initial acquisition and voluntary agreement of some can leave others, through no fault of their own, dependent upon charity for the satisfaction of their most basic needs. By contrast, according to the second account, initial acquisition and voluntary agreement can confer title of property on all goods and resources except those surplus goods and resources of the rich that are required to satisfy the basic needs of those poor who through no fault of their own lack the opportunities and resources to satisfy their own basic needs.

Clearly, only the first of these two accounts of property rights would generally justify the killing of the poor as a legitimate exercise of the property rights of the rich. Yet it would be unreasonable to ask the poor to accept anything other than some version of the second account of property rights. Moreover, according to the second account, it does not matter whether the poor would actually die or are only physically or mentally debilitated as a result of such acts of prevention. Either result would preclude property rights from arising. Of course, the poor may have no real alternative to acquiescing in a political system modelled after the first account of property rights even though such a system imposes an unreasonable sacrifice upon them – a sacrifice that we could not blame them for trying to evade. At the same time, although the rich would be disinclined to do so, it would not be unreasonable to ask them to accept a political system modelled after the second account of property rights – the account favoured by the poor.

Consequently, if we assume that however else we specify the requirements of morality, they cannot violate the *'ought' implies 'can'* principle, it follows that, despite what libertarians claim, the right to life and the right to property endorsed by libertarians actually support a system of welfare rights.

Nevertheless, it might be objected that the welfare rights that have been established against the libertarian are not the same as the welfare rights endorsed by welfare liberals. We could mark this difference by referring to the welfare rights that have been established against the libertarian as 'action welfare rights' and referring to the welfare rights endorsed by welfare liberals as both 'action and recipient welfare rights'. The significance of this difference is that a person's action welfare right can be violated only when other people through acts of commission interfere with a person's exercise of that right, whereas a person's action and recipient welfare right can be violated by such acts of commission but also by acts of omission as well. However, this difference will have little practical import. For once libertarians come to recognise the legitimacy of action welfare rights, then, in order not to be subject to the poor person's discretion in choosing when and how to exercise her action welfare right, libertarians will tend to favour two morally legitimate ways of preventing the exercise of such rights. First, libertarians can provide the poor with mutually beneficial job opportunities. Secondly, libertarians can institute adequate recipient welfare rights that would take precedence over the poor's action welfare rights. Accordingly, if libertarians adopt either or both of these ways of legitimately preventing the poor from exercising their action welfare rights libertarians will end up endorsing the same sort of welfare institutions favoured by welfare liberals.

In summary, it seems clear that in order to provide a libertarian justification for welfare rights we need only begin with a right to liberty or, alternatively, a fundamental set of rights like the right to life and the right to property, and then appeal to the *'ought' implies 'can'* principle. For given the fundamental character of this principle it seems impossible to reject it and the welfare rights it entails without rejecting what is essential to a moral point of view.

Finally, it is important to note that the libertarian argument for welfare rights that has been advanced in this paper is perfectly general. It applies both within a society and between societies as well. Of course, particular societies can legitimately give preference to the satisfaction of the basic needs of the members of their own particular societies. But when there exists in a society surplus resources beyond what is necessary to meet the basic needs of the members of that society surely the members of other societies can lay claim to such resources as a legitimate exercise of their action welfare rights. Needless to say, affluent societies can, and usually do, effectively prohibit the exercise of such action welfare rights, but, as we have seen, these prohibitions lack any moral justification and, consequently, we can not blame the poor for trying to evade them whenever possible.[13]

NOTES

1 Robert Nozick, *Anarchy, State and Utopia*, New York, 1974, p. ix.

2 Murray Rothbard, *For a New Liberty*, New York, 1978, p. 148.

3 See, for example, my article, 'Neo-libertarianism', *American Philosophical Quarterly*, XV, 1978, pp. 17–19; Ernest Loevinsohn, 'Liberty and the redistribution of property', *Philosophy and Public Affairs*, VI, 1977; David Zimmerman, 'Coercive wage offers', *Philosophy and Public Affairs*, X, 1981. To limit what is to count as coercive, Zimmerman claims that in order for P's offer to be coercive: "it must be the case that P does more than merely prevent Q *from taking from* P resources necessary for securing Q's strongly preferred preproposal situation; P must prevent Q *from acting on his own* (or with the help of others) *to produce or procure* the strongly preferred preproposal situation." But this restriction seems arbitrary, and Zimmerman provides little justification for it. See David Zimmerman, 'More on coercive wage offers', *Philosophy and Public Affairs* XII, 1983, p. 67.

4 It might seem that this second approach could avoid this difficulty if a restriction of liberty is understood as the curtailment of one's prima-facie rights. But in order to avoid the problem of a multitude of conflicting liberties, which plagues the first approach, the specification of prima-facie rights must be such that they can only be overridden when one or more of them is violated. And this may involve too much precision for our notion of prima-facie rights.

5 Isaiah Berlin, *Four Essays on Liberty*, London, 1969, pp. xxxviii–xl.

6 On this point, see Maurice Cranston, *Freedom*, London, 1953, pp. 52–3; C. B. Macpherson, *Democratic Theory*, Oxford, 1973, pp. 95–7; Joel Feinberg, *Rights, Justice and the Bounds of Liberty*, Princeton, N.J., 1980, ch. 1.

7 See John Hospers, *Libertarianism*, Los Angeles, 1971, ch. 7.

8 Alvin Goldman, *A Theory of Human Action*, Engelwood Cliffs, N.J., 1970, pp. 208–15; William Frankena, 'Obligation and ability', in Max Black (ed.),*Philosophical Analysis*, Ithaca, N.Y., 1950, pp. 157–75. Judging from some recent discussions of moral dilemmas by Bernard Williams and Ruth Marcus, one might think that the *'ought' implies 'can'* principle would only be useful for illustrating moral conflicts rather than resolving them. (See Bernard Williams, *Problems of the Self*, Cambridge, 1977, chs. 11 and 12; Ruth Marcus, 'Moral dilemmas and consistency', *The Journal of Philosophy*, LXXVII, 1980, pp. 121–36. See also Terrance C. McConnell, 'Moral dilemmas and consistency of ethics', *Canadian Journal of Philosophy*, VIII, 1978, pp. 269–87.) But this is only true if one interprets the 'can'

in the principle to exclude only 'what a person lacks the power to do'. If one inter-prets the 'can' to exclude in addition 'what would involve so great a sacrifice that it would be unreasonable to ask the person to do it' then the principle can be used to resolve moral conflicts as well as state them. Nor would libertarians object to this broader interpretation of the principle since they do not ground their claim to lib-erty on the existence of irresolvable moral conflicts.

9   See my paper, 'Is there a rationale for punishment?', *The American Journal of Jurisprudence*, XXIX, 1984.
10 Obviously, the employment opportunities offered to the poor must be honourable and supportive of self-respect. To do otherwise would be to offer the poor the opportunity to meet some of their basic needs at the cost of denying some of their other basic needs.
11 The poor cannot, however, give up the liberty to which their children are entitled.
12 See John Hospers, 'The Libertarian Manifesto', in James P. Sterba (ed.), *Morality in Practice*, Belmont, N.Y., 1983, especially p. 26.
13 One of the most popular ways the poor have of evading these prohibitions in con-temporary societies is illegal immigration.

Reflections on injustice and international politics*

MOORHEAD WRIGHT

University College of Wales at Aberystwyth

Thinking about justice in international politics is a particularly frustrating activity for a number of reasons. In the first place, there is the problem of demarcating justice from other moral concepts such as benevolence and charity and defining the respective spheres of these concepts. Too narrow a band for justice will tend toward cynicism, too wide a band will tend to equate justice and morality. In the second place, there is an enormous literature from Plato and Aristotle onwards on justice in social and political philosophy which ought to be explored before applying the concept to international politics. Decisions need to be made about which parts of it are relevant to international politics, i.e. what structural features there are in international politics which are analogues to community or society in domestic contexts. Thirdly, there is little evidence that justice actually plays a role in the deliberations of statesmen and political leaders.

It may be helpful therefore to approach this problem with an emphasis on injustice, whose presence can be readily identified by the resentment which it arouses. That the connection between injustice and resentment is a close one is indicated by the definition of resentment in the new *Longman Dictionary of the English Language*: "a feeling of bitterness or persistent hurt and indignation at something regarded as an insult, injury or injustice". As the qualification "regarded as. . ." suggests, resentment is not an infallible index of injustice or legitimate grievance, but provides grounds for further investigation. In addition such an approach leads us into a slightly different literature on the subject which may provide fresh insights, principally the work of Barrington Moore, Jr.

Injustice has therefore the advantage of being what A. D. Woozley, following J. L. Austin, calls the 'trouser word' when compared with justice.¹ We will nevertheless be driven back to justice in the end. There is both a logical and an empirical necessity for this. Logically, injustice is the contrary of justice (as Woozley himself points out), i.e. an absence or denial of justice where it should be present. Empirically, the only

* This essay also appears in the *Review of International Studies*, vol. 12, no. 1, January 1986, whose editor has granted permission for its publication in this colloquium.

remedy for injustice is justice, so eventually one has to look for a positive theory of a just international system or order. There is one other charge which could be brought against an approach which emphasises resentment – that of reliance on the now discredited emotivist theory of ethics. This is not well-grounded, however, as I hope to demonstrate in exploring the rational grounds of justice based on a modified social contract theory.

The problem of justice in international politics has been much discussed recently. I must briefly set my proposal in this context although at considerable risk of over simplification, given the constraints of space. The traditional view, associated with Hobbes, Pascal and other realists, is that the notion of justice is inapplicable across state boundaries in that no-man's-land of 'the state of nature', marked by conflicting value systems and no settled overarching political authority and law enforcement. If we take justice to be epitomised in the titles of such key official roles as Justices of the US Supreme Court and Justices of the Peace in the advanced legal systems of states, the international equivalents are so few and marginal that we may be forgiven for siding with the realists. There have been roughly two strategies for avoiding this impasse, neither of which I find entirely satisfactory. One is to invoke the traditional distinction between formal and material or substantive justice. This is the approach adopted by Terry Nardin and Frederick O. Bonkovsky in their recent works.[2] Nardin's is the most elaborate defence of this view, based on Michael Oakeshott's theory of civil association in which rules are agreed upon to facilitate the diverse purposes of the individual members. International justice in this sense consists in compliance with the formal, non-instrumental 'rules of the game' of the international system. Nardin's opponent here is what he calls an "enterprise" association, which has by definition a unity of purpose. It must be conceded that Nardin builds an impressive case for his approach from the historical and legal argument which forms the substance of his book, but it seems questionable to argue that there is no deeper purpose behind even the most formal rules, and that the model of civil association is the most appropriate for international society.

The second approach is the resort to the idea of cosmopolitan justice as advocated for example by Charles Beitz.[3] An equally distinguished tradition dating from the Stoics lies behind this approach, but in attempting to reconcile the claims of partial communities such as nation-states with those of mankind or humanity, it makes too many demands and overlooks the genuine social bonds which tie people together in groups and the distinct social arrangements which they evolve. For cosmopolitans, as Thomas J. Schlereth points out in his study of eighteenth-century *philosophes*, groups intermediate between individuals and humanity considered as a mass are seen as obstacles to progress, although some saw validity in the idea of a "tolerant citizenship".[4] From the point of view of the basic structure of the international system, Nardin's approach is essentially 'conservative', the cosmopolitan perspective on justice is basically radical. The conception which I would commend here is based on a number of overlapping 'justice-constituencies' among which there is a continuous process of conflict and accommodation. Julius Stone defines a 'justice-constituency' in terms of "the claimants and beneficiaries of justice in concrete times and places, with their biological endowments and social inheritances, their physical and social environments, and their limited and tentative envisionings of the future".[5] That such 'justice-constituencies' are so often coterminous with states in the modern world does not exclude their coexistence with other, more inclusive ones, including what Stone calls a "postulated justice-constituency of mankind".[6]

Against this background we can turn to the Harvard sociologist Barrington Moore for his study of the roots of "moral anger and the sense of injustice" in the common experiences of people in society.[7] These reactions are produced by the failure of society to meet their expectations or to fulfil the basic purposes of society: the furtherance and protection of a given population's control of and adaptation to its environment, and the promotion of a distinctive culture or way of life which the people find satisfying. The most common forms of injustice which give rise to these reactions are violent death, hunger and other forms of physical deprivation, tyranny, oppression, alienation and exploitation.[8] That moral outrage or resentment is directly experienced by victims of injustice and provides the motivation for disobedience and social reform and in the extreme case revolution is the main thesis put forward in *Injustice*. What interests us in this context is the empirical evidence which Moore finds in a variety of cultures for the existence of recurring elements in moral codes, i.e. for what he calls a "natural morality" which transcends social differences. In other words, there is a core of inarticulate agreement among human beings as to what constitutes unjust treatment of themselves and their fellow human beings. The basis of this is what Moore calls the "implicit social contract" underlying all societies. When one or other party violates its obligations under this contract injustice occurs and rectification is called for. An example Moore gives is "a strong inclination of human beings to develop a rough conception of the just and proportionate relationship between what they invest in a task and the profit or benefit they ought to get from executing it".[9] The core meaning of justice here is the receipt of that which is due or owing in an exchange between equals.

In this connection a distinction is often made in the literature on justice between comparative and non-comparative justice, notably by Joel Feinberg.[10] If we were to accept this distinction, the violations of the implicit social contract referred to above would tend to be placed in the latter category. I do not myself think that this is a significant distinction in this context, for what causes resentment is the comparison with treatment which others in like circumstances have received in the past or are receiving at present in other societies. It is the perceived disparities between expected and actual treatment which ignite the sense of injustice. So in this sense all justice is comparative. As Woozley argues, that is what injustice fundamentally is: "the affront done to a man as a human being by not treating him in the way that he can expect to be treated".[11]

If this sense of injustice is to be articulated into a set of principles for political and social action, it will be necessary to go further into the idea of the social contract. This is by now so well known a tradition of political thought that I need not detail its history or features. The relevance of some of its applications to international politics has been called into question by a number of writers, including recently myself.[12] Here I propose to adapt to my purposes one of the most convincing accounts of the contractualist theory of morality – that of Thomas Scanlon.[13] He argues that the most plausible account of moral motivation is the desire to secure agreement on basic principles, i.e. that people generally feel the need to justify their actions by reference to principles which would command general assent, or put negatively, which no one could reasonably reject. Scanlon in fact stresses the negative aspect of his theory in order to sidestep one of the frequent criticisms of social contract theory, namely that it demands an unrealistic level of agreement among individuals or groups with very diverse purposes or interests. In trying to avoid Rawls's device of the 'veil of ignorance', he is content with the negative form of rational justification. It is also important to stress, as do Moore and others, that there is no actual agreement but an implicit or hypothetical one. I do not claim that the negative and hypothetical nature of Scanlon's version of contract theory gets around all of the difficulties of this approach, but at least it has a better chance of success.

Adapting Scanlon's contractualist approach, we can define injustice as the denial of the legitimate interests of human beings and the groups of which they are members. 'Legitimate interests' are those which all members of a given 'justice-constituency' would reasonably accept as the grounds for claims against each other, including those responsible for managing its affairs. The legitimate interests include but are not necessarily limited to the following: (1) survival; (2) physical and mental well-being; (3) personal autonomy or freedom; (4) fair compensation for one's contribution to the social product and/or the common good; (5) participation in those decision-making processes which substantially affect their other 'legitimate interests'. These correspond to the major forms of injustice mentioned earlier. They are closely interrelated and some are clearly of greater importance than others. Nor do I underestimate the problems of actually determining the boundary between justice and injustice in some of them, e.g. where it is a matter of degrees of well-being and autonomy. What constitutes 'fair compensation' is another notorious problem. I am also not unmindful that the fifth interest comes perilously close to Western democratic norms and would not be accepted by a theocratic system, for example. But the point I wish to stress here is that prima-facie no one could reasonably reject them as the basis for social arrangements.

This view of the social contract implies that legitimate interests can be provided for one individual or group without sacrificing those of others, but in the real world the picture is complicated by the prevailing conditions of scarcity of and competition for most of the states of affairs which we value. What matters however in this context is the claim that the nation-state is only one possible type of 'justice-constituency' and hence that, for allocation of some goods at least, belonging to one such nation-state may not be a relevant criterion on the presupposition of a 'natural morality' common to all humanity.

One prominent source of injustice is the predatory or oppressive person or group which violates these legitimate interests for its own aggrandisement. A less salient but equally important source is found in those interpretations of the common good which define it as something which can only be gained at another's expense. Security, which is a basic objective of societies in both their internal and external aspects, is especially vulnerable to such interpretations. Accumulation of wealth, arms, etc. is inevitable in conditions of scarcity, so the argument goes. And 'we' must have more in order to protect what we already have.

Considerable inequalities can however be regarded as just, i.e. those which fall within tolerable limits, provided that 'differential treatment' is based on relevant differences. These limits are constantly being renegotiated: in other words the social contract is not a once-and-for-all thing. As Moore points out, there is a constant probing and testing of these limits. C. H. Whiteley characterises the social contract as "a continuous set of adjustments of claims and concessions made by real people already living together, already having settled interests, and already differing from each other in their interests and in their influence and bargaining power."[4]

At this point the familiar distinction between utility or the social good and justice becomes relevant. The former requires a positive congruence of ends, and is an aggregative concept. The latter accepts a diversity of ends provided that A's pursuit of his ends does not harm or impede B's pursuit of his ends. Therefore justice, which is concerned with the rights and entitlements of individuals and groups considered as ends-in-themselves, has to be kept separate from individuals and groups as means to the common good. Both are important facets of morality, but have quite divergent implications for distributive justice, particularly the equality issue: as means to the social good individuals are unequal, as ends they are equal. So justice requires proportionate compensation of contributions to the common good (based on criteria of merit, ability, desert, etc.) whereas justice based on individuals as ends calls for strict equality since all humans are presumed equal in their basic or minimum needs.[15] These sorts of considerations apply no less to nation-states in international society than to individuals in domestic society, once we accept the thesis that it is meaningful to talk about a global common good. The extent of inequality we are presently facing is indicated by World Bank estimates that 75% of the world's people produce and consume 21% of the world's product. And specific comparisons over time show this even more dramatically. The US per capita income grew by an average 2% per annum from $7,030 to $11,560 in 1980 dollars from 1955 to 1980. India's per capita income grew by about 1.7% per annum from $170 to $260 in 1980 dollars over the same period. So the gap actually widened: US average income increased from 41 times India's to 44 times over the period.[16]

On this analysis the excessive concentration of wealth in a few rich countries of the world and the parallel maldistribution of wealth within the poor countries are clearly violations of the principle of proportionate rewards. Nor can they be justified on the grounds of social utility. From the point of view of domestic society the argument has always been that inequalities provide the incentives which entrepreneurs and business men need to expand the economy, thereby benefiting everyone. The most sophisticated recent rationalisation of this view is of course Rawls's "difference principle" which sanctions inequalities as long as they benefit the least well off.[17] But it is doubtful whether this principle can serve as a principle of distributive justice for the poorer, agrarian-based economies of the Third World. Nor does it seem to be a viable principle of the world economy, although it may have limited applicability.

What is often overlooked in discussions of distributive justice is that it is just as much concerned with the distribution of burdens as with benefits and with the relationship between the two, which should be one of proportionate equality. Moore's discussion of injustice concerns authority and the division of labour on an equal footing with the allocation of goods and services. The same point is made by Oscar Schachter, who argues that in satisfying basic needs as a matter of equity or justice "the relationship between donor and recipient is seen as a matter of mutual rights and responsibilities". Charity implies inequality and submissive or dependent behaviour on the part of the recipient.[18] One criticism of this thesis might be the following: that what is owing to others is entirely independent of what they do themselves. Against this criticism we can cite the strong natural disposition to link rights and performance. It is for example plausible to argue that part of the reluctance of developed countries to bail out the economies of poor Third world countries stems from the latter's failure to do all they can to solve their problems. Corruption, economic mismanagement and ecological short-sightedness are often cited in this context.

Finally I must anticipate some objections which may be brought against my approach. The test of injustice, which we have found in Moore's analysis to be "moral anger", can be easily detected in specific cases of domestic injustice, and Amartya Sen has produced a rigorous and telling economic analysis of 'entitlement systems' as a primary cause of famines.[19] In international affairs it is more difficult to locate specific sources of injustice. Certainly there is considerable evidence for 'moral anger' or resentment behind the drive for a New International Economic Order and associated institutions such as UNCTAD. Cynics have of course derided these pressures as simply another set of predatory motives countering those of the advanced industrial nations. It is no doubt difficult to know where justice resides in the clash of partisan demands and claims, for the idea of neutrality or impartiality is central to our concept of justice and strictly speaking can only be located in officials or third parties who have no interest in the matter at issue. But the fact that there is considerable empathy or 'vicarious' moral anger in the developed world is good evidence of the justness of the Third World cause: an example would be the Western reaction to the 1984 famine in Ethiopia. In social contract terms this empathy supports claims for the fulfilment of the legitimate interests of human beings.

The 'moral anger' approach has the advantage of highlighting injustices but it tends to produce excessive, often violent actions, which in turn prompt counter-reaction by the conservative, 'have' forces. It may be argued that the resulting clash is unlikely to lead to progress, but the idea of the ongoing implicit social contract as the continuous process of testing limits of toleration would imply the possibility of evolution or progress. The main value of Moore's work for the problem of international justice is to highlight the historical importance of evolving standards of condemnation and principles of social reform within the context of domestic society, and to demonstrate the recurring or cross-cultural elements in moral codes. To these considerations we can add some cautious grounds for optimism, e.g. the internationalisation of some standards of condemnation in human rights instruments. A world without blatant injustices is not a utopian vision, though a world of perfect justice is.

NOTES

1   A. D. Woozley, 'Injustice', *Studies in Ethics, American Philosophical Quarterly* Monograph No. 7, Oxford, 1973, p. 109.
2   Terry Nardin, *Law, Morality and the Relations of States*, Princeton, N.J., 1983; Frederick O. Bonkovsky, *International Norms and National Policy*, Grand Rapids, Mich., 1980.
3   Charles Beitz, *Political Theory and International Relations*, Princeton, N.J., 1979.
4   Thomas J. Schlereth, *The Cosmopolitan Ideal in Enlightenment Thought*, London, 1977, especially ch. 5.
5   Julius Stone, 'Approaches to the notion of international justice', in Richard A. Falk and Cyril E. Black (eds.), *The Future of the International Legal Order*, vol I, *Trends and Patterns*, Princeton, N.J., 1969, p. 425.
6   Stone, 'Approaches', p. 437.
7   Barrington Moore, Jr., *Injustice: The Social Bases of Obedience and Revolt*, London, 1978, especially chs. 1–3.
8   See Moore's earlier *Reflections on the Causes of Human Misery and upon Certain Proposals to Eliminate Them*, London, 1972.
9   *Injustice*, pp. 43–4.
10   Joel Feinberg, 'Noncomparative justice', *Philosophical Review*, LXXXIII, 1974, pp. 297–338.
11   Woozley, 'Injustice', pp. 121–2.
12   Moorhead Wright, 'Central but ambiguous: states and international theory', *Review of International Studies*, X, 1984, pp. 233–7.
13   Thomas Scanlon, 'Contractualism and Utilitarianism', in Amartya Sen and Bernard Williams (eds.), *Utilitarianism and Beyond*, Cambridge, 1982, pp. 103–28.
14   C. H. Whiteley, 'The justification of morality', *Philosophy*, LVII, 1982, p. 442.
15   D. D. Raphael, *Moral Philosophy*, Oxford, 1981, p. 79.
16   World Bank, *World Development Report 1984*, Oxford, 1984, p. 6.
17   John Rawls, *A Theory of Justice*, Oxford, 1972.

18   Oscar Schachter, *Sharing the World's Resources*, New York, 1977, p. 9.
19   Amartya Sen, *Poverty and Famines: an essay on Entitlement and Deprivation*, Oxford, 1981.

Programme of the colloquium

Friday 28th September

5 p.m.   *Session I. International affairs and the theory of justice*

Speaker:	Respondent:	Chairman:
Prof. James Fishkin	Prof. Antony Flew	Mr Renford
University of Texas	York University,	Bambrough
at Austin	Ontario	St. John's College,
		Cambridge

Saturday 29th September

10 a.m.   *Session II. Intervention and the sovereignty of states*

Speaker:	Respondent:	Chairman:
Mr Jeff McMahan	Prof Neil MacCormick	Prof. Stephen R. L.
St. John's College,	Edinburgh University	Clark
Cambridge		Liverpool University

8 p.m.   *Session III. Duties of rich countries to poor*

Speaker:	Respondent:	Chairman:
Prof. Brian Barry	Prof. Robert	Dr John Harris
California Institute	Fullinwider	Manchester
of Technology	University of	University
	Maryland	

Sunday 30th September

10 a.m.   *Session IV. Nuclear deterrence*

Speaker:	Respondent:	Chairman:
Dr Anthony Kenny	Arthur Hockaday	Dr Henry Shue
Balliol College,	Commonwealth War	Center for Philosoph
Oxford	Graves Commission	and Public Policy,
		University of
		Maryland

2.15 p.m.   *Open session (i)*

'The self, morality and the nation-state'
Dr Brian Baxter, University of Dundee

'Is enduring good order between states really possible?'
Dr Peter Ingram, Queen's University, Belfast

'Equal pay for equal work in the Third World'
Professor Hugh Lehman, University of Guelph, Ontario

'Institutional rights and international duties:
  a critique of Shue's argument'
Professor David S. Scarrow, Kalamazoo College, Michigan

8 p.m.   *Open Session (ii)*

'Multinational decision-making: reconciling international norms'
Professor Thomas Donaldson, Loyola University of Chicago

'Conflicting conceptions of deterrence'
Dr Henry Shue, University of Maryland

'The poor against the rich: the case for action welfare rights'
Professor James P. Sterba, Indiana University

'Injustice in international politics'
Dr Moorhead Wright, University College of Wales, Aberystwyth.

List of Participants

Mr R. A. Akanmidu, Department of Philosophy, University of Birmingham.

Dr Robin Attfield, Department of Philosophy, University College, Cardiff.

Dr W. H. Balekjian, Department of European Law, University of Glasgow.

Mr Renford Bambrough, St. John's College, Cambridge.

Professor Brian Barry, California Institute of Technology, Pasadena.

Mrs Joanna Barry, California Institute of Technology, Pasadena.

Dr Brian Baxter, Department of Political Science and Social Policy, University of Dundee.

Miss Bonnie G. Bird, London.

Dr Antony Black, Department of Political Science, University of Dundee.

Mr Christopher Bryant, Department of Moral Philosophy, University of St. Andrews.

Dr Anthony Carty, Faculty of Law, University of Glasgow.

Professor Stephen R. L. Clark, Department of Philosophy, University of Liverpool.

Mr Christopher Coope, Department of Philosophy, University of Leeds.

Mr S. L. Cowper-Coles, Foreign and Commonwealth Office, London.

Mr Roger Crisp, Oxford.

Miss Frances DiCesare, Lincoln College, Oxford.

Mr Alex Donald, Department of Moral Philosophy, University of St. Andrews.

Professor Thomas Donaldson, Department of Philosophy, Loyola University of Chicago.

Mr Michael Donelan, London School of Economics.

Mr Timothy Duffy, Edinburgh.

Mr A. Edwards, Department of Government, University of Manchester.

Mr Anthony Ellis, Department of Moral Philosophy, University of St. Andrews.

Mr Gavin Fairbairn, Manchester.

Mr Bruce D. Finley, Lincoln College, Oxford.

Professor James Fishkin, University of Texas at Austin.

Professor Antony Flew, York University, Ontario.

Miss Michele A. Flournoy, Balliol College, Oxford.

Mr Ian Fowlie, Department of Moral Philosophy, University of Aberdeen.

Capt. & Mrs J. Franklin, Fulbright Commission, London.

Professor Robert Fullinwider, Center for Philosophy and Public Policy, University of Maryland.

Mrs G. Garthwaite, Leeds.

Dr Gordon Graham, Department of Moral Philosophy, University of St. Andrews.

Mr John Hall, Department of Moral Philosophy, University of St. Andrews.

Mr Richard Hamilton, Department of Philosophy, University of Edinburgh.

Dr John Harris, Department of Education, University of Manchester.
Sir Arthur Hockaday, Commonwealth War Graves Commission, Maidenhead.
Mr Brad Hooker, Oxford.
Dr Peter Ingram, Faculty of Law, Queen's University of Belfast.
Miss Jennifer Jackson, Department of Philosophy, University of Leeds.
Dr Anthony Kenny, Balliol College, Oxford.
Mr Stanley S. Kleinberg, Department of Philosophy, University of Stirling.
Miss Paulette Kurzer, London.
Professor Hugh Lehman, Department of Philosophy, University of Guelph, Ontario.
Mr Peter Long, Department of Philosophy, University of Leeds.
Professor Neil MacCormick, Faculty of Law, University of Edinburgh.
Professor D. M. MacKinnon, Aberdeen.
Mr Jeff McMahan, St. John's College, Cambridge.
Professor Bernard Mayo, St Andrews.
Mr David Midgley, York.
Mrs Mary Midgley, Newcastle-upon-Tyne.
Mrs Gillian Peake, Manchester.
Mr P. E. Phillips, Faculty of Law, The Queen's University of Belfast.
Lady Anne Piper, Oxford.
Professor David S. Scarrow, Department of Philosophy, Kalamazoo College, Michigan.
Mrs Janet Scarrow, Department of Philosophy, Kalamazoo College, Michigan.
Dr Henry Shue, Center for Philosophy and Public Policy, University of Maryland.
Mr David Spiro, London.
Professor James P. Sterba, Department of Philosophy, University of Notre Dame, Indiana.
Mr Luke Swinhoe, Twickenham.
Miss Amy Toh, Pentre Broughton, North Wales.
Mr Colin Warbrick, Faculty of Law, Durham.
Dr Moorhead Wright, Department of International Politics, University College of Wales, Aberystwyth.

Index of Names

Subject Index

absolutism, 9, 10, 111
Afghanistan, 82
aid, 85-7, 89-91, 167f, *see also* famine relief
Angola, 82
autonomy, national, xii, 30-42, 45, 46, 48, 51n, 52, 55, 56f, 58, 143-5, 148, 151, *see also* sovereignty
autonomy, personal, 19f, 29-30, 32-3, 114-26, 144f, 145, 154n, 217

bad faith, xii, 111f
Bangladesh, 160
bluff, 103, 106f, 172, 173

Campaign for Nuclear Disarmament, 96
Canada, 159
Categorical imperative, 64
Chad, 132
Chile, 25, 138
CND, *see* Campaign for Nuclear Disarmament
coercion, x, 24-60 *passim*, 70, 74, 76f, 81, 85f, 88, 142-53 *passim*, 154n, 165f, 174, 202-12 *passim*
Colombia, 138
colonialism, 33, 46, 82, 123f
compliance, problem of, ix, 61-91
Congo, 154n
consent, 32, 34, 36, 40, 43, 50n, 78, 141, 142, 154n
consequentialism, xi, 1-23, 43, 45
conventionalism, 75
Cuba, 24, 49
cut-off for heroism *see* heroism
Czechoslovakia, 98, 154n

Day After, The, 104
decision theory, 74f, 76
democracy, 29, 31, 32, 36, 144, 217
deterrence, *see also* nuclear deterrence, 92, 171-201
difference principle, 16, 75, 155, 159f, 161, 218
diplomacy, 141, 147
discrimination, rule of, 106, 107, 108
EEC *see* European Economic Comunity

egoism, 116, 117
El Salvador, 24, 27, 37, 49, 51n, 82
emotion, ix, 213
equality, xi, 1, 3, 7, 14, 16, 17, 18, 129, 218, 219, 155-62 *see also* inequality
Ethiopia, 219
European Economic Community, 77, 78, 80, 91, 138

famine relief, *see also* aid, 1, 2-9, 11n
feelings, *see* emotion
flexible response, 94

game theory, 74, 76, 80, 187
Germany, 77, 199n, 201n
Great Britain, *see* United Kingdom
Grenada, 26, 82
Guatemala, 26

heroism, 2, 4-11, 12, 23, *see also* supererogation

impartial spectator, x, 3, 15
impartiality, x, xi, 1-23, 32, 35, 73-6, 81, 87-9, 154n, 219, *see also* impersonality
impersonality, 113-26, *see also* impartiality
India, 127, 134, 218
indifference, *see* zone of indifference
inequality, xf, 15, 16, 17, 21f, 81f, 128, 139n, 155-62 *passim*, 202-12 *passim*, 217, 218, *see also* equality
injustice, *see* justice
intention, xif, 102, 104, 107-9, 111f
international law, 28, 50n, 57f, 60, 68, 69, 80, 141-55 *passim*, 214
intervention, x, xii, 24-60, 82
intuitionism, 1, 4, 8f
intuitions, 132, 134, 156f, 159
Israel, 82
Italy, 129, 132, 133, 134

Japan, 78, 176, 199n
justice, 1-23, 39, 46, 66, 72ff. 89f, 91, 116, 139n, 155, 159, 160f, 161, 171, 204, 208f, 213-21

Korea, 129